To the shining lights in my life,
Susan and Shane,
who make coming home the very best part of any road trip.

And to the memory of my wonderful mother, Sandee,
who took her longest road trip way too soon.

On the Road *Again*

On the Road *Again*

The Triumphs & Follies of the 1999 Toronto Maple Leafs

Howard Berger

Warwick Publishing
Toronto Los Angeles
www.warwickgp.com

On the Road *Again*
© 1999 Howard Berger

We acknowledge the financial support of the Government of
Canada through the Book Publishing Industry Development
Program for our publishing activities.

ISBN: 1-894020-62-6

Published by Warwick Publishing Inc.
162 John Street, Toronto, Ontario M5V 2E5

Design: Kimberley Young
Photos: Dan Hamilton, Vantage Point Studios

Printed and bound in Canada

Table of Contents

Acknowledgments

This project came together quite suddenly and with some arm-twisting from Warwick publisher Nick Pitt, who deserves most of the credit (blame?) for its manifestation. I thank him, as always, for his resolve, and confidence in me.

Though they surely will not delight in, or agree with, all of the sentiments in this book (perhaps even some of their own), I couldn't have executed much of it without the independent cooperation of Ken Dryden and Mike Smith. More of an odd couple you will not find. Individually, and apart from one another, they are both quality people.

Scott Taylor, the witty and often wacky sports columnist at the *Winnipeg Free Press,* was an invaluable research aide, and, as always, a good friend.

A heartfelt tip of the hat to my fellow workers at The Fan-590, who possess a similar passion for yakking endlessly about the Maple Leafs. People like Doug Farraway, Dan Dunleavy, Stormin' Norman Rumack and Gord Stellick. And to a former colleague, and one of my favorite co-workers of all time: Charles (Spider) Jones.

A sincere and overdue debt of gratitude to my employers at the radio station for according me the privilege of traveling with the Maple Leafs, full time, since 1995. I won't mention any names (Doug Ackhurst and Nelson Millman . . . ooops!), but you know who you are.

And no project of this magnitude is even remotely possible without the unwavering patience and devotion of a better half — in this case, two better halves: my beloved wife, Susan, and my three-year-old son, Shane. After being away for half the winter, it is patently unfair to curl up next to a computer and virtually ignore family life throughout the ensuing summer. But that's what my wife and little boy endured for much of 1999, and there are precious few words of gratitude that can truly portray how I feel about them.

They've heard it before, and I'll say it again:

"I love you both with all my heart."

Introduction

It is interesting to try and determine where you might place the 1998–99 Toronto Maple Leafs among the great teams in franchise history.

Certainly not among the eleven Stanley Cup winners — for seizing the ultimate prize in hockey ranks alone in terms of achievement, even when done so in unexpected fashion (like Punch Imlach's over-the-hill gang of 1967). And, it's often a fruitless exercise to compare eras. Who could possibly conclude, for instance, that the 1954–55 Maple Leaf squad which lost in the semifinals under coach King Clancy was better or worse than the 1998–99 team that did the same under Pat Quinn? Opinions, of course, will vary, but hard facts are unattainable.

It might even be a stretch to compare the current Maple Leafs to the good but not-quite-good-enough teams of the early '90s that twice made it to the final four. Simply because there has since been a complete overhaul in personnel. It is, however, plausible to believe that the 1993 Toronto club — with a bit of luck — might have ended the franchise's post-expansion Cup drought. We could, quite conceivably, be discussing the turn-of-the-century Maple Leafs in the context of trying to stop a seven-year championship dry spell, rather than one of 33 years.

Toronto hockey fans can thank Wayne Gretzky for the variance. His overtime goal in Game 6 of the Campbell Conference final (aided, many still believe, by a non-call from referee Kerry Fraser), and his virtuoso exhibition in the deciding seventh match two nights later at Maple Leaf Gardens, singularly shattered the fantasy of blue-and-white supporters. Had the '93 Leafs — inspired so magnificently by Doug Gilmour — gotten past the L.A. Kings in that ultimate match, and played off against the equally startling Montreal Canadiens . . . well, it still pains dyed-in-the-wool Torontonians to imagine what might have been.

Exactly where the '98–99 Maple Leafs rank will likely require the further passage of time. Clearly, this was among the most surprising of Toronto teams, as even a moderate gain in the standings was considered remote prior to the season. The additions, however, of three significant individuals — goalie Curtis Joseph, head coach Pat Quinn, and veteran winger Steve Thomas — proved that weak teams in the current-day National Hockey League can take giant leaps.

The dramatic Maple Leaf improvement — as you'll discover — took place under less than ideal circumstances. Though they have now gone their separate ways, it is an oblique credit to president Ken Dryden and former associate GM Mike Smith that they managed to isolate their vitriolic conflict from the on-ice affairs. At no juncture in Maple Leaf history has the club prospered — shoulder to shoulder — alongside such bitter executive warfare.

All of this occurred in a season replete with nostalgia. There was a time not long ago when the mere notion of the club vacating Maple Leaf Gardens was considered laughable. No one drives a car without a steering wheel; how could the Maple Leafs possibly play their games anywhere but in the enduring shrine at Church and Carlton? Times change. As did the Leafs' homestead. The name of an airline now adorns the façade of Toronto's hockey centrepiece. On February 20, 1999, the venerable Gardens gave way to the Air Canada Centre — 1.5 miles south as the bird flies, yet eons removed from the history and reverence of the hockey club born of Major Conn Smythe.

The transition, however, was truly marvelous, as generations of Maple Leaf heroes assembled to bid adieu to the old, and welcome the new. From Red Horner, to Teeder Kennedy, to Johnny Bower, to Darryl Sittler, to Doug Gilmour — they all played roles in a week-long celebration that will stand alongside any of the grand narratives in Maple Leaf annals.

It has been my delight and privilege to carry out a lifetime dream over the past six NHL seasons: traveling with and covering the Maple Leafs for a Toronto media outlet, The Fan-590 — our country's first all-sports radio station. That such a unique (and, at times, bizarre) story developed with the 1998–99 Maple Leafs, led me right into a trap — the intrinsic, pain-in-the-neck exercise of chronicling events in book form.

This is my third such venture devoted to the Toronto Maple Leafs. It follows *Maple Leaf Moments* — a 30-year reflection on the hockey club, published in 1994, and *On the Road* — a journal-type observation of the team that skated through the lockout-shortened season of 1994–95. As with the others, this was a labor of love, one that I trust you'll find some enjoyment in.

Howard Berger
Toronto
September 1999

Chapter 1

Branches Fall from the Tree

As the Maple Leafs toiled in wondrous if not spectacular fashion through the 1999 Stanley Cup playoffs, confusion and turmoil gripped the club's executive plane.

An inevitable showdown between the two dominant figures in the hockey administration lurked perilously — its onset delayed only by the unanticipated developments on the ice. Furthermore, the escalating mutiny between president/general manager Ken Dryden and associate GM Mike Smith impacted heavily on head coach Pat Quinn, and threatened to gravely polarize the company's high command — its six-man board of directors and chief executive officer. A full-scale palace revolt was at hand.

Prior to and during the season, free agent acquisitions and trades helped fan the flames of animosity. Potvin, Joseph, Thomas, Schneider, and Karpovtsev — they all became sideshow acts in the dysfunction that gripped the front office.

Within a month of the Maple Leafs' elimination by Buffalo in the Cup semifinals, the uprising came to a climax: Smith was gone, Quinn looked to be placated, and the "search" for an all-encompassing GM barely extended beyond the front door of the Air Canada Centre.

Toronto: Summer 1999

After a season of unforeseen and startling renaissance, the Toronto Maple Leafs staged a frightening replication of their dubious past. The messy turf war that yielded the annulment of Ken Dryden and Mike Smith evoked images of an era not so long ago, when disorder governed all aspects of the hockey club.

That Smith was banished by Dryden after a rocky, 22-month alliance came as no surprise; the two men had grown to detest one another. That the breakup occurred scant weeks after a 97-point season was a tragedy, but typical of recent Maple Leaf lore. Not a decade has yet passed since the demonic reign of Harold Ballard and its constant, debilitating upheaval. Memories endure, and the most recent Maple Leaf mishap served as a nostalgic high-stick to the head.

It culminated just prior to the annual NHL entry draft — an interval during which, in recent years, commotion in the hockey club has flourished. The 1999 draft took place at Boston's Fleet Center, and reporters in town from Toronto had a couple of full-course meals on their plates. Seventeen-year-old Luca Cereda, an obscure prospect from Ambri-Piotta of Switzerland, became the Leafs' first-round selection, but the youngster had to share, minimally, the spotlight with the executive-level earthquake that erupted three days earlier.

While on the surface it appeared to impact solely on the two principals, grievous undertones evolved that threatened to disable the club's infrastructure. Exposed was a deep-rooted enmity — paradoxical to all of the good things the club had began to accomplish on the ice.

The root of the discord, apart from innate personal antipathy, lay in the vagaries in title and role between Dryden and Smith. And the Herculean clash of egos that resulted. From the outset of their regime, Dryden insisted on the tag of general manager. Smith was hired under the sobriquet *associate* GM, even though he handled all the nuts-and-bolts labor of the position. He basically ran the hockey department — fielding and initiating correspondence on player movement. The title designation by Dryden seemed peculiar and mysterious — rife with the potential for conflict. It spawned an upper-echelon tug of war that resulted in loathsome feelings among more than just the two primary figures.

But the burgeoning strife was met with a shrug by many of those who had chronicled the recent history of the team. Consider the following:

Two years earlier — at the '97 draft in Pittsburgh — the newly appointed Dryden had been adamant in renouncing speculation that he was trying to lure veteran executive (and former Montreal Canadiens teammate) Bob Gainey from the Dallas Stars. A week later, Dryden convened a news conference to explain why Gainey had rejected his offer to become the Leafs' new general manager.

And the '98 draft in Buffalo occurred the day after Dryden had ended the longest charade in the club's annals. Pat Quinn was hired as head coach, and Mike Murphy fired, almost four months after the Leafs had fundamentally decided (during a grim executive caucus in March 1998) that Murphy would no longer be their man behind the bench. In an unreasonable act for which he later expressed regret, Dryden forced Murphy to dangle in misery as he quietly pursued Marc Crawford — newly estranged coach of the Colorado Avalanche. Rather than allowing Murphy to seek other avenues of employment, Dryden strung along his ill-fated coach in the implausible event that all potential replacements demurred.

When NHL commissioner Gary Bettman placed inconceivable restrictions on Crawford — ruling that his pact with the Avalanche had not been voided by his voluntary departure from the team — Dryden still withheld Murphy while Smith first interviewed Terry Murray, then Quinn. Only when the latter's appointment became inevitable did Dryden visit Murphy at his home in Aurora, Ontario, and deliver the grossly overdue news. It was June 24, 1998 — more than 12 weeks after Murphy's fate had been determined by the club's hierarchy. At least Dryden had the courage and integrity to do the deed in person.

The most recent front-office tumult was just as virulent. Three weeks prior to his dismissal, Smith went public with an ultimatum that all but assured his demise. While conducting his post-season review with the media at the Air Canada Centre, he confirmed rampant speculation that he'd abandon the Maple Leafs upon the June 30 expiration of his contract if not empowered with the full general manager's portfolio. It's a posture he claimed to have assumed when Dryden hired him in August 1997, though he admitted the Leaf president granted him no assurances — verbally or contractually.

Less than two years after their icy relationship began, Smith was insisting on unequivocal jurisdiction over team matters that were Dryden's domain — a preposterous request given their contempt for one another.

Compounding the strife was the knowledge that each had been procuring endorsement among the board members of Maple Leaf Sports & Entertainment Ltd. — the parent company that runs the hockey club, the Air Canada Centre, and the Toronto Raptors of the National Basketball Association. Smith was said to be pulling rank by maligning Dryden, claiming the Leaf president had increasingly infringed on his area of responsibility, and others in the hockey chain, including Quinn.

This backroom soliciting gave rise to a full-scale skirmish — kind of a Texas cage match in suits — pitting Dryden, MLS & E chairman Steve Stavro and director Brian Bellmore (Stavro's long-time counsel and Dryden's boyhood chum) against part-owner Larry Tanenbaum, company CEO Richard Peddie and the powerful Ontario Teacher's Pension Plan Board — represented on the MLS & E board by director Robert Bertram. Though often featured in the main event, Smith was nothing more than a potentially gainful accessory.

Insiders claim that Peddie — with Tanenbaum's crucial backing — went to Smith and assured him that he'd be named full-time GM. Derisively nicknamed "Slick Dick" — less for his manicured appearance and stylish wardrobe than his perceived caginess — Peddie envisioned himself as the grand beneficiary of the Dryden-Smith quarrel by leading an internal coup d'état that would effectively oust the Maple Leaf president. Others say that Peddie was content with Dryden being president, but fought to have his managerial authority within the hockey department nullified. Regardless, his weight (and that of Tanenbaum's) did not carry with the full board, and Dryden maintained his standing, while prevailing over Smith. Peddie fell into profuse disfavor with Stavro's camp and some observers (both in and outside the Maple Leaf organization) were surprised that he did not lose his job. His keen budgetary eye and, obviously, his alliance with Tanenbaum were factors, but Peddie was deeply wounded by the outcome, and one can only imagine the sour taste that lingers.

Smith apparently triumphed to some degree in his own efforts. Though their agendas may have differed, Peddie, Tanenbaum and the Teachers believed that Smith's role in the Maple Leafs' dramatic improvement warranted a contract renewal. Or at least an aboveboard attempt by Dryden at a workable compromise. Neither seemed remotely possible.

But the Leaf president is a company man, and early in June he did offer his incompatible associate a contract to become full-time GM — though it was one he surely had to know Smith would not accept. Dryden contends it encompassed the "traditional boilerplate general manager's authority." But Smith was quick to disagree. "In my view, in the job Ken offered, he would be very hands-on," Smith claimed after his dismissal. "I wasn't prepared to compromise anymore in terms of what I believed a manager's job should be."

Accordingly, Smith presented Dryden with a counter-offer that likely caused the Maple Leaf president symptoms of apoplexy. Buoyed by the Tanenbaum-Peddie "guarantee," Smith tendered that he become an alternate governor of the Leafs (along with Dryden and Bellmore) while, essentially, gaining full authority on all matters pertaining to the on-ice operation of the hockey club. He would effect this status by way of a cunning scheme that instantly placed a red flag in front of Dryden.

Smith proposed that he report equally to Dryden and Peddie. That would be like reporting equally to Bill Clinton and Slobodan Milosevic — staff at the Air Canada Centre would be ducking bombs left, right and center. Dryden knew that Peddie was, ostensibly, a Smith ally, and the counter-motion would have reduced his influence to that of an inconsequential middle man. Or, perhaps, removed him from the scene altogether (as Peddie had been plotting to do). Full-scale executive warfare was underway.

Dryden — clearly mortified — prepared his selected platform and submitted it during a lengthy and rancorous board meeting the third week of June. Though obviously lacking unanimity, he received adequate approval to withdraw his initial offer to Smith. Acting quickly, he dialed up Smith's cellphone while the latter was driving his ailing wife, Judy, to chemotherapy treatments at a Boston-area hospital. He abruptly informed his ex-associate that no further negotiations would take place between them. Their partnership had officially been dissolved.

When the details surfaced a few days later, the Maple Leaf president was pilloried for the insensitivity of his timing. According to Smith, Dryden was fully aware of the purpose of his trip to Boston. "He had talked to my secretary [Maria Tomasevic] and knew where I was going, and why I was going there," Smith said. "[Maria] told him he could get a hold of me on my cellphone."

From Dryden's standpoint, there was little to accomplish by waiting for a more appropriate time to contact Smith. The Maple Leafs were too deep into their off-season to continue messing around. Knowing the depth of their discord, Dryden may have acted with excessive zeal, but it's unlikely he was sinister enough to purposely await the most emotionally wrenching juncture to spring the news on Smith. Dryden might still require some managerial acumen; he may have a problem in his Maple Leaf post with ego or insecurity, but from my point of view, he is not an ogre.

The concept of timing, however, has not been among his virtues. At least, not according to conventional standards. Dryden clearly operates at his own pace, which is abundantly more deliberate and fraught with perplexity than others'. The expulsions of Murphy and Smith, for instance, occurred many weeks later than they reasonably should have, for the writing was clearly on the wall in both cases.

Dryden never believed Murphy possessed the qualities of a sound head coach, but he simply appointed himself general manager of the Maple Leafs too late in the summer of '97 to find a qualified replacement. He then displayed a lack of both administrative aptitude and basic goodwill by needlessly ruining so much of Murphy's summer the following year.

The Smith example was even more profound. The former associate GM claimed he spent endless hours acting as a buffer between Dryden and Quinn, as the Leaf president grew insatiable in his lust to review and influence every aspect of the hockey operation. Smith believed this was Dryden's frenetic response to a lack of recognition for the club's improvement — credit that increasingly went to Smith himself, and to Quinn.

"Ken's ego was out of control," Smith said. "Around mid-January [of the 1998–99 season], the situation began to grow intolerable. The team was having success that nobody predicted and it was killing Ken to see the accolades I was getting. Of course, I never walked around looking for credit; I don't do that type of thing. It just worked out that way. To me, our accomplishments resulted from the efforts of everyone in our office. I told Pat [Quinn] to just concentrate on coaching the team and let me worry about dealing with Ken. But it got to the point where Ken was holding hockey-related meetings without me. That was the truest indication of where he stood."

This hypothesis, of course, belongs to Smith and is naturally fraught with bias. He said the more Dryden interfered, the further apart they grew, and their parting once his contract expired became inevitable. Dryden said he dodged the issue of Smith's future during the playoff run to preclude distraction — a plausible claim. But you have to believe that if a man were in place whom he truly wished to retain, Dryden could have quietly worked out a deal and made a positive, up-beat announcement that would've troubled no one. Smith, however, was figuratively gone long before the deed actually occurred — his counter-offer to Dryden the proverbial lid on the coffin.

"It was a question of trying to do what was right for the Toronto Maple Leaf organization," explained Brian Bellmore. "An offer was made, and the conditions that came back were not the kind that any functional organization could work with. So, a decision had to be taken and it was."

That decision surely required minimal forethought. Though he would never admit so publicly, Smith had to see the end coming long before it actually arrived. One clear indication of this was Dryden's choice — in February 1999 — to attend league GMs' meetings in California. Smith handled the day-to-day chores of the hockey club, yet Dryden saw fit to represent the team at the GM level — his prerogative based on title, but a clear affront to Smith. The Leafs were in Florida to play the Panthers on February 3, and while the Zamboni circled the ice before the game, I casually sauntered over to Smith's private booth in the National Car Rental Center. The associate GM was leaning on his elbows with a long face, and I inquired as to why *he* was not at the meetings.

"Ask Ken . . . he's the big boss," came the less-than-enthusiastic reply.

Apart from weakly disclaiming media indictments of their animosity, Dryden and Smith hardly extended themselves to put on a happy face in public. They never sat anywhere near one another during hockey games. The club's hierarchy watched the action from a private booth at the far-south end of the press box in Maple Leaf Gardens. Dryden, Bill Watters, Anders Hedberg, Nick Beverley, George Armstrong, Floyd Smith, Darryl Sittler . . . they were all regular occupants of the booth, while Smith perched himself on a steel-loft outside the enclosure — often alone. At the Air Canada Centre, the private booths are in the second level of the press box, up behind the media. Dryden and Co. sat in a booth located just inside the west blueline, while Smith's domain overlooked the east blueline. Unlike the games themselves, there was plenty of territory in the executive neutral zone.

During the '99 playoffs, in Pittsburgh, I was situated in an auxiliary press box in the southeast corner of the Civic Arena, just in back of a row of spectators. It was up behind, and to the right of Kevin Hatcher's "phantom" goal in Game 3 of the Maple Leafs-Penguins series. During intermissions, I would regularly cavort in the concessions area to the rear of my location, and was stunned, one time, to notice Smith leaning against a nearby wall, eating a hot dog. While the rest of the Maple Leaf executive staff sat in a glass-enclosed booth at one end of the main press box, high above the ice, Smith had found himself a ticket in the corner seats.

Late in the 1998–99 season, the media caught on to this polarizing, and accurately sensed it to be an embodiment of the Dryden-Smith coalition. It even became the subject of a feature column in the April 9 edition of *The Hockey News* by associate editor Bob McKenzie. And it proved the extent to which Dryden and Smith would publicly contradict the truth. McKenzie wrote:

> There have been reports that Dryden and Smith don't get along. The story goes that Dryden and Hedberg are close and that Smith is anything but with either of them. Smith usually sits by himself, far from the rest of the management team.
>
> "I wouldn't read anything into that," Smith said. "I've always watched games by myself."
>
> Toronto newspapers highlighted the fact Smith and Dryden didn't sit together during a pre-game meal in the media room at Madison Square Garden. Both scoffed at that having any significance whatsoever.
>
> "That's totally out of whack," Smith said.
>
> "[The relationship] has been fine," Dryden said. "The only question that needs be asked . . . is what are the results? We're getting them. We're getting there."
>
> "I've worked with Ken as president," Smith said. "I've kept him fully informed as to what we're doing."

Naturally, all of this proved to be poppycock. A more accurate depiction of the faulty relationship surfaced during the opening round of the Stanley Cup playoffs. On April 28, 1999, Smith told the *Philadelphia Inquirer*, "I won't be back as associate GM next year. I don't have a sense of whether they'll offer me the GM job and I don't have a sense of what my answer would be." When asked the following day about the *Inquirer* story, Smith had no official comment, though he told me privately the quote was accurate.

Of course, there was nothing left to repudiate by the time Dryden made the official announcement of Smith's expulsion, during a hastily arranged news conference, June 23, at the Air Canada Centre. The accompanying press release read:

> The Toronto Maple Leafs announced Wednesday that they have withdrawn a contract offer made to associate general manager Mike Smith last week and that no further attempt will be made to renew

his contract. Smith was informed by the club Wednesday morning that negotiations with him have concluded. The team will immediately commence a search for a general manager.

"The decision wasn't easy. We have made some progress as a team these past two years, and Mike has done his part, as others have done theirs," said Leafs President Ken Dryden. "This past season was exciting, but more than 'A season to remember', it was 'A year to build on', for we still have a long way to go to become the team we want to be. We're more likely to get there, I believe, if we take another path.

"The road to the top is not easy. It's never a straight line," Dryden added. "There are lots of bumps along the way. No one person can get you there. On the ice and off, you need to work together, and support each other, to make each other better and stronger, because you need them and they need you. Because only together can you lighten the load enough to get it there.

"I thank Mike for his efforts these past two years, and I wish him well."

The press release was classic Drydenspeak, so much so that he actually read his comments verbatim from the sheet to begin the news gathering. He was then bombarded with questions about his onerous relationship with Smith, and Smith's insoluble quarrel with assistant GM Hedberg, who later resigned his post with the Leafs, but would have done so earlier if Smith were retained.

While not denying the allegations, Dryden typically attempted to soften them. "This was something that wasn't going to work out," he admitted, implying that Smith's presence had created a lack of equanimity in the club's front office. "Yes, there was a difficult relationship. But you still [try to] find a way. I never felt there was a rift, that's too strong a word. At times, it got uncomfortable." Just *how* uncomfortable became more apparent later that same afternoon, during Smith's rebuttal to reporters via telephone conference call.

When choosing not to speak candidly, Smith can be the undisputed master of implication. He won't articulate exactly what he's thinking, but his insinuations — often teeming with sarcasm — are unmistakable. Such was the tone of his conference call. Recounting the normally long-winded Dryden's cellphone missive that he was fired, Smith deadpanned, "It was quite abrupt for Ken. So, actually, it was fairly pleasant." About Dryden's acknowledgment of a "difficult" relationship between the two, Smith dryly said, "I seem to remember him dancing around in the playoffs [when the Maple Leafs were succeeding]. Things didn't seem difficult then."

The raillery and invective gushed through the phone lines during the entire half-hour call, fully exclaiming the incompatibility between Smith and Dryden, and increasing wonderment at how these primary figures in the Toronto organization co-existed for almost two years. It also underlined the chaos and disorder that frequently prevailed as a result of their alliance.

Two fundamental examples occurred in July 1998, during the club's triumphant pursuit of unrestricted free agents Curtis Joseph and Steve Thomas.

The Maple Leafs' saga with Joseph helped to stir the club's smoldering executive pot. Dating as far back as the midway mark of the 1997–98 season, the Leafs vowed to be aggressive players on the following summer's free agent market. Something of a radical nature was required to amend a stale, uninspired roster nose-diving to its second idle spring. Inept offensively, it appeared the club would focus its designs on a scoring winger to team with Mats Sundin, whose $6.3-million stipend was proving to be extravagant waste.

As such, Rick Curran — representing veteran free agent John MacLean — spent the first week of July exhaustively negotiating a contract with Smith, and virtually everyone in the Maple Leaf organization (including Dryden) figured the deal to be a slam-dunk. After spending 14 productive seasons in New Jersey, MacLean, 34, had been dealt to San Jose as part of a four-player trade in December 1997. Once a free agent, he sought to move his family back east, and through Curran, the Oshawa native made it known that Toronto was his preferred locale. Remuneration had been agreed on, but Smith remained inordinately headstrong on the length of contract — refusing to add a third year to the Toronto offer. Though acutely disappointed, MacLean took his act to Broadway and signed with the New York Rangers.

The Maple Leafs made casual to moderate inquiries about veteran defencemen Jyrki Lumme (who signed with Phoenix) and Uwe Krupp (landed by Detroit), but were not in the financial ballpark with either man. Once MacLean opted for New York, it seemed Toronto's pledge of a free agent assault was nothing but hot air.

Smith had made a comment on the second day of bidding that appeared to support that claim. Declaring that he would not partake in an escalating salary war for any player, I wondered how he expected to maintain the club's assurance that it would aggressively pursue free agents. "All I can say right now is that even the middle-range players are outside our financial reach," he explained to me on the air. As one might imagine, the remark served only to heap fiery criticism on Smith and the entire Maple Leaf ownership for a barbarous sham.

But two things happened later that week. Hell was raised at an impromptu board meeting, and Dryden decided to go on a late-night ice cream prowl with his wife, Lynda, and son Michael.

Insiders claim that members of the Maple Leaf board, including those vacationing within reach of Toronto, were summoned for an emergency session. And that during an intensely hostile exchange, Stavro underscored just how much of a shit-kicking the team was taking in the media and the call-in shows. "We promised we were going to make some improvements through free agency and we've done nothing," he griped. "Let's get off our duffs and get busy."

But with most of the players the Leafs had been pondering already under contract elsewhere, no discernible back-up plan existed. That's when Dryden's sweet tooth came to the rescue.

Later that same night, the Maple Leaf president drove his family to the Hasty Depot convenience outlet on Davenport Road in midtown Toronto. As Dryden pursued the ice-box at the rear of the store, super-agent Don Meehan (and co-hort Wade Arnott) happened upon him, Meehan looking for bottled water in a nearby aisle. Dryden and Meehan chatted casually and the agent inquired as to Dryden's prevailing sentiment on the free agency issue. He was told the Leafs had nothing of an imminent nature in the works and began to sense an opportunity. Meehan quickly extolled the virtues of his prize client, Curtis Joseph, who had single-handedly lifted Edmonton beyond the first round of the playoffs the previous two springs. Dryden listened intently.

During the ensuing 90-minute palaver, Lynda and Michael Dryden had sufficient time to devour the entire ice cream cabinet (they didn't), while their husband and father gained plenty of ammunition to contemplate Joseph as a free agent (he did). Fate had seemingly intervened on the Leafs' behalf.

The new-sprung strategy was at least partially borne of desperation and strife, but it did make tangible sense. Less than three weeks into his coaching reign, Pat Quinn had perused the Maple Leaf roster and was pondering a more assertive offensive tack — one that would require the presence of an unwavering consistency between the pipes. Skepticism abounded as to the worthiness of the incumbent goaltending arrangement.

Felix Potvin had been the starter during the previous six Leaf seasons but appeared to be if not in decline, then certainly in some sort of performance oblivion. Toronto's second-round draft choice in 1990 had burst splendidly on the NHL scene in the 1992–93 season, allowing GM Cliff Fletcher to smartly exchange veteran Grant Fuhr for Buffalo Sabres sniper Dave Andreychuk. The tandem of Andreychuk and Doug Gilmour meshed spectacularly with a dependable array of defencemen and Potvin's unexpected brilliance. The result: consecutive advances to the Stanley Cup semifinals in 1993 and '94.

In the summer of '94, however, a pair of maneuvers by Fletcher severely depleted the Toronto blueline and contributed to a spiraling nose-dive from which the team — and Potvin, in particular — did not recover. Trustworthy defencemen Sylvain Lefebvre and Bob Rouse, stalwarts on the two successful playoff teams, went elsewhere: Lefebvre to Quebec as part of the multi-player deal that brought Sundin to Toronto, and Rouse to Detroit when Fletcher failed to retain him as an unrestricted free agent. Potvin would never be the same.

Whether he suffered irreparably from the defensive losses, or merely had two flash-in-the-pan seasons, will be largely determined by the remainder of his career (now with the New York Islanders). His performance declined in lock-step with the team in front of him, which makes it difficult to conclude exactly what came first — the cart or the horse. Indisputable, however, was Potvin's growing unreliability. He developed a perplexing tendency to offset stretches of brilliance by allowing soft goals — the emotional scourge of any hockey team. His confidence, and the declining faith of his teammates, suffered irreversible harm on the night of November 17, 1997, at Maple Leaf Gardens.

The Leafs and St. Louis were deadlocked at 2-2 in the dying seconds of regulation time when Blues defenceman Al MacInnis fired a harmless shoot-in from center-ice. The puck took one bounce and skipped past a startled Potvin with only 1.8 ticks left the clock. It was a shocking illustration of his plight and it absolutely horrified his teammates, who privately admitted in later months that their trust in him fizzled. When the vitriolic frenzy from fans and media intensified after the first week of free agency — and Dryden fortuitously ran into Don Meehan — the winds of change began to blow.

Curtis Joseph, however, was not prepared to fling himself into the Maple Leafs' lap. A native of Keswick, Ontario, 60 km northeast of Toronto, he was genuinely hoping the Leafs would show interest in him, but the value Meehan established was prohibitive — between five- and six-million dollars (U.S.) per season and a minimum commitment of four years. There was also intense competition from opposing teams with deep pocketbooks: the New York Rangers, Philadelphia, Florida and Anaheim. Additionally, two other high-rollers were testing the waters: John Vanbiesbrouck and Mike Richter. Joseph initially leaned towards the Flyers, but GM Bob Clarke could not raise the ante close to either the Rangers or Toronto. Having grown up a huge Leaf fan, Cujo gave Meehan plenty of rope in bartering with the unhurried Toronto management. His forbearance, and the Leafs' willingness to pry open the vault for Meehan, secured the deal.

In the end, all three goalies signed contracts within a span of 24 hours, and Joseph received the most money. Urged by Meehan not to procrastinate any further, the Leafs inked Cujo to a four-year pact on July 15, at a 1998–99 stipend of $5,500,000 (U.S.). Richter re-signed that same afternoon with the Blueshirts for a '98–99 salary of $5,100,000 while the Flyers grabbed Vanbiesbrouck the next day from the Panthers for a mere pittance: $4,004,445.

The Maple Leafs had finally made their avowed big splash on the free agent market, silencing their critics. A beaming Joseph donned his new Toronto uniform at a packed news conference in the Leafs' dressing room at the Gardens. Disclaiming speculation that a trade with Montreal had been in the works, Smith pledged to deal Potvin as soon as a palpable offer came his way. "There is no deal in place but we'll see what falls into place in the next several months," said the associate GM — words that were certain to make Potvin nauseous.

Reached at his summer cottage near Magog, Quebec, the beleaguered goalie could only shake his head and hope for the best. "I talked with Mike [Smith] and he was saying there wouldn't be a trade soon," Potvin lamented. "This has been a tough day; I need some time to clear my head. Like a lot of people, I figured that Mike Richter would either stay with the Rangers or go to the Flyers, and that Curtis would go to the other team. I was surprised when I heard the Leafs were going to sign Curtis. I'm sure I'll be thinking about this a lot for the next while."

The Joseph acquisition raised obvious questions about the quandary that training camp would present if Potvin was still around. "The fact is, I have three NHL goalies now [including Glenn Healy]," shrugged Pat Quinn. "It's not a great situation and I'm hoping it will be resolved before camp begins. But if not, as a coach, I'll have to handle it."

Just more than two weeks later, the Leafs brought Steve Thomas aboard as almost an afterthought. When the MacLean negotiations broke off, sources claim Smith had no reserve scheme in place. Smith then apparently caused a further uproar in the front office by wrongly accepting credit for landing Thomas. The story goes that Leafs contract guru Bill Watters — frustrated by the loss of MacLean — did some brisk homework with the club's director of pro scouting, Nick Beverley. When told that Beverley actually had Thomas rated *ahead* of MacLean (another example of communication deficit), Watters privately called Thomas's agent, Larry Kelly, who confirmed that his client was aching to return and play in his home town. Choosing not to further extend his neck, Watters suggested that Beverley inform Smith and within minutes, Smith was on the phone to Watters asking for Thomas's representative.

On July 30, the Maple Leafs inked the 35-year-old winger to a two-year deal worth $5 million. MacLean actually took less money per season from the Rangers ($6.9 million over three years), but got the contract term Smith had denied him. The Leafs wound up getting slightly more bang for their buck in the 1998–99 season. Both players scored 28 goals but Thomas skated on Toronto's top forward unit with Sundin and recorded 18 more assists for a 73-point campaign. It was his highest output since 1993–94 with the Islanders, and 15 more points than his *combined* total of the previous two seasons in New Jersey. Thomas's courage was evident in the latter half of the Maple Leafs' march to the Conference final. Numbed by hypodermic needles, he played with a fractured collarbone and partially separated shoulder suffered in the Eastern semifinal victory over Pittsburgh.

MacLean's 28-goal performance was impressive at 34 years of age, but the Rangers failed to make the playoffs for the second consecutive year.

While the Maple Leafs came tantalizingly close to a trade with Florida in late-summer, Potvin not only wound up attending training camp, he remained Toronto property for nearly six full months after the signing of Joseph. The Leafs bungled a deal with the Panthers that — in hindsight — they should have jumped at. Florida GM Bryan Murray believed he was in such dire straits for a goalie that he agreed to send the Leafs a couple of brilliantly promising youngsters — center Rob Niedermeyer, 24, and defenceman Rhett Warrener, 22. The Maple Leafs would part with Potvin and former first-round choice Jeff Ware, a defenceman who was not in their plans.

But Niedermeyer had suffered a sequence of concussions and his long-term serviceability was a question mark. In the Panthers' opening game of the 1997–98 season, at Philadelphia, he was bulldozed by Eric Lindros and knocked silly. He missed the following 10 games and never felt particularly right when he returned. In mid-March, Niedermeyer got involved in a scrap with Vancouver's Brad May and his head bounced off the Miami Arena ice when the two players fell. The second concussion finished his season, and he sat out the Panthers' final 16 games. He missed an additional 15 games with a dislocated thumb and eight more due to arthroscopic knee surgery. But the head injuries were the ones that lingered and produced the ailment the Maple Leafs were most concerned with — post-concussion syndrome.

The Leafs had recently witnessed, first-hand, the debilitating effects of a serious brain injury. Veteran Nick Kypreos, a scrappy role-player, was expected to contribute to the 1997–98 Toronto team. But during an exhibition game in New York prior to the season, he was knocked unconscious in a fight with Ranger farmhand Ryan VandenBussche — ironically, a Maple Leaf draft choice in 1992. Kypreos plummeted to the ice, face-first, spilling a ghastly, enlarging pool of blood around his head. It was one of the most gruesome sights I'd ever witnessed. Kypreos never recovered sufficiently to resume his career. For months, he'd awaken in the morning feeling nauseous, and bouts of fatigue were random and unpredictable. He retired from hockey before the season ended.

Niedermeyer represented an infinitely larger investment to the Leafs, and Mike Smith and Co. were entirely justified in confirming his health status before pulling the trigger. But why they waited till the eleventh hour is a mystery that even Smith could not explain. The trade negotiations had been occurring, on and off, for more than a month, and sound reasoning would suggest Niedermeyer's health should have been the *first* item on the Leafs' agenda. The big centerman had confessed to experiencing fairly persistent side effects throughout the summer of '97, but some speculated he began embellishing his complaints to undercut the deal. Niedermeyer did not want to leave Florida, and his agent, Mike Barnett, stooped to lying on his behalf — telling me several times that the Panthers were not attempting to deal him. Which was nonsense.

But the 1998–99 season proved the Maple Leafs may have gone too far in their zeal to have Niedermeyer examined. The trade with Florida fell apart when Smith — uncharacteristically acting on orders from above — insisted that the Leafs be allowed to send Niedermeyer to the renowned neurologist, Dr. James Kelly, in Chicago. The Panthers' medical staff had given Niedermeyer clearance to play, insisting he would have suited up in the previous season's stretch drive if the club had been in playoff contention. Maple Leaf doctors were consulted and granted the same information. It wasn't solid enough for Toronto ownership, however, and when Murray was told of the Leafs' request, he grew indignant.

Under no circumstances would the Florida GM consent to the independent exam. He knew that Niedermeyer and Barnett were scheming to scuttle the trade and he absolutely teed off on Smith, claiming he had leaked the names involved to the media (Murray obviously didn't know Smith very well). Murray told reporter Michael Russo of the *Fort Lauderdale Sun-Sentinel* that permitting autonomous medical exams "would allow players to control trades. If they've had past injuries, all they'd have to say is, 'Yeah, doc, I get a bit of a headache once in a while', and it would scare off the other team." He blamed Smith for sabotaging the deal.

Unfazed, the Leaf associate GM shrugged and said, "I've been accused by other GMs of doing that, too, but that's not my style. Some of the things I've been accused of leaking were not part of any conversations I've had [with reporters]. They were things the print and radio guys ferreted out themselves."

The upshot is this: as the Florida team doctors insisted, Niedermeyer was indeed healthy and he played in all 82 games for the Panthers during the 1998–99 season. On a bad team he put up decent numbers, with 18 goals and 33 assists for 51 points, and his up-side remains boundless. The Panthers ultimately gave up on Warrener, trading him to Buffalo (along with a fifth-round draft choice) for behemoth defence-man Mike Wilson. But challenged in a lengthy playoff run, Warrener blossomed into a superbly poised defender for the Sabres, before breaking his ankle in a post-game mishap during the Stanley Cup finals.

In summation: the Florida deal looks like it could have been a thorough plunder-ing by the Maple Leafs, had they chosen to make it.

Incredibly, the Potvin saga had scarcely begun. The veteran goalie, as he promised to do, reluctantly appeared at the Leafs' training camp in Hamilton and tried to keep his chin up. "Sometimes things happen and you just have to deal with them," he shrugged upon reporting to the Copps Coliseum. "I hope that by coming to camp, it will not only speed up the process [towards a trade], but also tell other teams that I'm going to be ready rather than sitting at home for a month doing nothing."

The irony of Potvin's remarks would flourish with a blaze in future weeks, as his personal vigil dragged on with no resolution.

Trade rumors were in abundant supply. Smith was blasted by Vancouver's newly appointed GM Brian Burke, of all people, for shooting off his mouth — the rough equivalent of O.J. Simpson admonishing another person for lying. The rumored swap had Potvin and defenceman Mathieu Schneider heading to the Canucks for some sort of package involving Alexander Mogilny, hot-shot junior prospect Josh Holden or defenceman Bryan McCabe.

"Vancouver's general manager said he would never talk to me again," Smith smirked, "which is quite a pleasant notion when I think about it."

The New York Islanders had long been in the Potvin sweepstakes, and they twice offered their captain, Trevor Linden, to Smith in a straight-up swap. Twice they were refused. Montreal GM Rejean Houle readily admitted during the '98 pre-season that he was often in touch with Smith, and had asked, in effect, to allow him to match any trade offer. But free-agent winger Brian Savage was said to be the best Houle could come up with, and Smith wasn't interested.

A wild one had Potvin going to Colorado (Patrick Roy was still unsigned) for Claude Lemieux and Craig Billington, then the Leafs peddling Lemieux and Billington to Edmonton for unsigned players Ryan Smyth and Janne Niinimaa. Glen Sather was said to be retching uncontrollably upon hearing that report.

Potvin was later devastated over a six-player trade between Montreal and Chicago (November 16), in which goalies Jeff Hackett and Jocelyn Thibault exchanged uniforms. It essentially eliminated two more teams from the Potvin hunt, as both had been talking to the Maple Leafs.

With the bulk of playing time obviously committed to Joseph, Pat Quinn realized he had a less-than-ideal situation on his hands, but he claimed he would spot-start Potvin, and he kept his promise. Between October 16 and November 20, 1998, Potvin played in five out of seventeen games and won three of them. Two of his victories were walks in the park: a 7-3 romp at Calgary and a 10-3 United Center annihilation of the Chicago Blackhawks.

But his consternation grew exponentially with each passing hour and it began to affect his play. Application and focus were difficult to maintain. He fought the puck more patently than usual. What turned out to be his final appearance in a Toronto uniform was a nightmarish 4-1 loss to Buffalo at Maple Leaf Gardens. In a microcosm of his struggles, Potvin seemed to be off in some distant locale. He allowed three soft goals and was harshly booed almost every time the puck came his way. Composed and laid-back as he appeared, an emotional turning point seemed imminent. When Joseph played the following six games in a span of twelve days (winning five of them), Potvin cracked.

His Boston-based agent, Jay Fee, made one of several visits to Toronto and watched the Maple Leafs beat the Los Angeles Kings, 3-1, at the Gardens, December 2. The next morning — a Thursday — he met with Bill Watters and informed him that Potvin had reached the end of his rope. With the Leafs' next game slated for two nights later in Montreal, Fee explained that Potvin was going to move his family to his parents' home in Anjou, Quebec — a Montreal suburb. He would not be attending that day's scheduled practice at the Gardens. Watters immediately contacted Smith, who advised Fee not to take any drastic measures. A potential trade with Tampa Bay seemed promising, but Fee had heard that song before.

It was agreed that the Leafs would issue a public statement saying Potvin had been given permission to go to Montreal early, and would meet the team for Saturday's morning skate at the Molson Centre. The irritated goalie even played along with the smokescreen. "I've been in limbo for 4½ months, so it's the least they could do," he told reporters. "I hope I'm not a Leaf all season because that means I'll probably miss the whole season."

Trade talks with Tampa Bay GM Jacques Demers had indeed become intense and were centered around the Maple Leafs acquiring veteran Mikael Renberg, a right-winger of moderate scoring ability. *Toronto Star* hockey writer Ken Campbell reported a possible three-way swap involving the Leafs, Tampa and Philadelphia — Renberg's original team. It had Potvin going to Tampa Bay, Renberg back to the

Flyers, and Chris Gratton to the Leafs (Campbell would be close). "The ball is in our court," Demers said of negotiations with Toronto.

The Tampa GM quickly called Smith after hearing about Potvin's "trip" home. Renberg and Sundin had frequently meshed well with Sweden's national team on the world hockey stage, and Demers — practically in heat over Potvin — felt he could satisfy Smith's requirements.

Behind the scenes, on Friday, Smith had to formally suspend his AWOL goalie. Potvin had resolutely made a decision to leave the team and Fee was preparing a public statement on his behalf. The agent told Smith that if a trade for his client was not consummated by game time the following night, he would release the statement. The gig was up.

Somehow, none of this had managed to leak out, which made Saturday, December 5, 1998, one of the busiest days I've experienced while covering the Leafs.

I sat in the Air Canada boarding lounge at Pearson Airport early in the morning with NHL referee Bill McCreary, who was on his way to Ottawa for that night's Senators-New York Rangers game. A Potvin admirer, he seemed quite intrigued over the goalie's saga, and we both sensed that a breaking point was imminent. Scanning the morning papers, it was obvious the Potvin story dwarfed all other sports news in the city.

The *Toronto Sun* had taken to running a derisive graphic, entitled "Waiting On A Trade." Facial mugs of Potvin and Toronto Blue Jays pitching star Roger Clemens were placed side-by-side along with a numerical contrast of the days since Joseph's signing (143), and Clemens' demand for a trade (4). In a rare column, *Sun* hockey writer Dave Fuller emerged squarely in Potvin's corner:

> Potvin's critics argue that anybody making $2.7 million US a year, living every Canadian boy's dream, should shut up and do as he's told. But this isn't another example of a spoiled athlete wallowing in his own greed and self-pity. It's the story of a humble man who refuses to let Leafs' owner Steve Stavro and his management cronies steal his dignity.

I went to Montreal on an 8 a.m. flight and checked in roughly 90 minutes later at the Marriott Chateau Champlain, the venerable hotel partly owned by former Canadiens defence great Serge Savard. As soon as I walked through the door of my room, the phone rang. Scott Metcalfe, my boss at the radio station, was on the line saying that Watters had just told our weekend morning host, Dan Dunleavy, that Potvin would not be attending that morning's Maple Leaf skate.

The proverbial fecal matter had hit the fan.

I hurried up the street to the Molson Centre and ran into Leafs media relations manager Pat Park, who confirmed Potvin's non-appearance and the summoning of Francis Larivee, a goalie on the club's American Hockey League affiliate in St. John's, Newfoundland. The official party line was that Potvin had been given further allowance to skip the team skate, but was expected to be at the arena for that night's game. Pat Quinn went along with the balderdash in his post-skate gathering with the media. "My understanding is that he's been told to be here tonight," the coach said, clearly annoyed at having to address the situation on a game day. Unofficially, and after some nosing around in the Leaf dressing room, it became clear that Potvin had chosen to remain AWOL.

On the record, many of the players were openly impassioned. "He's been my team-mate a long time and I certainly hope things finally work out for him," said captain Mats Sundin. Added Joseph: "This isn't the most comfortable situation I've ever been in, but I'm just trying to concentrate on my job and play well for the guys. Felix has been a real pro through the whole thing and it would be nice to see him get his wish."

Somehow, there was time for a bite of lunch that day at the Place Ville Marie food court. Otherwise, it was all about Potvin. Having reported the cryptic messages from several of the players, I headed back to the Molson Centre around 4:15 p.m. — an hour earlier than I'd normally arrive for a seven o'clock road game. Ten minutes later, Tie Domi came in alone and I taped an interview with him for my pre-game show. Domi and Potvin were particularly close friends and the Maple Leaf enforcer laid it on the line. "Felix has had enough," he told me. "It's been a really tough go for him and his family and everyone has a breaking point. All the guys in the room are just hoping his situation gets settled soon."

As if he hadn't provided enough of a clue, I asked Domi, flat out, if Potvin would be showing for the game. "Not a chance," he replied.

The large Toronto media contingent slowly assembled outside the room, await-ing the arrival of Mike Smith. Looking haggard, the associate GM held an impromp-tu scrum and verified what, by then, had become obvious: that Potvin had chosen to not honor his contract and was thus under suspension. "I don't agree with it," Smith said. "He is a professional athlete who is being paid a fair amount of money. Unfortunately, the job he's been asked to do is *not* play."

Smith refused to comment on why the much-speculated deal with Tampa Bay hadn't materialized, saying only that the right offer had not come his way. He spoke briefly and with palpable chagrin about his wife's cancer diagnosis, and how it had become public in recent days. He had been at her side at Massachusetts General

Hospital in Boston for much of the previous two weeks as she recovered from surgery. I remember a sudden feeling of guilt coming upon me, as perspective entered the picture. I asked Smith how difficult it had been to concentrate on his job while so naturally gripped with emotion. "I've had better weeks," he said. "It sure makes all this daily crap seem pretty meaningless. But that's part of life and so is this. You just carry on."

Buried in all the commotion of that evening was an absolute monster of a hockey game. After a scoreless first period, the Leafs and Canadiens went back and forth through the final 40 minutes. Daniil Markov and Dimitri Yushkevich gave Toronto a pair of leads in the middle frame, but Shayne Corson and Patrick Poulin answered each time. Martin Rucinsky's floating wrist shot beat Joseph at 7:22 of the third, and the Habs tried to protect their one-goal lead against a Leaf squad maintaining its tenacity.

There was a fair amount of pandemonium at my end of the Molson Centre press box in the dying moments. *Montreal Gazette* feature writer Dave Stubbs was seated a few feet to my left, and with 2:30 remaining on the clock, he called me over to look at his lap-top computer. The statement Jay Fee had been preparing on Potvin's behalf had been sent out over the wire. Just as I started to read it, an uproarious cheer erupted in the building. Instinctively, I looked down at the ice, figuring the Canadiens had scored again. But no. It was the numerous Maple Leaf fans who were wildly lauding Domi's game-knotting marker — the result of a blatant defensive-zone giveaway by Montreal's young rearguard Brett Clark. Quickly heading back to Stubbs' computer, I perused the remainder of Potvin's official declaration of abandonment:

> As a member of the Toronto Maple Leafs organization for the past eight years, I have given my maximum effort each day and have always been proud to be a member of this great city's hockey club. Today, however, it is with great regret that I have chosen to leave the organization. After extensive deliberation with family and friends, I have made this decision despite whatever financial consequence might arise.

That consequence would be oppressive, considering his $2.7 million (U.S.) salary. Every day he remained under suspension, Potvin would forfeit $14,063 (U.S.) — the rough equivalent of $21,000 in Canadian currency. His conviction in the matter was quite obviously firm.

Rookie Tomas Kaberle's slapshot from the point found its way through traffic and past Jeff Hackett at 34 seconds of overtime, giving the Maple Leafs a stunning 4-3 victory over the Habs, and providing some diversion from the day's events.

Afterwards, the talk once again centered on Potvin. "Felix has obviously reached a breaking point," Smith acknowledged. "What we've asked of him has been extremely difficult. I don't know of a No. 1 goalie in this league who could have gone through what he has." Added Quinn: "He's a good person and he has been a good person through this whole thing. The players want what's best for him and while he was here, they tried to make him feel a part of things, even though *he* didn't feel that way."

Potvin's close pal, Domi, said, "I think everyone respects Felix for fighting it out until now. I talked to him today and I can assure you this move is not about money. Felix just wants to get on with his life. I wish nothing but the best for him and his family. And the fans of Toronto should appreciate what he has done for this team over the years."

Smith made a point of assuring everyone that he would not be the least bit pressured into consummating a careless deal by Potvin's drastic maneuver. "Nothing has changed at this end," he said. "We've identified the kinds of players we want on this team and I won't make a trade until someone comes around with what I'm looking for. The same thought would have prevailed if Felix stayed. We're not going to make a deal that's only going to help us for one or two years, and we're not going to make one that helps us only in the future."

Word had leaked out that Smith was asking Tampa for defenceman Cory Cross and a draft choice, in addition to Renberg, and the subsequent request was bogging down the deal. Jacques Demers was looking to do a straight-up swap, with the possibility of including stale defenceman Karl Dykhuis — a player the Leafs had no interest in. Smith got ballsy and suggested the teams exchange first-round draft choices in '99, thus garnering Toronto a virtually certain lottery pick. Demers almost took a paralytic stroke before hanging up the phone.

Once back at the Chateau Champlain, I made a chance call to Demers at the Drake Hotel in Chicago, as the Lightning was there for a game against the Blackhawks the following night. To my surprise, he answered the phone and we talked for about 10 minutes. Demers told me he was still quite enamored with the idea of acquiring Potvin. After some considerable prodding, he acknowledged that Renberg was the player he was offering, but was adamant he would not surrender anything more to Smith.

"Potvin for Renberg is a fair deal for both teams," he said. "We get the goalie we want and Toronto gets itself a pretty accomplished shooter. I don't know what's holding up Mike, but I hope he re-considers the offer soon. Potvin's the guy I want but there's another team interested in Renberg."

Demers was referring to the Philadelphia Flyers, Renberg's original club. Flyers

GM Bobby Clarke had grown exasperated with Chris Gratton, the big, scrappy centerman he had procured from Tampa Bay as a restricted free agent in August 1997. The acquisition cost him $16.5 million over five years and Gratton was playing more like someone worth $165. Two years removed from a 30-goal season with the Lightning, he was mired in a frightful slump with only one goal in the Flyers' first 26 games. But Demers figured a reversal of scenery might snap him out of it, and Philadelphia wanted Renberg back. Only Demers's infatuation with Potvin kept the Flyers in a waiting mode.

The cat-and-mouse game continued the following night (Sunday), when Maple Leafs director of player evaluation (and Smith's right-hand man) Joe Yannetti was spotted in the United Center press box — presumably not for the spectacle and artistry of the Chicago-Tampa game. He was there to keep visual tabs on Renberg on a day when no talks were held between Smith and Demers.

Meanwhile, the columnists were having a field day with the Potvin story. In the *Star*, Rosie DiManno all but applauded the goalie for his stance:

> We scold athletes for their lack of integrity when they think only of the money, yet we're now bashing Potvin for deciding that the money isn't worth the mortification of a permanent seat on the bench. What hypocrisy. Those who have spent time around the Leafs this year know Potvin has been a cordial and good-natured part of the team, despite his burdens. He has not been a divisive or corrosive element. If anything, Potvin has shown a fatalistic sense of humor that has amused his teammates, even as they pity him.

DiManno's colleague, Damien Cox, showed compassion for Smith:

> One can certainly criticize Smith for not being forthcoming about Potvin's actual situation, for creating a smokescreen that had no logical purpose. But one must also commend the man for trying to do his job in the face of a personal crisis. He could simply have dumped Potvin for 80 cents on the dollar days ago, freeing him to attend to his wife. One could have even forgiven him for having a harsh word about Potvin [Saturday], but such was not the case.

Toronto Sun sports editor Scott Morrison denounced both sides of the Leafs-Potvin dispute for the charade, but he felt most for the goalie:

In truth, the Leafs had hoped they could arrange a deal with Tampa Bay, or maybe even Vancouver, before his absence became an issue. But when another trade didn't materialize (apparently because the Leafs' demands were excessive), Potvin finally took matters into his own hands. And who can blame him? It's a story of a salt-of-the-earth guy, well-liked by his teammates, who tried it the Leafs' way for five months, and will now try it his way.

The Toronto–Tampa Bay bantering continued for the rest of that week. Looming was an eight-day roster freeze (December 19–27) designed to prohibit players from being traded in the heart of the Christmas-holiday season. As well, Tampa had maintained its serious trade discussions with Philadelphia. The Leafs were whipped, 6-2, by the Rangers at Madison Square Garden on Monday night (December 7). Smith resumed talks earlier that day with Demers from his home in Martha's Vineyard, Massachusetts, then flew to New York with nothing new to report. Relenting on his earlier suggestion, he had asked Demers to swap *second*-round draft choices in the Potvin-Renberg deal, but there was no way. The Lightning had already traded that pick, and Demers began to grow agitated.

"There will not be any draft picks involved," he told hockey writer Roy Cummings in the *Tampa Tribune*. "And, we're not giving up on any 19-, 20- or 21-year-olds. We're going to take our time, there's no panic. People say Jacques Demers is impulsive; the minute things go bad, he makes a fast decision. That's not how it works in the GM business."

Potvin, having kept his lip buttoned since defecting, decided to get a few things off his chest, and held a press conference on Wednesday afternoon at the Chateau Champlain hotel. Seated next to Jay Fee, he outlined his feelings with uncharacteristic emotion.

"I know it's hard for some people to understand why I did this," he said. "But I'm the one who had to deal with the feelings of not being wanted, and not being part of the team. Since day one, I tried to be patient, but I just reached a point where I talked to my wife and told her I couldn't handle this anymore.

"I was completely miserable. After practice, I was going home in a bad mood and not wanting to be around my family. It became a terrible situation for them, and that probably bothered me more than anything else. Knowing that we aren't going to be in Toronto, but not knowing where we're going to end up was very difficult, especially with two kids, and my wife pregnant. So, I felt the best thing to do was eliminate having to come to the rink.

"You see in the paper that trades are made, but you're not part of them, and it makes it hard to accept. The bottom line is, I didn't ask to be traded. They said they were going to trade me so I don't know why it takes so long."

Fee expounded on Potvin's remarks. "The main thing is he's happier to be out of that environment," the agent said. "People wonder why you're leaving when you have a contract. But I don't think any contract ought to present the kind of psychological and mental abuse that can mount on a player. What we want to do is stabilize Felix's environment. He's much more comfortable being away from the Maple Leafs."

The Leafs moved on to Chicago late Thursday afternoon for a game with the Blackhawks the following night. Smith went back to Martha's Vineyard and continued talking to Demers on the phone, but would not soften his demand that Tampa Bay relinquish more than just Renberg for Potvin.

Cliff Fletcher, the former Maple Leaf GM and now senior advisor with the Lightning, admonished Demers for persisting with the Toronto discussions, figuring that dealing with Smith was a lost cause. Like Demers, he felt that Renberg for Potvin, straight up, was a fair exchange and if the Leafs were looking for more, Demers should look elsewhere. A close friend of Bobby Clarke's, Fletcher believed Tampa Bay could improve in another significant area by re-acquiring Gratton, and urged Demers to forget the Leafs and deal with the Flyers. Demers slept on it for the night, then called Smith a 8:30 Friday morning to say he was pulling out of the talks.

"I told Mike the price is too high for us," he said, frustrated. "At this time, negotiations are no longer on-going."

Equally annoyed was Jay Fee, who growled, "The Leafs danced with Tampa for more than a week and they couldn't creatively close their differences once again. They waited too long and the thing fell apart. At this point, I'm not surprised. How could anybody be?"

Smith had to be reaching some form of exasperation as well, but he remained outwardly impassive. "The talks with Tampa have cooled," he said, offering a bid for understatement of the century. "I'm beyond the point of being encouraged, discouraged or surprised anymore. There are other teams involved [in the Potvin hunt], but the talk is at the staging level — building a platform for a deal. I've not commented on which teams are involved since this whole thing started and I see no reason to start now.

"It's my sense that Tampa Bay wanted a decision right away, and it wasn't there for us. The talks were good but the timing was a problem."

The Flyers were in Toronto on Saturday morning (December 12) for their final visit to Maple Leaf Gardens. Demers and Clarke concluded their negotiations and announced a two-for-two deal: Gratton and checking center Mike Sillinger going to the Lightning for Renberg and center Daymond Langkow — Tampa's first choice (fifth overall) in the 1995 entry draft.

"We got a player we can build a franchise around," Demers said when asked if the trade with Philadelphia was Plan B. "There has always been an interest in Felix Potvin, our thinking hasn't changed on that. But Toronto's price was just too high. This morning, we had one player to build around — Vincent Lecavalier. Two hours later, we have two guys — Lecavalier and Gratton."

Interestingly, Demers did give up the 22-year-old (Langkow) he vowed he wouldn't, but there was an obvious burden on him to close a deal.

Reaction in Toronto to the latest Potvin false alarm was typical. The *Sun*'s Al Strachan, a relentless critic of Smith's, put his own spin on the matter:

> [Tampa Bay] had all it could handle of Mike Smith's dithering. Tampa had offered Renberg straight up for Potvin, a deal that hockey professionals felt was fair. Said one: "Look at Toronto's left side. There's nobody there who could do what Renberg can." Smith varied his demands for Potvin, but basically he wanted Renberg, a defenceman and a high draft pick. He might as well have asked for them to throw in the White House.

Another opinion came from Ken Campbell of the *Star*, and was typical of the consternation that most were feeling about the prolonged matter:

> Exactly when are the Leafs going to realize that the market just isn't a seller's one when it comes to goalies? When this whole thing started, [Mike] Smith steadfastly maintained it would take a top-five player from another team to get Potvin because that's the price you pay for a top-eight goalie in the league. It was a highly debatable notion then, and as Potvin sits at home and his value plummets, it's not even a debate worth having anymore.

With the Tampa Bay possibility now ended, much of the trade speculation surrounding Potvin ceased, especially during the Christmas roster chill. Other, more traditional stories took merciful precedence. The New York Rangers and Wayne Gretzky made their final appearance at Maple Leaf Gardens December 20, and many figured it to be Gretzky's last waltz in the hockey shrine. On Boxing Day (December 26), the Montreal Canadiens bade the Gardens farewell by downing the Leafs, 2-1. Hockey legends Maurice (Rocket)

Richard and Teeder Kennedy performed the ceremonial opening face-off in the building where they'd squared off in numerous acts of malevolence. On January 5, the Leafs held their first-ever practice session at the Air Canada Centre before an enormous media throng.

During this stretch of roughly four weeks, Potvin's name hardly ever surfaced, even in casual conversation — an ominous silence to be sure. But the goalie was a very hot topic behind the scenes, where Smith had entered into serious trade discussions once again. As the former associate GM later told me: "The deal we wound up making for Felix was small in comparison to one we very nearly made."

The Leafs were in Boston January 7, and I was extremely busy covering the game for both The Fan and the *National Post*. Prior to the game, I had spoken privately with a Maple Leaf player, who dropped a bombshell by revealing that the team was potentially very close to one of two trade possibilities involving Potvin — a blockbuster with the Calgary Flames and something on a lesser scale with the New York Islanders. He offered me the name of a player agent for verification and upon arriving in the Fleet Center press box, I promptly phoned that agent, who corroborated the player's facts. I then called in the news to our radio station, sparking intense discussion the rest of the night. Was the Potvin saga finally coming to an end?

The proposed mega-swap with the Flames would feature Potvin heading west and Theoren Fleury coming to the Leafs. There had been much discussion around the league about Fleury, the pepperpot winger who would become an unrestricted free agent the following July. Through his agent, Winnipeg-based Don Baizley, Fleury made it clear that he was fully intending to explore the free market and that he'd almost certainly not commit himself to any team before then. He was, however, an intriguing possibility on even a rental basis for his potential augmentation of a Stanley Cup contender. As well, a club trading for Fleury would have the obvious head start in trying to convince him to stay put. The Leafs considered all of this and were contemplating several trade options.

The one reported to me was a six-player deal that would see Fleury and defenceman Todd Simpson (the Flames' captain) come to Toronto for Potvin, defenceman Jason Smith, and forwards Steve Sullivan and Todd Warriner. Smith was a player the Maple Leafs were actively thinking of dealing, for he appeared not to mesh with Quinn's wide-open offensive strategy (more on this later). At the time, Sullivan and Warriner were being offered around merely so the Leafs could open up a couple of roster positions. St. John's farmhands Lonny Bohonos, Ladislav Kohn, Jason Podollan, Yuri Khmylev and Kevyn Adams were among a group of players that Smith and Quinn wanted to audition at the NHL level. Incumbent bodies had to be sacrificed.

For reasons stated above, and despite its tantalizing specter, there was an inherent risk involved in obtaining Fleury. If the Leafs could not sign him before or during free agency, they'd have only Simpson to show for the loss of four NHLers. Unless Fleury — before leaving — single-handedly steered Toronto to its first Stanley Cup in 32 years, the trade would be looked upon as a total waste. Smith had all but cast his future on the Potvin deal, and had clearly stipulated his requirement that a player (or players) obtained for Potvin provide the team with vital, long-term benefits. As such, the second trade consideration appeared to be much less of a gamble.

For the previous four months, the New York Islanders had been hot on Potvin's trail, but had not pieced together an acceptable offer. The name of Bryan Berard had surfaced on several occasions dating back to mid-September, but the Isles were reluctant to deal a young defenceman of his potential — even though general manager Mike Milbury had lost considerable patience with him. Scott Morrison of the *Sun* pointed out another important factor in a January 3 column entitled, "Lots of Interest But No Cat Takers":

> There are the Islanders, who reportedly have been shopping the enigmatic Bryan Berard (who also is nursing a sore groin and is out at least another week) to several teams, although so much is wrong with the Isles it's hard to see that team ultimately pulling the trigger on a deal for Potvin, especially when they are going nowhere and have Roberto Luongo waiting in the wings. But then, stranger things have happened.

Indeed, the presence of Luongo seemed to negate all but the immediate benefit of acquiring Potvin. The Isles had chosen the celebrated prospect from Val d'Or of the Quebec junior league fourth overall in the 1997 draft, and Luongo stood as their puckstopper of the not-too-distant future. But the problem Milbury faced was the present. As one Maple Leaf official so eloquently verbalized: "The Islanders had shit the bed and Milbury was feeling the heat." As of January 8, New York had, in fact, succeeded in only three of its previous 19 games (3-13-3) — one of the victories occurring in Los Angeles, ironically, on a Berard overtime goal. With an already tenuous ownership structure above him, Milbury knew he had to accomplish something fairly drastic to enrich his own employment prospects. That, despite a foolhardy contract elongation granted him the previous summer.

Therefore, as Mike Smith recalls, "there was nothing of an exceptional nature that brought the trade discussions to a head. The timing was right for the Islanders, and we were finally offered a player that met our requirement of helping in the short term and the future. It was a matter of pulling the trigger."

The Maple Leafs returned to Toronto on Friday morning after their 2-1 loss to the Bruins the previous night. The initial plan was to charter home immediately following the game, but the club's aircraft suffered a mechanical malfunction, forcing the entire Leaf entourage to check back into a Boston airport hotel and stay the night. Some late scrambling turned up enough seats on an Air Canada departure at 9:20 a.m. Friday — the flight I was on.

Naturally, the morning papers were brimming with denials from Ken Dryden about the reported speculation from the previous evening. A sidebar in the *Toronto Sun* headlined "FLEURY FOR POTVIN RUMOR DENIED" was particularly amusing, as it had Lance Hornby quoting Dryden saying that, in fact, no trade discussions were underway with anyone — an absurdity.

"'Nothing's going on,' Leafs president Ken Dryden said last night in Boston when asked if there was anything to report from the trade front."

In fact, the exact opposite was true. Smith had concluded his negotiations with Milbury and was merely waiting for the Islander GM to call back with an agreement. Milbury contemplated several other trade options involving Robert Reichel and Bryan Smolinski, a pair of forwards he hoped to peddle. That took pretty much all of Friday. On Saturday morning, Milbury phoned Smith to say the Islanders and Maple Leafs had a deal.

A full 178 days after the signing of Curtis Joseph, Smith followed through on his pledge to find Felix Potvin a new home. The Potvin-Berard swap included an exchange of sixth-round draft choices and landed the Leafs an unrefined, but skilled defenceman, only 21 years of age, and less than two years removed from winning the Calder Trophy as the NHL's top rookie (1996–97 season). The Leafs were at home that night for a rematch with Boston, and a rather smug-looking Smith held court with the media in the club's executive offices two hours before the game.

"I think this trade will work out but I've been wrong so many times, it could be a long shot," he sniped, tongue-in-cheek. "Actually, it's been a long, slow dance but [the Islanders] finally made Bryan available. This was probably the best offer we received, though there were others that were close to being equal to what we got here. Some we came close to making [Fleury from Calgary], some fell apart at the last minute [Niedermeyer from Florida]."

The Islanders were in Montreal that Saturday to meet the Canadiens — an obvious convenience for Potvin, still in exile there. He drove to the Molson Centre and met his new teammates, then suited up (wearing No. 55) as back-up to Tommy Salo.

Berard, sidelined with his groin injury, caught an 8 p.m. flight to Toronto and met the media after the Leafs' 6-3 win over the Bruins. A seemingly eternal wait was finally over.

As elated as anyone was Jay Fee, who later told me: "Most people would have been surprised at just how many offers the Leafs received for Felix — the vast majority of them unknown and unreported — and how incredibly particular Mike Smith had been. There wasn't nearly as much inaction as he tried to let on publicly; he was always talking to teams about Felix. I respect the job Mike had to do but it wasn't the way I'd have gone about it.

"Hockey can be a cruel business but I think I'll always resent the Toronto organization for what they did to that family. Having to drag those poor kids in and out of schools; getting all of their hopes up and then botching up a perfectly good deal [with Florida for Neidermeyer]. It was a bit puzzling to be sure."

Reaction in Toronto to the deal was mostly favorable, though Berard arrived as a relatively unknown entity. In the *Star,* Damien Cox tabbed the trade a reasonable risk for Toronto, and posed some two-sided possibilities:

> [Berard] could be the slouchy, droopy-lidded, Kurt Cobain-styled, tattooed dude that sauntered into the NHL four years ago and told the Ottawa Senators to find another franchise player. Or he could be the conservatively attired, self-effacing young man who marched into a post-trade press conference last night sailing on a wind of hopeful change.
>
> He could be the powerplay quarterback that turns the Maple Leafs from an intriguing mid-season surprise into a serious challenger, or he could be the element that disrupts the positive chemistry of a team that refused to be distracted during seven months of waiting for this deal to happen.

It was actually less than six months, but who was counting?

In the *Sun,* Al Strachan brought up an interesting point:

> The curious aspect of this trade is that the Leafs had nothing kind to say about Mathieu Schneider and gave him away at a bargain-basement price. But they have now traded for a kid who is a Schneider in the making. In many ways, the two have similar backgrounds and similar approaches to the game. They're even close friends.

Strachan re-opened a can of worms that had slithered through the Maple Leaf training camp four months earlier. Amid all the petty disagreements and skirmishes for territory, the Leaf executive cadre had found unanimity in one respect — a singular lack of endearment and regard for Schneider, the veteran defenceman Cliff Fletcher had acquired in a largely contentious deal with the Islanders. On March 13, 1996, Fletcher made a seven-player swap with Milbury essentially to re-acquire favorite son Wendel Clark, lost to Quebec two years earlier in the deal that brought Sundin to the Leafs.

Conventional theory has always been that Maple Leaf chairman Steve Stavro prodded Fletcher into making a deal he opposed. In fact, Fletcher made the trade very much on his own, hoping that Clark's return would ignite a team racked with turmoil after the firing, a week earlier, of head coach Pat Burns. And reverse the tone of apprehension and dismay among the city's hockey fans. The extent to which Stavro influenced the deal was rather trivial: the Maple Leaf owner would occasionally tell Fletcher that Clark was a popular subject among patrons of his grocery store chain. "He's the only player people ask me about," Stavro would say. Fletcher did the rest.

Schneider and defence prospect D.J. Smith also came over in the re-acquisition of Clark, while the Leafs practically sold the farm. They discarded highly touted blueliner Kenny Jonsson (their first pick in the '93 draft) and their 1997 first-round choice, along with checking forward Darby Hendrickson and Detroit junior star Sean Haggerty, a 60-goal shooter that season. Ironically, the Islanders would draft Luongo with the first-rounder obtained in the deal, but the Leafs — in that No. 4 position — would have had a crack at both Sergei Samsonov and Marian Hossa, a couple of potential superstars.

Schneider had been a fixture on the Montreal blueline in the first half of the '90s — a key member of the '93 Stanley Cup champions. He had some offensive flair, as evidenced by a 20-goal, 52-point output in the 1993–94 season. Dealt to the Islanders in April 1995, along with Kirk Muller, for Pierre Turgeon and Vladimir Malakhov, Schneider played in only 78 games for Milbury before his transfer to the Maple Leafs. He arrived in Toronto with a well-heeled, but mostly unsubstantiated reputation as a hard liver, modern legend accusing he and Muller of closing more bars in the New York area than the majority of people visit in a lifetime.

He played 115 games in a Toronto uniform, and his two-plus seasons as a Leaf were dotted with controversy and misfortune. In a game at Anaheim on November 13, 1996, a backpedaling Schneider stuck out his right elbow and nailed an on-rushing Paul Kariya directly in the snout. The Mightiest of Ducks floundered on the ice for several minutes and left the game with a slight concussion. For his misdemeanor,

Schneider was suspended for three games by Brian Burke, then the NHL's disciplinary poobah.

But Schneider's real problems began at the end of that month, when an upper-groin strain forced him out of the lineup. He played in pain for seven days, then sat out from December 6 to January 31. Returning for two weeks, Schneider then shut it down for good on February 13, undergoing corrective surgery in March. The injury cost him 53 games of service in the 1996–97 season.

A dubious story about Schneider from the '97 All-Star break has become a part of inner-sanctum Leaf lore. Required to check in regularly with the club's training staff for treatment of his groin injury, the defenceman failed to show up one day. Instead, he left a rambling, muddled telephone message that worried the team's brass. According to those who heard it, Schneider seemed "spaced out on something" — slurring his words and pausing awkwardly. His reputed lifestyle again came into question.

There was suspicion and much intrigue surrounding the break-up of Schneider's marriage. His wife, Yvonne, was from Calgary and the couple had a son, Jordan, in 1994. When the Maple Leafs played the Islanders at Uniondale in October 1996, Yvonne and Jordan attended the morning skate at the Nassau Coliseum. Mathieu stayed by their side at ice level until he had to go into the dressing room and get his gear on. Little Jordan walked out onto the ice with Bill Watters and they passed a puck back and forth. The Schneiders seemed to be one happy family. But not long afterwards came word of an acrimonious separation. While cloaked in mystery, Schneider was alleged to have walked away from the marriage. Why? Nobody seemed to know.

In Dryden's first summer at the controls (1997), the Maple Leaf president raised eyebrows by offering Schneider to Dallas for Bob Gainey — eight years after Gainey's playing career ended. Schneider was to be compensation for Dryden's acquisition of Gainey as general manager, an unheard-of condition at the time. Of course, several such deals have since transpired: the St. Louis Blues yielded draft choices to acquire coach Joel Quennville from Colorado and GM Larry Pleau from the Rangers. And, more recently, the Tampa Bay Lightning sent Rob Zamuner — a member of its original team in 1992–93 — to Ottawa as a reimbursement for luring president/GM Rick Dudley away from the Senators. Gainey chose not to join Dryden in Toronto, but Schneider had yet another "X" beside his name.

The '97–98 campaign was a disaster for the entire Maple Leaf team, and Schneider was the defensive poster boy for the club's misadventures. The only wheel on a slow and aging blueline, he often tried to compensate by lapsing into a pauper's imitation of Bobby Orr — his attempted rink-length dashes regularly aborting at either his own blueline or in the neutral zone. The resultant turnovers led to odd-man rushes the other way, and all too frequently culminated with Schneider sprawled on his belly in a futile attempt to recover his position.

Despite that, he finished with 11 goals and 26 assists for 37 points — the fourth-highest regular-season total of his career, and the best, by far, on the Leaf defence corps. He took a wicked and careless stick in the face from Vancouver forward Dave Scatchard in a late-November game at the Gardens that required a fair bit of reconstruction, and showed a goodly amount of courage by skipping only two games. In February, he appeared slow, small and generally out of place on the U.S. blueline at the Winter Olympics in Nagano.

Most irritating for Maple Leaf management, however, was the perception that the carefree Schneider seemed unaffected by the team's plight. He spoke his mind impetuously and had the same, glazed-over smile and golly-gee inflection in practically all situations, no matter how contentious. Personally, I thought he was great. From a media standpoint, Schneider always made himself available, and his comments were often thought-provoking. It was impossible to piss the guy off, at least in public. I could hit him with every unsavory allegation that came to mind, and he'd smile, shrug, and discard the claim. But there clearly was no long-term future for him in Toronto.

Schneider's contract was up for renewal in the summer of 1998, and the Leafs were in no hurry to re-sign him. The defenceman similarly appeared to be biding his time, as he refused to take the club to salary arbitration. He was part of a large array of restricted (Group II) free agents that included Sandis Ozolinsh, Rob Blake and Scott Niedermeyer. Through his agent, Tom Reich, Schneider made it known that he was seeking roughly $2.7 million (U.S.) per season over three years, while the Leafs countered with a qualifying offer of $2.2 million. The two sides would never come close to narrowing the gap.

Schneider followed through on his vow not to attend training camp without a contract (a stance the Leafs endorsed). "Toronto has to make up its mind if it wants to trade me or sign me," he said in early September. "If they want to sign me, the deal could get done in a day. It's a no-brainer. I know the numbers I'm comfortable with. There won't be a lot of negotiating."

He wasn't kidding. The two sides remained locked in a stalemate throughout camp. Hardly a word was exchanged between Reich and Bill Watters. When they did talk, their conversations were abrupt, as neither man was willing to budge off his monetary figure. The numerous Group II free agents were hesitant to sign new deals, each waiting for the other to land a monster contract and set the standard. It didn't happen.

As the regular season began, the Leafs were actively shopping their unsigned defenceman. There was an unusual paradox in the fact the club no longer wanted Schneider, but nonetheless anointed him as its top blueliner, thus seeking a notable return. He was traded to the New York Rangers on October 14 for fellow defenceman Alexander Karpovtsev and a fourth-round draft choice in '99. The Leafs were on an early season western-Canada trip, and were staying at a lodge in Banff, Alberta, when the deal was made. Immediately, questions were raised as to why the Leafs believed they were getting equal or better value with Karpovtsev — a player who had teased Ranger management with flashes of excellence, but had not ascended to frontline status in five years with the team.

The 6-foot-1, 205-pounder from Moscow was infuriatingly erratic. On one night, he could stand up to and physically challenge Eric Lindros, while the next, he'd be overmatched by another club's 5-foot-9-inch third-liner. Though he had some offensive ability, his puck-handling skills and ability to make quick reads were both extremely suspect; Leaf fans would soon grow weary of watching him ice the puck when pressured, often times during a powerplay. Still, Mike Smith either saw an upside to Karpovtsev, or remained doomed by a fatal attraction to Russian-born players, regardless of competence.

"Potsy," as he is known, arrived in Toronto with a chip on his shoulder the size of Mount Everest. He had been assailed by the New York hockey media and had obviously been apprised of the negative response to his acquisition by his fellow Russians on the Leafs. When chosen by Pat Quinn to sit out a game in early November as a healthy scratch, Karpovtsev shocked reporters who casually approached him by angrily snapping, "No comment!" Though he had a better season than Schneider, Karpovtsev single-handedly rendered the plus-minus statistic meaningless. He led the entire NHL with a plus-39, occasionally had some physical presence in front of the net, but scored only three goals, and appeared miscast on the powerplay. His club did make the playoffs, however, and advance to the Stanley Cup semifinals. Conversely, Schneider had an ordinary season with the Rangers, accumulating 34 scoring points and a minus-19, while his team missed the playoffs.

* * *

The emotional spin-off from Mike Smith's termination in Toronto was swift and devoid of political decorum. It almost immediately led to Quinn adding the GM's portfolio (with Dryden's urging), and severely damaged any short-term belief and faith Quinn held in the club's president. Quinn practically fibrillated when initially told of the news by Dryden, having been duped — he claimed — into believing the matter would be resolved. Astounded, he stopped just short of flat out calling Dryden a liar, placing a further and more potentially damaging strain on the entire issue.

"I'm shocked at this turn of events," Quinn groused to reporters at the NHL Awards ceremonies in Toronto the following night (June 24). "Mike is the man who brought me here to coach. I reported directly to him and we had a sound relationship. And now, with Mike gone, I'm not sure of the next step. The way it affects me, clearly, is that a new general manager may not want me. Who knows? Usually the manager hires a coach. I don't have any answers, really."

Quinn pondered a potential breach of his contract and could not escape the sickly notion that he'd been used as a pawn in Dryden's quest to gain board approval for ousting Smith. The Maple Leaf president appeared to have been caught in a blatant fib when he told reporters that Quinn had been consulted throughout the process, to the point of discussing potential replacements. Dryden allegedly pacified his detractors on the board by claiming that Quinn was completely on side.

"That can't be true," Quinn flatly stated. "Ken called me late last week to say there'd been some difficulty in the negotiations, but that was it. I was led to believe an agreement would materialize. Now that it hasn't, I'm not sure where it leaves me. There are a number of things that need to be discussed."

The verbal dispute intensified in Boston during the two-day journey for the '99 NHL draft — Friday and Saturday, June 25–26. And it made for an extremely busy couple of days for reporters covering the team. Quinn flew in from Toronto early on Friday, while Dryden went to Boston later in the morning. I was on the same Air Canada flight as Dryden, and after arriving at the Boston Back Bay Hilton shortly after 1 p.m., I called Quinn at the hotel where the Leaf contingent was staying — the Marriott Copley Place. Thankfully, the coach answered his phone and after some arm-twisting and cajoling, he agreed to meet with me for a follow-up interview. Inquiring as to his frame of mind on the Dryden-Smith demise — he'd had a night to sleep on it — Quinn assured me he was not about to soften his stance. If anything, his indignation had grown.

I basically sprinted a half-mile to the Marriott and called Quinn's room when I arrived. The coach met me by the lobby elevators five minutes later and our conversation quickly centered on the highly contentious property of this matter: Dryden's apparent misleading of Quinn, the Maple Leaf board and the media about Quinn's role and depth of knowledge in the Smith negotiations.

"There's no way I could have misinterpreted the situation," Quinn told me, repeating his claim from the previous night. "The last time I'd spoken to Ken, he mentioned that the negotiations weren't going smoothly. But I was firmly advised that the board of directors wanted the matter resolved, and that ultimately it would be. The next time I spoke to Ken — three or four days later — he told me that Mike was gone. There was no communication between us before the final decision was made. And I suppose that's what bothers me."

Again, Quinn was essentially calling Dryden a liar. It was an implication the Leaf president would have to address — both privately and publicly. Quinn had become the focal point of the entire team, his popularity with Leaf fans commensurate with the club's 28-point ascent in the standings. To confound and alienate him would be abjectly stupid. Dryden's choice to jettison Smith had deprived Quinn of his chief ally, and the organization of its hockey point-man. The Maple Leaf president had grown reluctant to discuss the Smith issue, but there was no longer any way to avoid the tumult. He would have to explain his alleged deception of Quinn.

Including myself, there were nine hockey reporters from Toronto at the draft, and all of us wanted to speak with Dryden about the flourishing upheaval. The situation called for an organized get-together, and the Leafs' media relations manager, Pat Park, arranged for Dryden to be in the lobby of the Marriott early Friday evening. If the Maple Leaf president is anything, he's phlegmatic — able to create the illusion of stoicism when under attack. It's a quality that likely served him well during his playing days. And one that enabled him to fend off a volley of incriminating queries from the media horde in that Boston hotel lobby.

"This is typical off-season hysteria," he charged. "With not much else going on, there would be a lot of boredom to contend with."

It was poor strategy on Dryden's part. First of all, he was not going to succeed in having the media drop the story, which is what he desperately wanted. And secondly, there's no evidence to suggest that if the uprising had occurred in the middle of January, it would not have been gargantuan news around Toronto.

Pressed on the accusation of deceiving Quinn — and using that deception to sway his board of directors — Dryden slowly shook his head. "I never thought it was a problem," he said. "[Pat and I] spoke at some length a couple of times and all of it was brought up. We talked it through from beginning to end, in terms of where things stood, the fact they were uncertain, and that it may not work out."

Exactly the claim Quinn was so hotly disputing.

Of course, had Dryden chosen to get ugly, he could have countered by pointing out that Quinn's NHL slate was not exactly spotless. Back in the 1986–87 season, his third as coach of the Los Angeles Kings, Quinn made a clandestine arrangement with his Smythe Division foes in Vancouver. He accepted an under-the-table advance of $100,000 to become GM and coach of the Canucks the following season, when his

L.A. contract expired (the episode became known as "Quinngate"). It was a blatant act of tampering by Vancouver and a dishonorable, unscrupulous move by Quinn, particularly in light of the fact the Kings and Canucks were battling for one of the final playoff spots in '87 (L.A. edged out Vancouver by four points). Substantial fines were levied by NHL president John Zeigler, and Quinn — though allowed to join the Canucks as GM — was banned from coaching the team until the 1990–91 season.

Dryden refrained from any mudslinging, even though his motives came under heavy suspicion the moment he fired Smith. What those who were critical of him — including myself — failed to acknowledge is that he was perfectly within his rights to divest himself of someone he believed he could no longer work with. Like it or not, he is president of the hockey team and has the autonomy to decide such matters. Additionally — as you read on — you'll discover that Smith is no choirboy.

But Dryden generated incredulity and distrust on several counts. His unprincipled handling of Mike Murphy convinced some that he simply lacked any form of people-relations skill. A number of those in the Leaf office would talk secretly about his apparent thirst for power and control, though — as mentioned — any sum of control he wished to assert was his prerogative. But more than anything else, there were charges that Dryden simply did not have a feel for running a hockey office after being out of the game for 18 years.

From my perspective, Dryden had been a success at every one of his known pursuits:

- He was an outstanding goalkeeper for the great Montreal Canadiens teams of the 1970s. His stunning ascent to stardom with the '71 Habs — whom he backstopped to a Stanley Cup — is still marveled at a generation later.
- He'd studied for and acquired a law degree during his playing days.
- The book he wrote on his final season in the NHL — *The Game* — is universally recognized as hockey's finest literary work.
- It was Dryden who paired with ABC broadcaster Al Michaels during telecasts of hockey games at the 1980 Winter Olympics in Lake Placid. No one was closer to Michaels when he uttered his now-famous, "Do you believe in miracles . . . YES!!" as the U.S.A. men's team locked up an improbable gold medal.

Furthermore, during his first two years as president of the Maple Leafs, Dryden showed poignant versatility in handling a couple of dissimilar issues.

He shrewdly engineered the movement to have the Toronto franchise returned to the Eastern Conference for the 1998–99 season, four years earlier than the league's original blueprint. In this idea, Dryden foresaw a precipitous reduction in travel costs, the televising of many more Leaf road games in the eastern time slot (thus generating increased advertising revenue), and lastly (though it was most prominently touted), the re-establishment of dormant geographic rivalries with Montreal, Buffalo and Boston.

Realignment had traditionally been an arduous task for the NHL, but Dryden got the deed done practically overnight. And he did so in classic Dryden fashion. When the NHL governors asked him why they should vote to fast-track his club to the East, Dryden simply replied, "Why not?" The awkward silence and dumbfounded expressions that followed cinched the deal.

Dryden also reacted with noteworthy compassion to the grievous Maple Leaf Gardens sex scandal that became public early in 1997, several months before he was hired. On the heels of an horrific story revealed by NHL player Sheldon Kennedy — who, in January of '97, indicted his former junior coach, Graham James, for years of sexual abuse — a tormented ex-Gardens' employee, Martin Kruze, came forth with charges of a similar nature. Kruze alleged that a number of youthful workers in the building had been sexually violated through much of the previous generation. Three perpetrators, one of them deceased, have since been implicated in the atrocity, and Kruze — tragically — committed suicide less than a year after bearing his painful recollections by throwing himself off the Bloor viaduct, an elevated main-street overpass and subway-train corridor that rises above Toronto's Don valley.

The regime of Gardens chairman Steve Stavro reacted to the Kruze revelations with callous self-defence, its public statements designed solely to absolve the company of any legal culpability. Even the Maple Leafs' GM at the time — Cliff Fletcher — an otherwise respected and highly principled man, was reluctantly forced to toe the party line.

When Dryden arrived, he dedicated much of his energy to healing the open wounds. Clearly repulsed by the matter, his impassioned words bore no lawyerly significance — just tender, kindhearted sympathy for the victims and their families. He was the only Maple Leaf executive to attend Kruze's funeral and he later organized and took part in an open forum at the Gardens designed to create awareness for sexual-abuse victims. It was a proactive stance that showed Dryden's humane substance, and the Kruze family will never forget his heartfelt kindness.

Dryden has hosted several meaningful and highly acclaimed television documentaries. *The Home Game* — a thought-provoking examination of hockey as a Canadian staple — was brilliantly narrated, as was a 20-year reflection on the 1972 Canada-Russia hockey summit (Dryden was in net for Canada the day Paul Henderson scored the legendary series-winning goal in Moscow). Various levels of government have retained Dryden to investigate and report on hockey issues.

The Maple Leafs' mid-week telecasts took on an added dimension when Dryden strove to create a more intimate profile. Veteran producer Mark Askin left his long-time post at *Hockey Night In Canada* to work with Dryden, and he absolutely swears by the Leaf president.

"Ken's the greatest thing that ever happened to me, and to the fans who watch the Maple Leafs on TV," Askin says. "He has a great passion for television and believes it's the ultimate tool in marketing and creating awareness about the product. To Ken, the Toronto Maple Leafs are the New York Yankees of hockey and he will not stand for anything but the very best broadcast.

"I'll never forget a meeting we had prior to his first season as president. Though he admitted he hadn't watched many games in the previous five years, he talked about the importance of isolating players and covering the game from a lower angle, all of it aimed at bringing more of an intimacy to the telecast; more of an 'insider's' view. I sat there thinking, 'This is my dream come true.' All of the elements he mentioned were things I'd tried to implement, but had always been rebuffed. None of my bosses understood it until Ken came along."

Dryden's innovations have included (as Askin pointed out) showing more of the live action from lower down, thus conveying the speed of the game; giving the viewing audience more close-ups of the players; and placing a stationary camera in a high corner of the dressing room for intermission and post-game shots (this practice was halted by Quinn, who felt it was inappropriate). Dryden has also permitted Maple Leaf players to be miked for sound during the action, their comments edited and played back during the ensuing intermission.

"The encouragement and the attention I get from Ken about the telecasts is unheard of," Askin says. "Most team presidents wouldn't give two shits what you put on the air, providing it isn't negative. And that's another thing. During one of our initial meetings, Harry Neale asked Ken, 'What do we say and how do we approach the analysis if things are not going well?' He looked at Harry and said, 'You call it as you see it.'

"Of course, the first year under Mike Murphy, the team didn't have many good nights and there was a fair amount of criticism on the telecasts. But I can honestly tell you we never heard a peep of protest from Ken. To me, he's an absolute delight to work for and has given us the capacity to try and make the Maple Leaf telecasts the best in the business."

But none of this seemed to impress Harry Sinden when I spoke with him about Dryden in Boston the day before the '99 draft. The veteran Bruins GM and longest-serving hockey executive in the NHL held Mike Smith in high regard and couldn't fathom why Dryden would let him go. When I pointed out to Sinden that Dryden had prospered at practically all of his ventures, he grew indignant.

"What's he done?" Sinden asked incredulously. "I remember him being a good player in the NHL, and if you liked his book, I guess he was a good author. Other than that, he was out of the game for a long time and he's been fooling around at his current job for a couple of years. I'm surprised at the move he made because [Mike] Smith is a guy who knows what he's doing. He can answer to the essence of a general manager's job — who can play in the NHL and who can't. I'm not sure there's anyone else over there who can do that."

* * *

Though often linked by their perceived levels of intellect, Ken Dryden and Mike Smith were the absolute personification of oil and water.

Dryden is a conservative man — a lawyer by trade — who painstakingly measures his words, and speaks in rambling, protracted sentences, often using language that begs for a nearby dictionary. He dresses well, is usually amicable, but has grown decreasingly accessible to the media in his role as the Maple Leafs' president and (now former) general manager. When pressed on a matter, he tends to laugh nervously, then either issue a benign wisecrack or an answer that requires great imagination to comprehend.

While he appears calm and poised in most situations (who can forget how Dryden the goalie casually leaned on the top of his goalstick during breaks in the action), Dryden the hockey executive does have a boiling point; a competitive fire that can quickly become evident. When discussing a subject that irritates him — denying a report, for instance — his voice rises, his neck-veins bulge, and he becomes notably animated. He is an absolute bundle of tightly wound nerves while watching his Leafs play from the press box, and that is the only similarity he shared with Smith. Dryden will fiercely slam the palm of his hand on the table he's sitting at when the Leafs fumble a scoring opportunity. While in public, however, his conservative nature usually prevails.

Smith, conversely, is a rebel — a middle-aged hippie. A non-conformist of the highest order. His manner of speech is the polar opposite of Dryden's, often summing up his thoughts flatly, unemotionally, and with a minimum of words, as if under the influence of a calming agent. He is, however, much more direct than his former boss, and therefore easier to deal with from a media standpoint (though I'll probably get an argument or two on that one).

Smith possesses what many would define, in polite terms, a "quirky" personality, and is extremely difficult to gain a read on. He seems to revel in the fact that he's perceived to be different, and the more you may look at him like he's crazy, the more unconventionally he'll behave.

During his years with the Leafs, when asked to comment on information about the hockey club that might be accurate, he'd clam up rather than deceive. "I can't say anything about that," he'd often reply, which in many ways, was an answer in itself. Rather than planting himself for hours behind a cluttered desk — wearing a starched-up suit — Smith would occasionally work from a side-chair in his Spartan office, classical music scores emanating from a compact disc unit. Abundant greenery added to the earthy environment.

Throughout his tenure in Toronto, he was frequently mocked for his dress habits and unkempt appearance. Many of us have rolled out of bed first thing in the morning with hair more neatly coifed than Smith's at mid-day. His shirts often appeared baggy and messily tucked and he practically always loosened his tie, when he had one on. Nonetheless, it was a mystery why this became the focal point of anyone's reporting during the hockey season, though in relation to his counterparts around the league, Smith did invite such observations.

Unlike many of his colleagues in hockey management, he refrained from building chummy relations with the media, and never betrayed a trust in order to divulge inside information (at least, not for my benefit). Without fail, and in any circumstance, however, Smith returned phone calls from reporters, another manner in which he differed from Dryden.

There is also a purportedly dark side to Mike Smith, one that former hockey executive John Ferguson claims to have witnessed. In the 1976–77 season, Ferguson, the ex-Montreal Canadiens pugilist from the 1960s, was GM of the New York Rangers. He saw fit to hire Smith (a Syracuse University graduate) as an assistant coach specializing in conditioning and player development. When Ferguson moved on to the GM's role with the Winnipeg Jets in their inaugural NHL season (1979–80), he re-hired Smith to oversee the club's Central Hockey League affiliate in Tulsa, Oklahoma.

Smith later advanced in the Jets organization to become Ferguson's chief aide and assistant GM from 1985 to '88. At that point, and depending on whom you ask, Smith was said to initiate a corporate end-around that ultimately led to Ferguson's dismissal. The former Hab claimed that Smith and *Winnipeg Free Press* hockey writer Reyn Davis conspired to have him ousted, and believes he's been slowly pulling the shiv out of his back ever since.

Ferguson outlined his theory in his 1989 autobiography *Thunder and Lightning*, co-written with Stan and Shirley Fischler:

It's no secret that the Winnipeg Jets had their ups and downs. We were up there in 1981–82, '84–85 and '86–87. I believed we could straighten things out [in '88] but what I didn't bargain for was the behind the back shenanigans of my assistant, Mike Smith.

This was the very same Smith I'd hired for special assignments with the Rangers. This is the Smith whom I spent ten years grooming, only to get a knife in the back. I should've gotten a clue about Smith way back in the New York days. Mike was brought to my attention by a fellow named Ed Enos [*later to be athletic director at Concordia University*], who'd been working on conditioning with the Rangers. A year after we hired Smith, Mike was the one who made it quite clear that he didn't need the services of Ed Enos anymore.

Over the years, my trusted aides Charlie Hodge and Les Binkley would warn me to watch out for Smith — that he had the power of persuasion and that he had Shenkarow's ear [*Barry Shenkarow was owner of the Jets*]. I told them the last one I'm worried about is Barry Shenkarow; I trusted Barry but had come to realize that Smith was a detriment to the Jets organization. "Barry," I said, "we have one problem here and it's Smith. I have to replace him."

I knew that Mike was trying to get the GM job in Minnesota after Lou Nanne had moved up to the presidency [of the North Stars]. He didn't get the job and the rest is history. We started the '88-89 season and before October was over, Reyn Davis wrote a scathing column about me, full of lies. I had never before phoned a hockey writer to complain about a story [*a claim others scoff at*], but this time I felt I had no choice, and I told Davis exactly what I thought about him and his article.

Not long after that, I was history as general manager of the Jets. Shenkarow orchestrated the whole deal with the help of Smith and Davis. After ten years on the job, I was fired less than a month into the new season. You figure it out: if they liked me in the spring, how come they suddenly didn't like me in the fall?

To put it mildly, the episode left me with an absolute bitter taste in my mouth, especially as regards the work of Smith and Davis. It was Shenkarow's team and he could do what he wanted with it. He did. What I had to do is pick up the pieces and get my life back together.

I stewed when I thought about the Shenkarow-Smith scenario.

I'd recall how one week Smith would say something and a week later, Shenkarow would come in and say the same thing. I said to myself, "Jesus Christ, what's going on here?"

Smith survived the bloodletting, replaced Ferguson, and managed the Jets until his own dismissal midway through the 1993–94 season.

To this day, both Smith and Reyn Davis thoroughly dispute Ferguson's charges and believe he suffered an acute attack of paranoia and virulence. Davis remembers writing the column Ferguson referred to in his book, but he insists he does not recall any covert action by Smith designed to overthrow Ferguson.

"That theory is all wet," says the 56-year-old Davis, now retired. "Fergy was a folk hero in Montreal, but in Winnipeg, he was a ham sandwich. There were a lot of people in that city who didn't like his kind of hockey. He tried to mold a team in his own image — rough and tough. You have to look no further than the '79 entry draft. Look who Fergy took and look at the players who were still available to him."

Ferguson selected Jimmy Mann, a bellicose right-winger with almost indiscernible skills, in the first round, 19th overall. Indeed, the following players were among those he could have chosen: Michel Goulet, Mats Naslund, Neal Broten and Mark Messier (!). It must be pointed out, however, that Ferguson's selection of Dale Hawerchuk as the No. 1 overall pick the following summer set the Winnipeg franchise on a course of prosperity for more than half a decade.

"I always found Mike Smith to be forthright," recalls Davis. "Even Mike wasn't the darling of Winnipeg fans, but he brought a different, more modern approach to the game than Fergy. He had an appreciation of European players, and he foresaw the influence they were about to have on the game. Fergy never meshed with him in that regard; he even acknowledged that, and his romance with Winnipeg didn't last very long."

When reminded of Ferguson's 1989 book statements, Smith reacts with emotions ranging from apathy to agitation. He claims he heard a story that the lawyers for the publishing company were astounded when reading Ferguson's comments, believing them to be textbook defamation of character. And that they insisted the allegations be toned down.

"I have two things to say about John Ferguson," Smith begins, ominously. "When he got fired from New York [in 1977–78], he was so angry that he asked Tom Savage and me to 'throw' the draft [*Savage was the Rangers' director of player personnel*]. To make bad picks. I told him, 'C'mon, John, I feel badly about you being fired but I still work for the Rangers and I've got to do what's best for them.' And in the mid-'80s, when his assistant GM Mike Doran was in a coma for three-and-a-half years, John never once went to see him.

"That's basically all you have to know about John Ferguson the person."

Doran never regained full consciousness (though he lay in an eerie silence with his eyes open) after wrapping his car around a tree while en route to Peterborough, Ontario, to scout a Junior A game. He passed away in 1987.

As part of his alleged powerplay to overthrow Ferguson in Winnipeg, Smith was said to have gained the ear of Shenkarow by insisting he could operate the Jets on a tighter budget. Ferguson had always been a free spender and Shenkarow often admonished him to cut down. One story claims that just before he was fired, Ferguson chartered a limousine to take the entire Jets NHL staff from New York to New Haven, Connecticut, for an AHL game involving the club's Sherbrooke farm team.

Smith claims that wasn't true but when asked if he betrayed Ferguson's loyalty to him, he says, "Not a chance. I had nothing to do with John getting fired in Winnipeg. The only guy in the organization he trusted was me. I was watching Sherbrooke play a game in Rochester when I found out he'd been let go. They paged me over the P.A. system to come to the main office of the arena. The Jets were going to New York and New Jersey for their next two games and I was 100 percent positive it was John on the line telling me to bring [farm team goalie] Daniel Berthiaume to New York. But there was a message to call the office and I was told, instead, that they had fired John.

"I hung up and immediately called John. He simply asked me if I was taking over [as GM] and I said I didn't know anything about that; I'd just heard that he'd been fired. The next day, he began spewing the venom at me."

Smith claims that some months later, Ferguson sent a friend named Ted Foreman to him as a "peace emissary" — an attempt to bury the hatchet. Smith flatly refused the overture.

"John's problem was that he grew to despise anyone who was going to take his job," Smith continues. "He hated Fred Shero to his grave, because Shero became the Rangers' GM when John was fired. I used to tell Mike Doran that if John ever left or got fired, he'd be given the Jets GM job. And Mike would say, 'That's great. Then I'll have John hating me forever.' It's just the way John was. He was a hateful person.

"But I will admit that a lot of what I've learned in hockey came from John; how the business runs, how to look at young players, any number of things. I've never denied that."

* * *

Smith's 5½-year reign in Winnipeg was mediocre, at best. The Jets twice missed the playoffs and were eliminated in the opening round the other two years. When he was fired by Barry Shenkarow on January 19, 1994 — and replaced by John Paddock — the Jets were on their way to a disastrous record of 24-51-9, the 51 losses representing the second-most in franchise history for one season.

Smith's years running the Jets were marked by the same controversies that have dogged him — fairly or not — throughout his hockey career: an intractable, single-minded approach to his work; a general inability to work with and warm to anyone outside his tight inner sanctum; an insatiable yearning for power, manifested by the alleged disparagement of co-workers behind closed doors; and an absolute fixation on prospects of Russian descent.

The Jets' drafting record during his years ranged from impressive to comical. His first-round picks in the five drafts between 1989 and '93 were as follows: Stu Barnes (No. 4 overall in '89), Keith Tkachuk (No. 19 in '90), Aaron Ward (No. 5 in '91), Sergei Bautin (No. 17 in '92) and Mats Lindgren (No. 15 in '93). The latter three proved to be terrible choices, compounded by hindsight in the form of players still available when they were selected.

Ward, for instance, was chosen one pick ahead of Peter Forsberg — the best two-way player in the world today. For someone presumably up to speed on the Russian hockey landscape, Smith completely overlooked Dynamo Riga defenceman Sandis Ozolinsh in '91 (as did others; Ozolinsh wasn't drafted until the second round, 30th overall). Czech winger Zigmund Palffy was also there for the taking (the Islanders chose him 26th overall). Ward never played a game for the Jets and was traded by Smith to Detroit for Paul Ysebaert in June 1993. Upon the completion of the 1998–99 season, he had a total of 11 goals in 167 NHL games, all with the Red Wings.

The selection of Bautin in '92 was a total waste. Future stars Martin Straka and Michael Peca were still available, and Bautin quickly became just another blip on the hockey horizon, scoring a grand total of five goals in 132 NHL games with Winnipeg, Detroit and San Jose. Smith recovered somewhat in the second round of that draft by choosing defenceman Boris Mironov, but he was long gone from the Winnipeg scene by the time Mironov began to develop into an effective NHLer (having been traded to Edmonton two months after Smith's departure).

Mats Lindgren was part of that deal with the Oilers, made by Paddock. By choosing Lindgren in '93, Smith passed on several players who developed into solid pros, most notably Jason Allison, selected two picks later by Washington. Saku

Koivu, Jamie Langenbrunner, Janne Niinimaa and Bryan McCabe were also up for grabs when Lindgren went to Winnipeg.

During his five entry drafts at the helm of the Jets, Smith made a total of 63 selections. A full one-third of those draft choices were Russian-born players, most of whom were never again heard of once their names were called out on the draft floor. In '92 and '93, Smith went wild, choosing 16 Russians out of 25 total picks. Among them: Alexei Budayev, Ruslan Batyrshin, Ravil Gusmanov, Alexander Alexeyev, Artur Oktyabrev and Ivan Vologzhaninov. Broadcasting nightmares that never materialized.

Like most stories, however, there is a flip side. In 1990, Smith drafted Tkachuk in the first round and unearthed Alexi Zhamnov 77th overall. He came up with Igor Ulanov with the 203rd selection of the '91 draft. Nikolai Khabibulin followed in '92 as the 204th overall choice. Michal Grosek went No. 145 in '93. A nucleus of Barnes, Tkachuk, Zhamnov, Ulanov, Mironov, Khabibulin and Teemu Selanne (who John Ferguson selected in '88) would've more than likely become a formidable team — a point that Smith has frequently argued. Then again, can you imagine a team comprised of Forsberg, Palffy, Ozolinsh, Peca, Allison, Koivu, Niinimaa, Langenbrunner and McCabe — players Smith passed on? Hindsight is always impeccable, and few general managers make multiple good calls at the draft table, but reflection does offer evidence why Smith experienced limited prosperity during his years in command of the Jets.

Smith has also maintained a small posse of right-hand men, all of whom are competent. But they have been viewed suspiciously, and occasionally have been ridiculed for their ardent loyalty towards him. Three such individuals remained with the Maple Leafs after Smith was axed by Dryden.

Assistant coach Alpo Suhonen held the same position with Winnipeg in the 1989–90 and '92–93 seasons, and will forever be linked to an insensitive, albeit hilarious remark made by Don Cherry on his "Coach's Corner" segment. When Ron MacLean initially mentioned Suhonen's name to Cherry during a *Hockey Night In Canada* telecast in '92, Cherry said, "Alpo? Isn't that a dog food?" The Finnish-born Suhonen is recognized as a brilliant, multi-faceted individual, who has coached his country's national hockey team and has dabbled in European politics. He has a keen sense of offensive creativity, and was most certainly a vital component in the Maple Leafs' goalscoring enhancement of 1998–99.

But Pat Quinn could hardly recall Suhonen's name when Smith proposed that he consider the Finn for a second assistant coaching slot. Quinn had already hired one of *his* long-time cronies, Rick Ley, and was plotting to lure good friend Bob McCammon away from the Edmonton Oilers. Ultimately, Quinn acceded to Smith's request and interviewed Suhonen, whom he found to be both qualified and compatible. Alpo was hired on August 26, 1998.

About the only drawback to Suhonen was his thick Scandinavian accent. Most of the Leaf players warmed to him almost immediately, but were often seen cocking their heads in puzzlement when he spoke to them during practice. He was particularly difficult to understand when he had to bark out instructions. One day at Maple Leaf Gardens, Mats Sundin skated over to the boards, smiling, after one of Suhonen's commands. "I don't know what he just said, but it's working," the captain laughed.

Suhonen is very well-liked and respected, but will probably return to his native land after the 1999–2000 NHL season.

Another Smith ally is New England–born Joe Yannetti, the Maple Leafs' director of player evaluation. Smith hired him in Winnipeg as assistant director of scouting in 1989 — a position Yannetti maintained through the transfer of the Jets franchise to Phoenix in '96. Smith brought him to Toronto a year later, and he relied strongly on Yannetti's appraisals of talent at the amateur and pro levels. Yannetti was frequently dispatched around the NHL to evaluate players the Leafs were considering as trade material (e.g., Mikael Renberg in the Potvin saga).

I talked with Joe at the Leafs' hotel in Boston during the '99 NHL draft, two days after Smith had been jettisoned by Dryden. The man looked sad, and justifiably so. "I feel badly this has happened; Mike has been so good to me and has taught me so much about the game of hockey," Yannetti said. "But I have no hesitation about staying with the Leafs. Mike always said to be loyal to the organization you work for, and that's what I'll do. He wouldn't want me to do anything different."

The third member of Smith's coterie is Phil Walker, the Leafs' strength and conditioning coach, whose career path is almost identical to Yannetti's. The 33-year-old Newfoundlander also joined Winnipeg during Smith's first season as GM, coming aboard as assistant athletic trainer. Like Yannetti, Walker remained with the organization through its transfer to Phoenix, but the parallelism hit a speed-bump after that.

Smith attempted to hire Walker in Toronto for the 1997–98 season but was met with vehement opposition by head coach Mike Murphy. The Leafs already had two of the most respected athletic therapists in hockey, Chris Broadhurst and Brent Smith, whose roles encompassed strength and conditioning. Neither man was at all enthused about the addition of Walker, and Murphy put up enough of a challenge on their behalf that Walker was assigned to St. John's. He joined the Maple Leafs the following season.

The story is somewhat sad in that Walker is an extremely likable fellow, and perfectly qualified to handle his role, with a Bachelor's degree in physical education. But

Smith's perceived cronyism placed Walker in a difficult spot. The Toronto players shared an intense loyalty with Broadhurst and Brent Smith, and a number of them viewed Walker's hiring with bafflement and suspicion. What could he provide that the incumbents could not? And was he part of their scene purely because of his long-term alliance with Mike Smith?

In Philadelphia one day during the '99 playoffs, Pat Quinn got the players together in one of the hotel meeting rooms and said they were going to have an off-ice conditioning session. "Oh, we can't do that, Phil Walker's not here," came a sarcastic reply from the back of the room. Walker traveled with the team to all its road games and spent the vast majority of his idle time with the coaching staff (as per his title). While he did work closely with the players, he often seemed like an outsider, and appeared uncomfortable around the team. He was a victim of circumstance more than anything else, and he assuredly deserved better.

* * *

When Smith's two-year contract with the Maple Leafs dissipated — and his thirst for the full GM's duties intensified — a bevy of John Ferguson–type charges began flying his way. Like he'd done in Winnipeg 11 years earlier, Smith was alleged to be scheming to displace the man who had hired him. But just like with Ferguson, he flatly denies initiating any covert action in Toronto.

"People say I pulled a powerplay on Ken, but that's not true," he claimed after his firing. "It was a powerplay between Ken and Richard Peddie. I was just the tennis ball being pounded back and forth. In the end, Ken offered me a job that had almost no authority at all. Every decision I made would have to be fully approved by him, and no general manager worth his salt would agree to that.

"Ken's ego was so out of whack, he couldn't control himself. We worked out a contract that called for Pat to report to the person in charge of hockey decisions, and that was me," Smith claims. "At least, at the time it was. But Ken began assuming more of that authority as the season progressed, and I don't think Pat was happy with that arrangement."

As Smith indicated, the Dryden-Peddie tandem is also one that's been less than genial since the latter came aboard in March 1998, for Dryden believes Peddie was forced on him. Having fashioned a solid business reputation in his role as CEO of the Stadium Corporation of Ontario (which operates SkyDome) Peddie was hired, ostensibly, to oversee the Leafs-Raptors-Air Canada Centre transition. But as president of the umbrella company, he automatically became Dryden's superior.

The day after Peddie was appointed, the Maple Leafs were in Anaheim, and Dryden was having a particularly rotten few hours. During the afternoon, he sat in the lobby of the Westin Southcoast Plaza — the team hotel — and was grilled by the Toronto media contingent over the club's failure in his first season as president and GM. *Sun* columnist Al Strachan was notably aggressive, putting on a show and making valid points — though many of his questions could just have easily been raised in the privacy of a one-on-one telephone conversation.

While eating dinner a few hours later in the media lounge at the Arrowhead Pond, Dryden swallowed hard and disgustingly shook his head in defiance when asked if he would now have to clear hockey decisions through Peddie, who had no experience in the game. Only a 3-1 victory by the Leafs over the Mighty Ducks was able to salvage a portion of his day.

Dryden's choice in the late summer of 1997 to form a three-headed managerial pyramid became the crux of all the front-office mutiny. His earlier intentions were far different, but they failed to materialize. Named as president of the Maple Leafs in May of '97, and entrusted with the chore of hiring a general manager to succeed Cliff Fletcher, Dryden failed in his efforts at luring at least two men to the position.

As recounted earlier, Bob Gainey, a teammate of Dryden's on the Montreal Stanley Cup dynasty in the late '70s, politely refused the job, not desiring to leave his managerial construction of the Dallas Stars in mid-stream. He was also, at the time, dealing with severe personal issues, including the tragic death of his wife, Cathy, from brain cancer, and the consequential drug addiction of one of his daughters. As outlined, Dryden was so determined to try and free Gainey from his contract with Dallas that he offered the Stars — as compensation — Schneider, the Leafs' only front-line defenceman. But the timing was all wrong.

Dryden later held serious discussions with David Poile, a respected career hockey man who had recently been dismissed by the Washington Capitals after an unspectacular 15-year term as that club's general manager. Poile considered the Toronto job but chose, instead, to become executive vice-president/GM of the expansion Nashville Predators, which completed its inaugural NHL season in 1998–99.

Dryden also interviewed veteran hockey man John Muckler, and how ironic that seems in light of what ultimately transpired in Toronto. Muckler had been fired as GM of the Buffalo Sabres after a bitter feud with coach Ted Nolan, who was also terminated. Nolan was said to have elevated backstabbing to an art form never previously witnessed, and he and Muckler rapidly developed a relationship eerily similar to that of Dryden and Smith's.

Long-time Edmonton Oilers president and GM Glen Sather was frequently consulted by Dryden for advice and direction, and may have briefly discussed assuming the Toronto position himself. During their playing careers, Sather and Dryden were teammates for one season in Montreal (1974–75) and they struck up a long-standing, if odd, friendship (the sardonic Sather revels in poking fun at his erudite counterpart). Sather recommended Smith for the Maple Leaf job (some say as a practical joke) and remained in Edmonton.

With training camp for the 1997–98 season fast approaching, Dryden suspended his fruitless search and formed an ill-fated committee to run the hockey team. He anointed himself general manager (an explanation for which he presents later on); committed the blunder of placing antagonists Smith and Hedberg alongside one another in the hockey department — Smith as associate GM, Hedberg as assistant GM — and retained Bill Watters from the Fletcher regime as assistant to the president (in charge of contract negotiations and the St. John's farm team). There were shorter assembly lines at General Motors, but time was of the essence.

After an interminable wait, it was also confirmed that Mike Murphy would continue to coach the team in the final year of his contract, which turned out to be a grave error by Dryden. It had little to do with Murphy's capabilities (though he failed to guide the Leafs into the playoffs in his two seasons at the helm) and much to do with a singular lack of support for the man Cliff Fletcher had brought on board a year earlier. No one would personify the term "lame duck" to a greater, and more tragic, degree.

Murphy dutifully remained on the job at his Maple Leaf Gardens office throughout the summer of '97, completely unsure of his status for the coming season; a genuine afterthought in the minds of his new employer. He was kept in the dark on team matters, claiming to garner his only information from daily media dispatches. When it was announced, for instance, that Gainey would not accept Dryden's offer to manage the team, I stopped by Murphy's office for an off-the-record chat. But neither Murphy nor his assistants — Mike Kitchen and Terry Simpson — were remotely aware of the position Gainey had clarified with Dryden the previous night. What great communication, I thought.

Not surprisingly, the Maple Leafs endured a disastrous '97–98 season.

Clearly dying on the vine, Murphy tried to manufacture a brave front, but never allowed himself to be deceived by his situation. I'll not soon forget how he conveyed his anxieties to me as we sat in the lobby of the Ritz Carlton Hotel in Phoenix. It was late November — less than two months into the season — but the writing was on the wall. This would be a year of personnel assessment under a coach that played no long-term role in the process. Roster adjustments would be reserved for the following term, subsequent to the hiring of a compatible mentor — one current to the new managerial regime.

Worst of all, the players knew it. As I stretched my legs during the long flight back from that game in Phoenix, several of them called me over to spill their guts. They ached for Murphy, whose credibility had been obliterated. And they wondered aloud how they'd endure the bulk of a season that simply didn't matter. It was a dreadful circumstance, created by immature, loutish management.

The Maple Leafs' final road trip of the lost campaign was a mid-April journey through western Canada. During the first intermission of the season finale in Vancouver — and mindful of the nightmare Murphy had endured the previous off-season — I interviewed Dryden on his immediate plans for the hockey club. I had been told, second hand, that an official pronouncement of Murphy's status would follow within two weeks, and Dryden confirmed my information. "If not in two weeks, then shortly after that," were his exact words.

When two weeks became three . . . then four, I met with Dryden in his Maple Leaf Gardens office and was told — with no explanation — that the time-frame had been extended. Less than a week later, I received a phone call from an inside source who informed me that Murphy had been given the corporate deep-six at a recent board meeting (the validation of a verdict reached two months earlier), but that no public acknowledgment was on the immediate horizon. Presuming that Murphy had been somehow apprised of his impending doom, I called him at home for a reaction and was horrified to discover that he knew absolutely nothing about it. The bewilderment and alarm in his voice assured me that he wasn't covering for anyone; he simply hadn't been informed (another example of the communication chasm that existed with his employers). Feeling like a bag of shit, I apologized to him profusely.

But my source calmly reassured me that the deed had been done behind closed doors, and I reported my findings on the air. Predictably, they were met with blanket denials from Dryden in newspaper accounts the following day.

It soon became known to insiders that the Leafs were in a clandestine hunt for Marc Crawford, who was hotly rumored to be on the outs with Pierre Lacroix, his general manager in Colorado. Accordingly, in the third week of May, Crawford split ranks with the club he'd guided to the 1996 Stanley Cup, explaining that he had rebuffed a contract extension from Lacroix. But with a year still left on his initial deal, the Avalanche countered that Crawford remained under its employ, and the club would seek prodigious compensation if he were to join another team.

Within days, however, Lacroix promoted Bob Hartley from Colorado's American Hockey League affiliate in Hershey, and handed him Crawford's old job.

Immediately, Crawford and his representatives claimed that such action voided his contract, granting him total free-agency status. The Avalanche begged to differ and the matter was sent for investigation and resolution to the office of NHL commissioner Gary Bettman.

Dryden, meanwhile, was obviously in no position to discuss the Maple Leaf coaching conundrum with any degree of sincerity. Tampering penalties in the NHL are prohibitive and while there was no evidence to suggest he had contacted Crawford, his intentions had become rather apparent. Particularly in view of the fact he could offer no reasonable explanation for prolonging Murphy's uncertainty. "We're waiting for the landscape around the league to become more clear before deciding on our direction," was Dryden's vague response.

As the situation dragged on, Dryden became increasingly hesitant to address the issue. And it put a strain on my already tenuous relationship with the Maple Leaf president. Returning on June 1, 1998, from a 17-day vacation in Los Angeles — and with Murphy's fate still unannounced — I tried to arrange a short interview with Dryden, whom I hadn't spoken to in four weeks. Several calls to his secretary, Ann Clark, were fruitless, producing a bevy of banal excuses as to why even an abbreviated get-together could not be arranged. Sensing the old brush-off, I abandoned my attempt at due process and learned that Dryden would be at the Gardens for a meeting in the director's lounge early on the afternoon of June 3. It seemed to be my only chance.

I drove down to MLG and checked to see if Dryden was in his office. Clark told me he was having lunch outside the building, and she wasn't sure if and when he'd be coming back. But apprised of his scheduled meeting, I walked across to the west side of the arena and waited outside the director's lounge — with some apprehension. I figured Dryden would be less than thrilled to come upon me, but felt I was merely doing my job.

Several moments later, the Leaf president appeared at the far end of the corridor, walking in from the Wood St. entrance. If looks could indeed kill, I might not have been dead, but certainly on life support. Stating the obvious, I informed Dryden that I wanted a minute of his time, and he replied, derisively, "Yeah, Howard, I know what *your* minutes are like." Suppressing the urge to say, "Look who's talking," I asked Dryden, flatly, about his pursuit of Marc Crawford, knowing I would not receive a direct answer.

"Marc Crawford is under contract to another team, so I can't talk to him, or about him," Dryden correctly responded.

I then pressed Dryden on why he was again putting Murphy through hell, when it appeared obvious that he had no intentions of retaining the coach (a determination he'd long ago made). It was now more than six weeks since the end of the regular season, and roughly four weeks since Dryden had initially promised to announce Murphy's fate. While I endeavor to separate reporting from emotions whenever possible, this fiasco was starting to grate on my nerves. "If he's your coach, why don't you just say so — he obviously wants to keep the job," I inquired. "If you're looking elsewhere [*which he was*], why not let Murph get on with his life?"

It was an unwelcome line of questioning that prompted more appeals of patience from Dryden. But no answers.

Thanking him for his time, I felt obliged to explain, first-hand, what Dryden already knew — that I had tried on several occasions to arrange this session with Ann Clark, but had gotten nowhere. It was an opening the Leaf president seemed to be waiting for.

"You know, I don't understand this," he said. "There are all kinds of things going on in sports these days; the Stanley Cup finals [between Detroit and Washington] are about to begin; how important can this issue possibly be?"

Explaining, again, what I felt he already knew, I mentioned that — in Toronto — the Maple Leafs supersede any form of news in the hockey world.

"The sports fans of this city want to know what's going on with your team more than anything else, combined," I replied.

Dryden shook his head and said, "No, it's what *you* want to know," implying that I was chasing some form of personal glory by hounding him. He then rudely waved me off and walked into the director's lounge.

I shrugged and turned to leave, when I encountered Dan Wilkinson, the Maple Leafs' manager of event personnel, and a fellow I'd come to know around the building.

"Howard, you know better than to ambush a guy like that," he said.

Ambush? It's hardly like I sprung out from the nearby stairwell and pounced on Dryden. He clearly saw me standing outside the lounge from the opposite end of the corridor, and the fact it may have perturbed the Leaf boss wasn't high on my list of concerns.

"Just got a job to do, Dan," I said.

"I know it's your job, but I have to do mine as well," he replied, explaining his admonition.

The Marc Crawford vigil continued for another two weeks — an insufferable fortnight for Murphy. Finally, on the afternoon of June 19, Gary Bettman ruled that the former Colorado coach remained contractually bound to the Avalanche, and affixed him with the motherlode of compensation packages. It was a ponderous decree of escalating financial indemnities and draft-choice forfeitures that no team in its right mind would even consider — a blackballing of the highest order. To top it off, Colorado did not have to pay Crawford the final year of his deal. That the ex-coach chose not to combat the two-fisted ruling points to how desperately he wanted to rid himself of Pierre Lacroix's influence.

Meanwhile, it left the Maple Leafs in a temporary lurch. Crawford was the apple of their eye and no one had expected such a restrictive compensation edict. Former Philadelphia coach Terry Murray — whose reign ended when he accurately, but unwisely, said the Flyers had "choked" against Detroit in the 1997 Cup final — spoke briefly with Smith about the Toronto job, but was leaning towards joining the Florida Panthers, managed by his older brother, Bryan. He signed with the Cats two days later.

Devoid of any other serious candidates, the Maple Leafs were contacted by Flyers GM Bobby Clarke, who recommended they approach Quinn (Smith immediately endorsed the suggestion). A former Maple Leaf defenceman, Quinn was sitting at home in Vancouver, recovering from hip-replacement surgery, and collecting a million-dollar-a-year salary from the Canucks, which had fired him as GM the previous November. Clarke said that Quinn had all but rebounded from his operation and might be receptive to an inquiry. Quinn had been at the MCI Center in Washington the night Detroit won the '98 Stanley Cup (June 16), as a guest of Capitals GM George McPhee, his former assistant in Vancouver. He flew to Toronto the following day to attend the wedding of Cliff Fletcher's daughter, Kristy. Quinn played in Atlanta from 1972 to '77, when Fletcher was GM of the Flames, and the two had formed a close friendship.

Though he was entering his mid-50s — an age when coaches are not traditionally pursued — Quinn's credentials were enticing. He had twice guided teams to the Stanley Cup finals: in 1980 with Philadelphia and 1994 with Vancouver. The '79–80 Flyers, under Quinn, established an NHL regular-season record that may never be broken by fashioning a remarkable 35-game unbeaten streak. That club did not lose a hockey game between October 14, 1979, and January 6, 1980. Almost unthinkable. But the Flyers dropped the Cup final to the New York Islanders in six games on Bob Nystrom's now-famous overtime goal.

In the spring of '94, Quinn coached Vancouver to within a goalpost of playing overtime in Game 7 of the Cup final. Pavel Bure narrowly missed knotting the decisive match at Madison Square Garden, and the New York Rangers won their first championship in 54 years.

Though his appointment of rookie coach Tom Renney in 1996–97 had not garnered results, Quinn was deeply aggrieved by his dismissal in Vancouver. He had quarreled fiercely with that city's hockey media, forming a particular distaste for the

Vancouver Province's inciting columnist, Tony Gallagher. A sturdy and trusting bond with Arthur Griffiths — the owner who hired him — could not be maintained when multi-millionaire John McCaw and his Orca Bay group purchased the Canucks in 1994. Having endured painful rehabilitation from his hip surgery, there appeared to be two factors that would mitigate against Quinn returning to the game: his health and his state of mind. Was he fit enough to stand behind a bench for three hours a night, and did he possess the proper motivation to jump back into the fishbowl? The Leafs were sure interested in finding out.

Discovering that Quinn was in town for the Fletcher wedding, Smith contacted him by phone. On Friday, June 19 — the day Crawford's compensation ruling was announced — Smith met in his downtown-Toronto condominium with Quinn and Quinn's Atlanta-based lawyer, Dick Babush.

"I'd known Pat for a long time," Smith said. "When I was GM in Winnipeg, he was with Vancouver. Getting together that day in Toronto, I could immediately sense that he was interested in coaching the Maple Leafs. All it took was a bit of a selling job; a refresher course. He had played in the city many years before and I told him that nothing about the hockey atmosphere had changed. The depth of affection and interest among the fans was exactly as it always had been.

"Pat later told me that when he walked back to his hotel [the Eaton Centre Marriott] after our meeting, he was very excited about the whole thing."

Quinn went home to Vancouver and kept in touch with Smith over the phone. He returned on Wednesday of the following week and painstakingly negotiated a contract in meetings with Smith, Dryden and Babush. Smith could sense his own burgeoning conflict with Dryden and he had likely cautioned Quinn of the potential for a breakdown in the managerial pecking order. As a result, Quinn's contract talks centered not so much on money, but on how he would relate to the complicated power structure of the Maple Leafs. It was ultimately determined that he would report directly to Smith, and Quinn signed his four-year, $4.4-million deal only after cementing that particular clause.

An outspoken man who fears few reprisals, Quinn says what he thinks — often to the point of astonishment. After I'd gotten word that the Maple Leafs were interviewing him, I called Quinn in Vancouver and he detailed his progress in a forthright manner that many in his situation would avoid. I reminded him of a brief conversation we'd had back at the 1984 NHL draft in Montreal. The Leafs were in the market for a coach, having recently fired Mike Nykoluk. Quinn had been out of work for a couple of seasons after losing his job in Philadelphia and was sniffing out opportunities to get back behind an NHL bench. Remembering how fond I was of him as a rugged Maple Leaf defenceman in the late '60s, I approached Quinn on the floor of the Montreal Forum, introduced myself, and told him of my desire that he get the vacant Toronto job. He seemed very much enamored with the idea and thanked me for my wishes.

As it turned out, Quinn was hired to replace Roger Neilson as coach of the Kings. Almost 14 years later, when I reflected on that conversation, the big Irishman candidly told me why he didn't get the Leaf job.

"Ballard said he didn't want a 'Mick' behind the bench."

But the owner went ahead and gave the job to Dan Maloney, another Irishman.

With the Quinn negotiations fully out in the open, Dryden took the time to finally end Murphy's water-drip torture. On June 24, he assembled the media in the Hot Stove Lounge at Maple Leaf Gardens and announced he had fired the beleaguered coach. "I don't regret the process," Dryden said, using his favorite word, "but I do regret how this vigil played itself out for Mike and his family."

Later that day, Murphy entertained the media at St. Andrew's Valley Golf Club near his home in Aurora. Some of us expected an outpouring of invective, which would have been justifiable under the circumstance. Instead, Murphy maintained his decorum and thanked the Maple Leaf organization for allowing him to realize a dream. It was a noble and unselfish act.

With a bit of fortunate timing, and the help of noted Canadian football player-agent Gil Scott, Murphy soon bounced back and accepted a position as assistant coach of the Ottawa Senators under Jacques Martin. A valued and trusted member of Pat Burns's coaching staff with the Maple Leafs in the early '90s, Murphy proved to be an effective buffer between the players and their bombastic head man. There's no telling how large a role he played in the Senators' tremendous 1998–99 regular season and the ultimate naming of Martin as NHL coach of the year — winner of the Jack Adams Trophy.

Prior to joining Ottawa, Murphy had engaged in brief discussions with his close pal, Colin Campbell, the NHL's executive V-P and director of hockey operations. When Campbell coached the New York Rangers, Murphy was one of his assistants for two years (before Fletcher hired him as the Leafs' head man in 1996). In the summer of '98 — Campbell's first with the NHL — there was talk of creating an additional vice-presidential role in the league's Toronto office, and Campbell made it known to Murphy that he'd be his choice for the job once it materialized, likely in a year's time.

True to his word, Campbell hired Murphy away from the Senators as V-P of hockey operations on July 23, 1999, and assigned him to work with another Maple Leaf alumnus — former GM Jim Gregory, the league's executive V-P of operations and head of the Toronto office. Murphy and Gregory offer shining evidence that good things happen to good people and they should form a highly successful tandem.

Quinn arrived in Toronto with a sizable chip on his shoulder, courtesy of his onerous relationship with the Vancouver media. He was officially hired by Dryden in the wee hours of Friday, June 26 — one day before the '98 entry draft in Buffalo. I was mildly in awe of the new coach, as I could vividly recall his short Maple Leaf playing tenure in my pre-teen years (1968 to 1970). No Leaf fan of that era will ever forget Quinn's pulverizing bodycheck on the great Bobby Orr during the Toronto-Boston Stanley Cup quarterfinal of 1969. It has become a prime example of Maple Leaf lore, and its 30th anniversary was commemorated by a number of newspaper stories.

"Thirty years . . . it rolls off the tongue flippantly," Quinn smiled when asked about the incident.

Despite my long-standing admiration of the man, I was acutely aware of his attempted bullying tactics in Vancouver, and I wanted to feel him out for myself. During the Leafs' 1998 training camp, I approached Quinn in the lobby of the Edmonton Westin Hotel when the club was there for one of its first exhibition games. In my initial four years covering the team, all members of the Toronto hockey media had been granted full access to the team bus and, when occasionally necessary, team charter flights. The head coach makes the call on these matters, and it had not been an issue with Pat Burns, Nick Beverley or Mike Murphy. The bus was a welcome convenience when moving between hotels and arenas — particularly on game days, when the team held a morning skate — and I rode it more frequently than my colleagues.

There was a code of honor to follow, which specified that nothing overheard or overseen from players or management be reported, and it never was. For the purposes of writing *On The Road* in the lockout-shortened season of 1995, I first clarified my intentions with Pat Burns, and the Maple Leafs' director of communications at the time, Bob Stellick. I was granted permission by Burns to chronicle anything innocuous that might occur, but to use my judgment wisely. Which I believe I did, though Stellick — an adversary during our years together — chose to get all huffy once the book came out.

During training camp in 1997, Murphy called me over and politely reminded me to maintain the code of honor. No problems resulted until late in the season, when Casey Vanden Heuvel of the Leaf publicity staff misinterpreted something that occurred, and made a big stink out of it. We were in Phoenix on the day of the 1998 NHL trading deadline and the Leaf bus was rolling towards the America West Arena for the morning skate. I was seated next to Dennis Beyak, the Leafs' back-up radio voice, and in front of radio analyst Jim Ralph.

It had become clear by then that the Leafs — well out of the playoff hunt — were going to unload veteran defencemen Jeff Brown and Jamie Macoun before the end of the day. I was casually discussing the subject with Beyak, when Ralph leaned forward and told me he had noticed young rearguard Jeff Ware while having breakfast that morning at the Ritz Carlton. The inference, of course, being that Ware had been recalled from the Maple Leafs' farm team to replace one of the departing veterans for that night's game against the Coyotes. It was a much-appreciated and valued piece of information from a fellow media member, and I immediately notified the radio station via my cellphone.

When I hung up, Vanden Heuvel — seated across the aisle — turned to me and said, "I guess you've forgotten the rules." I asked him what he meant and he accused me of relaying information that Bill Watters had been discussing with Murphy at the front of the bus. I told Vanden Heuvel he didn't know what he was talking about and a minor argument ensued. It turns out that Watters and Murphy were indeed discussing Ware's promotion at the same time Ralph was telling me about it — four rows back. Even a dog wouldn't have been able to overhear the two Maple Leaf employees from that distance, given the constant drone of the bus's engine. Ralph and Beyak politely informed the perturbed publicist of the coincidence but Vanden Heuvel — obstinate at the best of times — would have none of it. He shook me off as I attempted to reconcile with him in the arena. (Macoun and Brown were indeed dealt later that day, and Ware did dress against the Coyotes.)

With Quinn now in charge, I was curious as to his policy regarding media on the bus. I asked him about it in the lobby of the Edmonton Westin and he launched into a dance routine that would've shamed Fred Astaire. First he said he hadn't thought about it. Then he mentioned that only the team broadcasters had been allowed on the bus during the bulk of his years in Vancouver.

"So what does that mean?" I asked.

"Well, we'll probably keep it the way it was here," he said.

"You're saying media will be allowed on the bus?"

"Oh, that's what happened previously?" he asked.

"Yes, in all of my years covering the team so far," I replied.

"Well, it's going to change now."

"So, your policy is not to have us on the bus," I re-confirmed.

"I'll have to check to see what management wants."

"C'mon Pat," I said, "the coach always makes that call, not management."

"Well, then consider yourselves no longer on the bus."

I resisted thanking him for his direct answer.

Nothing more came of the matter until the first road trip of the regular season, which, ironically, began back in Edmonton. I traveled on an Air Canada flight that left Toronto at the same time as a Canadian Airlines flight carrying the Maple Leafs. After three hours and forty minutes in the air, both planes landed in northern Alberta and luggage was dispensed, simultaneously, from opposite ends of the Edmonton airport terminal. To split the expense of the long trip into town, I shared a taxi ride with *Toronto Star* hockey writer Paul Hunter, who had been on my flight. Hunter's colleague Rosie DiManno had flown with the Leafs, and though we'd looked for her, she was nowhere to be seen.

After checking in 45 minutes later at the Westin, Hunter and I took another cab to the newly named SkyReach Centre for the Leafs' scheduled practice. It was there that I hooked up with Rosie and was told about her misadventure of the previous hour. Unaware of Quinn's change in media policy, the veteran columnist had gathered her luggage and casually stepped onto the team bus. Just like she'd done many times before. She was about to take a seat when Vanden Heuvel approached and told her to leave. Catching her completely off guard, he informed her of Quinn's edict, and Rosie — feeling thoroughly humiliated — asked the bus driver to retrieve her bag from the lower compartment. She then took a taxi into Edmonton.

Of course, the entire episode resulted from a dreadful lack of respect and communication. Quinn had evidently informed his media relations staff of the new bus policy, because Vanden Heuvel acted without hesitation when DiManno climbed on board. He was fully aware that the media were no longer welcome. Why in heaven's name the Leafs' P.R. staff chose not to send the media a written memo on the new policy was incomprehensible. If even the slightest level of common sense had prevailed, DiManno would not have been subjected to her embarrassment on that trip.

While leaving the Maple Leaf dressing room after practice, we passed by the door leading into the visiting coach's office. "If we had any guts, we'd go in there and confront Quinn over this," I said to DiManno. Well, that's all it took. My pal Rosie — figuratively — has bigger gonads than any reporter I've ever met. She laid a cursory knock on the door and barged into the room before a response. Luckily, Quinn and his assistants were in full dress, and she asked Quinn for a first-hand ruling on the bus issue. The brawny Leaf coach seemed to cower for a scant moment — not expecting such a vehement challenge from this plucky woman reporter. But he regained himself and said, quite mannerly, "There's no disrespect towards your profession, but my policy is to have only the team broadcasters on the bus. I hope you can understand."

We both did, of course, but something else was sticking in my craw. I couldn't help but once again think of the several horror stories I'd been told about Quinn's disrespect for the Vancouver media. To me, this bus ruling in Toronto was a pre-emptive strike by the new coach against a generally admiring and, to that point, passive throng of media. Solely a product of the monstrous chip on his shoulder. The acquisition of Quinn had been met with nothing but unanimous approval by all members of the Toronto press. Accolades poured off newsprint and over the airwaves.

His response? A collective kick in the ass.

For my own good — if no one else's — I decided to stake out some territory with the coach. How? The only way I could: by talking about his ruling on the air . . . repeatedly. Over and over again, I slammed Quinn for his unprovoked maneuver. I was ridiculed by some people who actually figured me to be upset at losing the bus privileges. A perceptive bunch, they were. Anyone with even a thimble-full of brains knew it was simply my way of showing Quinn that when he barked, I would not jump. And I think it served me well for the balance of the season.

Al Strachan of the *Sun* was one of the guys who needled me about my bitching and moaning. Even after I'd saved his ass. The morning after DiManno's bus episode, I got off the elevator at the Edmonton hotel and saw the Leafs were climbing on board for the ride to their morning skate. Strachan — completely unaware of Quinn's edict — instinctively began to follow the players and was about to step up onto the vehicle when I yelled out, "Hey Al, don't go in there!" He looked back at me with some confusion and I waved him over. I then explained how Quinn had changed the media policy, and we were no longer welcome on the bus. I did some hissing about the new rule and Strachan pulled an about-face. Whereas most people in his shoes may have offered some form of gratitude, Al typically shrugged it off.

"Ah, Howard, you should consider it a compliment," he said. "They don't want legitimate media on the bus. Stop bellyaching."

Silly me. I had a sudden relishing of hindsight, at that moment, to have witnessed Strach's mortification as he was shooed off the bus. But it was too late.

Once the season got rolling, I let the issue die, but I couldn't resist one further dig at Quinn. On October 29, a Thursday morning, the Leafs practiced at St. Michael's Arena in mid-town Toronto, prior to leaving for a road game the following night in Buffalo. While huddling with several of my colleagues in the frosty arena, the subject of the team bus came up and I began to consider making a wise-ass remark to Quinn in the post-practice media scrum, mainly to see his reaction. Egged on in sinister fashion by my cohort Paul Hendrick of the Leafs' television crew — a man thoroughly welcomed on the bus — I decided to go for it.

Quinn held his scrum outside the front doors of the arena on the cool and crisp autumn day. After the third or fourth question, there was a slight pause, and the mischievous Hendrick nudged me from behind. With the Buffalo road game looming, I looked at Quinn and asked, "Pat, are members of the media allowed to travel on the same highway as the team bus?" As my colleagues snickered, Quinn smiled and actually began answering the question seriously before he caught himself.

"What's *your* problem, did the lobotomy not work?" he thundered at me before shaking his head and walking away. Classic Quinn.

The big Irishman settled nicely into his role as coach of the Maple Leafs and the club's unfathomed success reflected brilliantly on him. From a media standpoint, he continued to be something of a paradox. As long as you asked Quinn questions that were perceived by him to be of a conventional nature — unsuspecting and non-confrontational — he would issue bright, thoughtful answers that were the envy of all hockey reporters. Once you stepped outside the lines, however, the bullying nature of the Maple Leaf coach would quickly emerge. It happened to me on several occasions, but one in particular stood out.

Defenceman Jason Smith, considered by many to be a cornerstone of the Leaf blueline, failed to grasp the system that Quinn had installed at training camp. Smith had proven to be adept at playing sound, positional hockey in his own end — providing he wasn't called upon to advance the puck with any regularity. Under Mike Murphy's conservative gameplan, Smith could simply dump the puck out of the defensive zone and allow his teammates to try and bottle up the opposition in neutral territory. The "trap," as it's called, was a scheme that Smith found comfort in, but one that proved to be highly ineffective. The Leafs couldn't put the puck in the ocean under Murphy, who had convinced himself that a singular lack of talent on his bench should preclude any thoughts of imagination.

Of course Murphy, as detailed earlier, found himself in an untenable situation during his final season on the job — completely the opposite of what Quinn would inherit. Murphy had quickly been made to feel impertinent by his new bosses, who had no long-term plans of retaining him. His every move was borne of desperation in the off chance that a new contract might come his way, and he was in a free-fall from the very outset of the Dryden regime. Under no circumstance could he afford to take a bold chance like Quinn ultimately did by loosening the offensive strings on a team whose collective hands seemed carved from stone. Perhaps Quinn had greater prescience, but he also had the security of a four-year contract, and the luxury of Curtis Joseph as his netminder.

As a result, Quinn possessed the latitude to see things differently. He analyzed his inherited roster and concluded there was more collective speed and skating ability than Murphy's concept permitted. In current-day hockey, he felt it would benefit his team (and provide entertainment for ticket-buyers) to try and beat the trap, and that's the direction he assumed from the outset. The Toronto coach staked his approach on the presumption that Joseph would perform to standard, and compensate for a generally soft defensive underbelly. The Leafs of Pat Quinn would take more chances with the puck, and thus create the potential for abundant disarray in their own zone. A sturdy backstop was essential.

Jason Smith was one of the players who Quinn believed was lagging in his adjustment. In Quinn's scheme, the Maple Leaf defencemen were called upon to initiate offensive forays by either lugging the puck out of their own territory, or passing sharply to attacking teammates. Smith appeared to lack the requisite combination of skill and tempo, and — curiously — his strong physical presence in the defensive zone withered. He wasn't the worst skater in a Toronto uniform most nights, but he clearly had regressed under Quinn.

In late February and early March, Quinn began sitting Smith out of games as a healthy scratch. Prior to a March 4 game in St. Louis, and depending on whom you ask, Smith was said to have thrown a loud tantrum in front of the coach when informed — after the warm-up — that he wouldn't be playing. The young rearguard sat out a stretch of seven consecutive matches just prior to the trading deadline, and there appeared to be little doubt the Leafs would attempt to peddle him. He clearly did not mesh with anything Quinn hoped to achieve.

The coach, however, began playing games with the media. Quinn's only tangible defiance of Mike Smith had occurred following Smith's acquisition of lead-footed, but large, defenceman Chris McAllister from Vancouver (for Darby Hendrickson in mid-February). Already saddled with an overabundance of blueliners, Quinn was loath to welcome another. However, McAllister — despite his obvious limitations — began playing regularly, as did promising rookie Tomas Kaberle, who'd been spotted by Quinn after a fast start. Jason Smith and Yannick Tremblay were the odd men out on defence (Tremblay would be chosen by the Atlanta Thrashers in the June '99 expansion draft).

But when asked about Smith prior to the trade deadline, Quinn strangely abandoned his traditional candidness and began going in circles. He'd say things like, "Oh, I feel badly for young Jason; he's still a big part of our team and he's not playing right now because I've got to look at some other people to see if they can cut it." It was a lot of malarkey. Smith was buried so deeply in the coach's line of performance that seven other defencemen were playing ahead of him.

Less than a week before the deadline, during a post-practice media scrum at the Air Canada Centre, Quinn again launched into one of his "We still love Jason Smith" monologues, and I'd had enough. Stepping outside that so-called line of tolerance, I basically told the coach he was full of crap.

"There's no way you still have any plans for him," I blurted into my microphone, drawing a death-stare from Quinn.

"What are *you* talking about?!" he shot back.

"It's obvious he can't play for you anymore," I replied."

"*What's* obvious??!!"

"It's clear that he's finished here —" and before I could say, "Why don't you just trade him?" Quinn roared, "*Nothing's* clear! Your *glasses* aren't even clear for cryin' out loud. Why don't you go back to school and learn the meaning of the word." Yadda yadda yadda! All the while, television cameras rolled and reporters in the scrum laughed obligingly with the coach. It made for great sound and the clip was played repeatedly throughout the remainder of that day.

Of course, it came as no surprise to anyone when Smith was traded to Edmonton at the deadline. The Leafs thought so highly of him, they passed on acquiring veteran Rob Zamuner's salary from Tampa and accepted second- and fourth-round draft choices from the Oilers. Essentially, they gave Smith away.

Though his actions were consistent with most of his colleagues, Quinn's disdain for the media was in evidence after games — particularly at home — and it spawned some heated emotions during the '99 playoffs. Media regulations in the NHL have become nightmarish for those operating on tight deadlines, as the league's general managers and coaches have willfully created a troublesome and forbidding climate for reporters. Exactly why, no one is sure, but it probably comes down to a form of control the GMs and coaches know they can exert. It is, nonetheless, an odd strategy by executives of a league that otherwise begs for attention in many areas of the continent.

Acting on these orders, the Maple Leaf publicity staff deliberately shielded the players all season long under Quinn — ushering them out for their post-game media sessions, one by one, on a request basis. If a particular player happened to be lounging in front of a TV set and didn't want to be bothered, the reporters waited — deadlines threatening.

In the spirit of media regulations, those covering hockey games have traditionally been permitted into the main dressing room 10 minutes after the final buzzer, and have had access to an "alternate interview area" — usually a sector of the back-room where the players dress at their individual lockers. It's long been understood and agreed upon that medical and training areas are off-limits to the media, yet the Leafs zealously guarded any and all turf outside the main dressing location.

In the old, smaller quarters at the Gardens, the players had an adjoining lounge in which they watched TV, got dressed, and partook in post-game snacks. Technically, media members were permitted to enter that room, but rarely did — opting to respect the players' quest for privacy. At the new Air Canada Centre, the athletes have a virtual fortress to roam around in, with private lounge, locker area, whirlpool-medical facilities, and weight and fitness rooms all tucked in behind and around the main dressing room, very much out of sight. The actual entrance to the main room consists of two electronically operated steel doors, accessed by a security card. I often think of the opening to the 1960s sitcom *Get Smart* when I see the doors swing into action. As well, there are a half-dozen exits sprinkled throughout the labyrinth of hallways which preclude players from having to walk past the ubiquitous reporters. One such exit takes them directly to the main elevators and the door leading out onto Bay Street.

As mentioned, access restrictions have become commonplace in a league mostly governed by dinosaur logic. The shining exceptions are the Edmonton Oilers and St. Louis Blues, which offer freedom of movement everywhere but the medical rooms. The Ottawa Senators have also chosen to abandon the stone age by allowing reporters to interview the players while they're going through their post-game "cool down" on stationary bikes. The rules are mostly shameful and unrelenting everywhere else, including Toronto.

Quinn has shown no desire to help facilitate anything for the media beyond his daily post-practice scrum and the obligatory sessions after games. And he's placed abundant strain on the Leafs' media relations personnel — in particular, manager Pat Park and his buzz-saw understudy Anthony Alfred. Both men are accommodating in most cases, but are hog-tied by Quinn's iron hand. Alfred is newer to the job than Park, and has not yet overcome his solicitude around the players. I've literally spent hours poking fun at Anthony and elevating his blood pressure, but he handles it well and has the perfect temperament for the job. As does Park, in a more refined (sometimes disquieting) manner. They are two decent guys in a generally tough situation.

This interminable struggle nearly boiled over in Pittsburgh moments after the Leafs' playoff elimination of the Penguins. The visitors' dressing set-up at the Civic Arena comprises two equal-sized rooms. The front chamber is open to reporters, while the rear one (where the players dress after showering) is off limits. In the delirium of the Leafs' post-season triumph, *Toronto Sun* sports editor Scott Morrison was standing near the dividing entrance of the two rooms, obtaining quotes from Gary

Valk, who had scored the overtime series clincher. Morrison was suddenly accosted and dragged beyond the off-limits zone by an ecstatic Steve Stavro, essentially the most powerful person in the hockey organization. The two were exchanging pleasantries when Alfred happened by and rather sheepishly asked Morrison to leave. The veteran reporter almost gagged at the request, but chose not to make a scene and walked out.

Moments later, the usually affable Morrison tore into Dryden in a corridor outside the dressing room. Excusing himself through clenched teeth for raining on the parade, Morrison told the unsuspecting Leaf president in no uncertain terms just how painfully farcical the situation had become. Dryden agreed to his request for a meeting, but it was a patronizing gesture. Under no circumstance was he about to instruct his head coach to alter the regulations.

In the grand scheme — and despite many of his bothersome nuances — I enjoy the presence of Pat Quinn as coach (and now GM) of the team I cover. I just wish he'd relax a bit and put his Vancouver experience behind him. He has an engaging personality and forthrightness that lends itself to a more amiable environment, yet he came here from B.C. with his guard up, and has not seen fit to lower it. It'll be interesting to observe how he reacts to fielding the questions we used to run and ask Smith. He's got two pretty large hats to wear now.

I went to see Quinn in his office the day after the Leafs were eliminated by Buffalo, just to let him know how outstanding a job I felt he'd done his first season. I told him I hoped that any words we'd had between us during the year were forgotten and that none of it was personal.

"Aahhh," he said with a grin, "you're one of the guys I can tell to go screw."

A compliment of the highest order.

* * *

On the Saturday morning of the '99 draft, a bombshell exploded in the form of a column by Rosie DiManno in the *Toronto Star.* Sensing that Mike Smith was a grenade waiting to be detonated, she flew to Boston a day early and met with the former associate GM at Massachusetts General Hospital while his wife underwent chemotherapy treatments.

As Rosie suspected, Smith was ready to vent. While obviously lacking any semblance of balance, her column revealed the following Smith charges:

- Just prior to the opening of the Air Canada Centre, Dryden had taken away the

Maple Leaf players' extra tickets for the inaugural game against the Montreal Canadiens. "I'd already told Ken in a meeting that the players had a right to those tickets," Smith said to DiManno. "[Ken] said, 'I don't care.'"

- Dryden attempted to block the trade that sent Mathieu Schneider to the Rangers for Alexander Karpovtsev and relented only after Smith threatened to resign.

- Despite the objections of Quinn and his assistant coaches, Dryden wanted to trade Felix Potvin for the Islanders' aging centerman Trevor Linden, rather than young defenceman Bryan Berard (Quinn's disapproval would have been noteworthy, as Linden had been captain of the Vancouver club he guided to the Stanley Cup final in 1994).

- A year earlier, Dryden had granted Smith complete authority to operate the hockey department without seeking his approval on matters. Assistant GM (and avowed Smith enemy) Anders Hedberg became petulant, and Dryden rescinded the control within six days.

- When Smith attempted to hold a "town meeting" the previous August with members of the Toronto hockey media, Dryden ordered the press conference canceled.

About the offer Dryden had recently made him to become GM, Smith told DiManno, "Basically, all decisions would have to be run through [Ken]; everything that would normally come under a GM's authority. And that's not the way things worked this past year, when I was only required to keep him informed. This has been a year of me ignoring Ken and finding ways to keep everything going forward. I couldn't go through another year like that."

On the personality contrasts between he and Dryden, Smith said, "Ken perceives himself to be the ultimate top guy. I perceive myself to be the leader within a group. If Ken and I had gotten to know each other in another walk of life, we wouldn't be close friends."

Discussing his thorough lack of relationship with Hedberg, Smith grew reflective. "When I came to Toronto, I thought we were pretty good friends," he told DiManno. "But Anders doesn't want anybody to know what's going on in his area. He doesn't share the [draft] list. How do you trade a player for a draft pick if you don't know the quality of player you're looking at in the draft? I asked that and never got an answer."

Smith concluded his diatribe by disclosing that communication had been nonexistent during his tenure as a Maple Leaf executive. "There were no interrelations between myself and the other hockey departments," he claimed. "And it was purposely set up that way. If there was a relationship problem, it existed at the upper echelons of the hockey department. It wasn't just based on myself."

Elaborating on his own difficulties with Dryden during a subsequent conversation with me, Smith said, "Every V-P in the company ignored Ken in order to get their jobs done, I wasn't the only one. If you didn't ignore him, there would be five-hour meetings at three o'clock in the afternoon, and you wouldn't get out of there 'til 8 or 8:30. That's not what people wanted to do."

* * *

Though the circumstances were less than ideal, Quinn's public outburst after the Smith firing all but assured him the double post of GM and coach. There was little reason for anyone to believe that Dryden would unearth someone agreeable to Quinn, and his so-called "search" for a GM all but ended when he first met with Quinn in Boston three days after gassing Smith.

That occurred at the Marriott hotel on the morning of the NHL draft. I deliberately went to the Fleet Center early to obtain a reaction from Quinn when he arrived at the arena. The beleaguered coach got off the third-floor elevator roughly 15 minutes before the day's events and appeared to be only slightly mollified.

"We didn't have a lot of time to talk today, what with the draft and everything that's happening," Quinn said as we hurriedly walked to the arena floor. "I still have a number of questions and concerns, and I'll meet with Ken again on Monday when we get back to Toronto. All I can say is that I'm prepared to move forward with the Maple Leafs."

The term "move forward" is one Quinn would use copiously through the remainder of the day. Coaches play the same role at entry drafts that GMs and scouts play in the middle of games: none at all. As such, Quinn had a heap of idle time to devote to his favorite recreation — rapping with the media. Actually, it took a bit of a ploy to lure the big Irishman away from the Maple Leaf table and towards the iron fence that separates reporters from the draft floor. The tables are arranged so that teams with the best records from the previous season are closest to the separation point. That has usually meant the Leafs were buried somewhere out of sight. But a fifth-place overall finish in 1998–99 had the Toronto contingent situated directly beyond the first row of media seating, quite a convenience for a reporter covering the team.

About 90 minutes into the draft, unqualified monotony had overcome practically everyone in the arena, as it typically does once the early first-round selections are made. Standing idly at the iron fence with DiManno — both of us seeking further detail on Quinn's frame of mind — I summoned the coach's attention while pointing to the *Star* columnist.

"Pat, this nice young lady would like to speak with you," I said.

DiManno gagged and nearly smacked me.

"Cut the shit, Howard," Quinn replied with that prankish smile we'd all come to know.

"Aw, c'mon Pat, you're not gonna turn down a lovely woman, are you?"

The coach rolled his eyes and hobbled over to the fence.

"What's it like to be a jerk all the time?" he asked, glaring at me.

I just grinned.

But the shenanigans quickly subsided once Quinn began enunciating his dismay. He confessed to thinking about the GM's role for himself, even though he had repeatedly declared all season long how thoroughly contented he was just being coach of the Leafs. "My intention was to coach, but circumstances have obviously changed," he said. "I'm going to have to think about whether or not I want to put my name in the [candidates'] hat. I might have to, just as an act of self-preservation."

The latter statement was easily the most revealing and would form the basis for Dryden's so-called search. Actually, it already had. Sources claim that as soon as Quinn broached the subject of taking over Smith's duties — during their Saturday morning, pre-draft parley — Dryden all but told him the job was his. For public consumption, the Maple Leaf president restated his intention to consider outside candidates — a process he claimed to have started at the draft. Dryden elevated the curiosity of several Toronto reporters when he chatted for a full half-hour on the draft floor with Doug Risebrough, Edmonton's V-P of hockey operations and Dryden's former Montreal teammate. Risebrough had been considered during Dryden's initial search for a GM, but he joined the Oilers when Glen Sather approached him.

Gallows humor quickly surfaced when it was suggested that Risebrough could become the first GM to re-build the Leafs on two separate occasions. He was, of course, the Calgary manager who traded Doug Gilmour to Toronto in January 1992, providing the Maple Leafs with two years of playoff glory.

A Saturday morning column in the *Sun* by Strachan detailed a list of potential replacements for Smith, ranging from agent Don Meehan and former Canadian Hockey League president Ed Chynoweth, to Jim Rutherford and Neil Smith, GMs gainfully employed by other teams in the NHL.

"I want to know the names on the list," Quinn mentioned at the draft. "It's an unusual situation. I've got to think about what's going to happen here," he said, failing to mention that some fairly judicial deliberation between he and Dryden had already taken place.

In the week after the draft, another scathing newspaper article appeared, very much in opposition to Dryden. In the June 30 edition of the *Globe and Mail,* hockey writer David Shoalts vilified the Maple Leaf president under the headline, "LEAFS NEED TO FIRE DRYDEN TO AVOID TOTAL CHAOS." Shoalts wrote:

> Ken Dryden's Toronto Maple Leafs are poised for a big fall in the next National Hockey League season.
>
> If the board of directors wants to avoid a likely disaster — in comparison to this charmed season — then it should separate Ken Dryden from Ken Dryden's Toronto Maple Leafs.
>
> For it was Ken Dryden's fierce desire to put his mark everywhere, to turn them into Ken Dryden's Toronto Maple Leafs, that has brought this team to a state not seen since the reign of one of his infamous predecessors. The chaos that has descended on the Leaf front office has too many uncomfortable reminders of Gerry McNamara's term as general manager in the 1980s under the bizarre ownership of Harold Ballard. . . .
>
> The worst damage has been to [Pat] Quinn's trust in Dryden, a fine state of affairs considering the coach is now the leading candidate to be the general manager, or has to be satisfied with whoever Dryden comes up with.
>
> For if Dryden cannot convince Quinn to buy into his program, what was the point of putting the shiv into the coach's friend, associate GM Mike Smith? . . .
>
> [No] credible outside candidate will be eager to step into what has clearly become a hornet's nest. . . .
>
> Looks like there's lots of reasons to stop looking for a GM and start looking for a president.

Amid all of this, Dryden pressed forward in secret negotiations with Quinn. On several occasions in the week following the draft, they met and put together the parameters of a deal that would transfer the official GM's duties to Quinn. According to insiders, the big Irishman was trapped in an emotional conundrum during these discussions. Tugging at him forcefully was a pair of contradictory sentiments: his desire to remain solely as coach of the Maple Leafs, and his irrepressible anxiety over having to answer to an incompatible GM. Quinn had no confidence at all that Dryden could locate a credible manager, and he harbored great suspicion as to the influence Dryden might exert on such a person if he were discovered.

As a safeguard, Dryden had held cursory discussions with three individuals: his long-time friend Risebrough, Dallas Stars assistant GM Doug Armstrong, and Vancouver Canucks V-P of player personnel Steve Tambellini. While all three are generally well thought of in the hockey community, it would have been nonsensical to place any of them above a veteran, experienced hockey man like Quinn. Dryden had prevailed in his quarrel with Smith but had done so without a viable alternative. He was trapped in a quandary of his own making and fully knew that Quinn represented his only tangible escape. Aware of Quinn's reticence, Dryden essentially pressured him into assuming the GM's portfolio by threatening to hire one of the above-mentioned candidates.

"Take it yourself, or work for someone else," warned the Leaf president.

Whether Dryden's strategy worked, or Quinn merely warmed to the idea of taking on added responsibility is a moot point. The bottom line is that Quinn was far and away the most highly qualified GM available, within or outside the Maple Leaf organization, and once Dryden heard Quinn ponder the potentiality of the double role, he knew not to look elsewhere. Had Quinn never broached the subject himself, Dryden may have been left in the lurch, but he took even the slightest inkling of allure from Quinn and ran with it.

Ironically, it cost Dryden even more of the hockey department influence he was so unwilling to yield to Smith. While Quinn, as GM, will technically report to Dryden the president, he has categorical authority on all hockey matters and is under no contractual obligation to consult with Dryden on anything.

The two met in Toronto on June 29, 1999 — three days after the draft — and fundamentally agreed that Quinn would be the GM. Quinn had minor surgery later that day (a large corn removed from his left foot), then flew to Nice, France, on July 2 with his wife, Sandra, to join former Vancouver Canucks owner (and Quinn's close friend) Arthur Griffiths on a yachting vacation. While at sea, Quinn kept in touch with Bill Watters by phone, as the period of unrestricted free agency had begun. Quinn voiced enthusiasm over the potential acquisition of defenceman (and former Leaf) Sylvain Lefebvre, and encouraged Watters to remain in solid but reasonable negotiation for the veteran free agent. While this was going on, my pal Tim Wharnsby, the *Toronto Sun*'s scoop-meister, got the official word of Quinn's generally presumed anointment, writing a front-page sports story. Dryden would not deny that he and Quinn had discussed the post in depth, only that no formal agreement had been reached. He was in final negotiations with Dick Babush, who stayed behind in Toronto.

On July 12 — a Monday morning — I received a telephone call at the radio station claiming that Dryden would officially announce Quinn's appointment as GM

during a press conference two days later. This seemed odd, because it had been widely reported that Quinn would not be back in town before the following week — July
19 or 20. Further investigation, however, revealed that Quinn was returning to
Toronto on July 13, only one day earlier than originally planned. It was learned that
the Maple Leafs had scheduled a budget meeting for the 15th, during which Dryden
and Quinn would go before the board of directors to outline the club's economic
requirements for the following year.

As such, Dryden called a press conference on Wednesday afternoon, the 14th, to
anoint Quinn. It would be held in the Bell Media room at the Air Canada Centre —
increasingly familiar territory for hockey reporters in Toronto, as Smith's season-ending mandate, then Dryden's official firing of Smith both took place there.

Appearing tanned and far more relaxed than during the hockey season, Quinn
entered the room with a sheepish-looking Dryden in tow. The Maple Leaf president
and no-longer GM made a lengthy opening address, and seemed both relieved and contented to have "a most difficult six weeks" behind him.

"I'm pleased to announce Pat Quinn as the new general manager and coach of
the Toronto Maple Leafs," Dryden began. "As general manager and coach, you not
only control the hockey operation of the team, you determine a 'Leafs way' of doing
things on the ice. You implement a style of play, then enhance it with the players you
draft and trade for.

"Pat is of the Leafs tradition. He embodies the hard work, discipline and rock-
ribbed defence of the Leaf championship teams of the '60s [*though he played on none
of them*] — and adds to that an ability to learn and adapt, incorporating the creative
possibilities of today's game, to generate a new Leaf style made for the present and
future. A style that can win."

Quinn said he became nostalgic while on his way down to the press gathering.
"As I was walking down the hall, I happened to see one of my heroes, I guess, and
the last man to hold both the GM and coach's job with the Maple Leafs — a picture
of Punch Imlach [*whom Quinn played for in 1968–69*]. Maybe times were different
then, maybe it was much more simple, but improvement happened from within and
under the direction of a coach who was able to influence the direction of the hockey
team through player transactions and development. That's the situation I have here
with the Maple Leafs now. It's an awesome task and one I don't take lightly.

"With the example I used of Punch, I certainly would strive to have his success, and
look forward to, perhaps, our first championship here in the not-too-distant future."

Quinn confirmed that Bill Watters would be among his chief lieutenants, assuming and carrying out many of the technical, day-to-day aspects of the GM's job while

he concentrated on coaching the Maple Leafs. Director of pro scouting Nick Beverley opted to stay with the Leafs (refusing an offer from Tampa Bay) with the pledge from Quinn of more influence in the hockey department. "I intend to be a coach who has the added responsibility of managing," he emphasized. "I can handle both jobs."

Dryden seemed to be, in a way, humbled by the events of the post-season. Not that he'd been arrogant beforehand, but the constant upheaval appeared to have taken its toll. He sat quietly through much of the press conference — quite content to let Quinn have his say. When questioned on a matter, his answers were shorter and more direct than usual. He seemed worn and exhausted.

* * *

It came as no surprise when the Maple Leafs were among the pioneers of a 1999 off-season that reeked of ownership collusion. When the subject of saving money arises in the Toronto organization, arm twisting is seldom necessary. The night after Quinn's official appointment, the club withdrew from the bidding for Sylvain Lefebvre. The Leafs would not budge off their submission of $2 million a season, while Lefebvre's agent, Bob Sauve, steadfastly remained at his asking price of $2.5 million: an amount he said the New York Rangers were willing to pay. Of course, very little shock value accompanied that claim, as the Rangers were in the midst of a frenzied attempt to purchase a playoff contender, having missed out on the post-season two years in a row.

Granted a colossal budget extension of $22 million, GM Neil Smith merrily went about rescuing his own job, and had already spent tens of millions on unfettered free agents Valeri Kamensky, Stephane Quintal, Theo Fleury and Kirk MacLean when Lefebvre was added to the stable. Scant months after NHL commissioner Gary Bettman "predicted" that salary inflation would discontinue, New York, interestingly, was the only team in the league to extend itself once the free agent season began. Merely one year after a bevy of well-to-do clubs waged economic warfare for players like Brett Hull, Ron Francis, Curtis Joseph, Mike Richter, Uwe Krupp, John Vanbiesbrouck, Doug Gilmour, John MacLean and Jyrki Lumme, all competition suddenly ceased. The Rangers effected a one-team scramble for talent, raising eyebrows among those of legal discernment.

When Boston's Harry Sinden became the first GM in the annals of the current collective bargaining agreement to exercise the "walk-away" clause — on August 17, he refused an arbitrator's requirement to pay forward Dimitri Khristich $2.8 million for the 1999–2000 season, thus granting the talented and still-young player unconditional free agency — the suspicion intensified. And when none of the other 27 teams moved to offer 80 percent of the arbitrator's figure — roughly $2.24 million (and no further player compensation) for a 29-goal, 71-point scorer: quite reasonable in today's NHL economy — suspicion turned to disbelief.

Did Toronto's choice of backing off from Lefebvre ultimately fall under a covert, league-wide accord to quell salary escalation? A similar course of action cost major league baseball owners $280 million in damages less than a decade ago, so few would expect another clandestine attempt at collusion. Nonetheless, the abrupt revision in spending policy across the NHL raised more questions than answers.

From a position of sheer personnel strategy, Lefebvre would have been a superb addition to the Maple Leafs, and both he and his family wanted to return to the city in which they lived from 1992 to '94.

A poised, classy veteran, and member of the '96 Stanley Cup champions from Colorado, there's no telling the positive influence Lefebvre may have had on young Maple Leaf blueliners like Bryan Berard, Daniil Markov and Tomas Kaberle. While it might be wishful for anyone to expect the Maple Leafs of 1999–2000 to receive duplicate production from their forwards, it was the club's defensive work that proved to be the previous season's chief shortcoming. Lefebvre would have added more than a touch of stability and self-assurance to the blueline, but the Leafs maintained all along they were not going to involve themselves to any degree in the free agent market, and they kept their word.

They did so despite a pure profit intake of roughly $1 million per game in the '99 playoffs — $9 million over nine home dates — and another significant ticket-price gouge (between eight and thirteen percent) for the '99–00 campaign. Maple Leaf fans were put off, wondering (like so many times previously) why a team that demands top dollar from its patrons would refuse to spend even mid-range money on a player the caliber of Lefebvre. The lone departure from this pattern of frugality had occurred the previous summer, when the club shelled out $8 million (U.S.) for the 1998–99 services of Joseph and Thomas. The nine subsequent playoff dates alone more than compensated for the layout, as the Leafs improved by leaps and bounds.

Why (apart from sharing in collusion) the club decided to return to its prior strategy — proven to be highly ineffectual over numbers of years — is a mystery, and one that could very well stunt its progress. Sure, the Leafs will say that the Rangers were the only team to avail themselves of free agency, pointing out the fiscal restraint of the rest of the league. But that doesn't adequately rationalize why a moderate expenditure (by today's standards) — one that would've landed Lefebvre — failed to pass. It proves that some lessons are not easily learned.

As such, it is commonly fair for any fan of the Maple Leafs to ask him or herself: "Does this hockey team really want to win?" When posed rhetorically, the answer is obvious — no one in his right mind strives to be looked upon as a loser. But the commitment to winning in professional sports often disturbs the balance between desire and fiscal responsibility. The Maple Leafs — like all pro teams in Canada — are hamstrung by the de-valued loonie. Maple Leaf Sports and Entertainment Ltd. is privately financing the Air Canada Centre (if gouging from helpless season-ticket holders can be considered a private exercise). Taxes in Canadian cities are more prohibitive than in most U.S. markets. So, yes, there are restrictions that cannot be ignored.

But do the Leafs honestly possess any sort of legitimate blueprint for winning the Stanley Cup? The Toronto Blue Jays won consecutive World Series titles in 1992 and '93, but only after years of teasing their faithful supporters to the point of anguish. While researching his bestseller on the Jays, *Diamond Dreams,* veteran author and *Globe and Mail* columnist Stephen Brunt discovered a rather shocking strategy. He obtained a copy of four budget plans considered by Blue Jays president Peter Bavasi in 1981, aimed at balancing finances and prosperity. The plans essentially ranged from fielding an average team and raking in bushelfuls of profits, to obtaining top-salaried ballplayers with the intention of winning a championship, and likely losing money in the process.

Fans of the baseball team who read Brunt's book were probably surprised to discover that Bavasi chose a middle-range option — with the ultimate goal of a World Series triumph not among his priorities. Brunt wrote:

> By following that plan, the Blue Jays could aspire to being a good baseball team, maybe even a very good baseball team. And from a bottom-line point of view, that's exactly where Bavasi wanted them — good, but not great. In the era of free agency, the same dictum applies in all professional sports: the most lucrative course is to contend, year after year, to play at a .500 clip or better, but never to win it all. Championships cost money. . . .
>
> Stay in the hunt enough to whet the fans' appetites. But don't blow your brains out to win, since that short-term glory, and the short-term satisfaction, will soon-enough be replaced by all kinds of red ink.

It's difficult to argue whether the Maple Leafs possess the same theory, simply because — unlike the Blue Jays of the 1980s and early '90s — they have been mostly inept. In the 32 NHL seasons since the Leafs won their last Stanley Cup, the franchise has finished above the .500 mark only 13 times. It has missed the playoffs 11 times, and has been eliminated in the first round on 11 of the 21 occasions in which it qualified. In five consecutive springs between 1975 and '79, the Maple Leafs prevailed in best-of-three preliminary round series. Once into the "real" opening round (the best-of-seven quarterfinals), they were banished four out of five times. On only four occasions in 32 years have the Maple Leafs advanced as far as the Stanley Cup semifinals (1978, '92, '93 and '99). And they have not yet made it back to the big dance.

So, the Leafs would have to raise the bar merely to match the Blue Jays' 1981 objective of moderate success. At the root of the issue is the undeniable fact that the Maple Leafs simply do not *have* to win. Over the span of decades, there has never existed even the slightest correlation between on-ice achievement and unconditional reverence. The club, frankly, has it all: an immense, wide-ranging sphere of truly resilient and unwavering devotees — steadily evolving from one generation to the next — which never stops doling out ungodly sums of money to watch it play, buy its licensed merchandise, or (quite evidently) patronize the sponsors of its telecasts.

The Leafs could lose all 82 regular-season games (they came closest in 1981–82 and 1984–85, winning only 20), and still emerge virtually unscathed. The fans and media would gripe 24 hours a day, but the arena seats would be paid for (accruing interest), broadcast rights would remain astronomical, and fathers would still purchase Maple Leaf paraphernalia for their children. Saturdays would linger as the domain of *Hockey Night In Canada*, attracting hundreds of thousands of blue-and-white zealots, preparing for their hearts to be wrenched yet again. This is not merely conjecture — it has actually happened on numerous occasions throughout the recent history of the franchise.

And yet, the return has been so pathetically marginal. When Maple Leaf ownership increases its already lofty ticket stipend an average of 10.5 percent across the board (as it did in the summer of '99), and then sits on its collective ass in the off-season, is it thumbing its nose at its faithful and enduring fans? Those who run the team, of course, will say no, but they may as well tell you the sky is green and the grass is pink. Words cost nothing.

Crying poor, conversely, is an art form: There's an arena to be paid off; the Canadian dollar is weak; other teams around the league aren't spending; the club was active in the free agent market the previous year. I have said it many times on The Fan-590 — no team in hockey is more adept at coming up with reasons *not* to do things.

Which often leads one to ponder what would happen if its patrons assumed a similar stance, and decided *they* could not spend excessively for a period of time. Don't people operate on budgets too? Evidently, that has never been even a slight consideration among those who run the hockey club. Every summer, like clockwork, Maple Leaf ownership places a greater financial burden on its season-ticket holders — practically daring them to turn elsewhere (which they don't). And, as few Leaf fans need be reminded, most summers follow seasons of mismanagement and failure. When the club decides — roughly once a decade — to re-pay the investment (as it did by signing Joseph and Thomas), the well runs dry once again. After all, there's a budget.

Of course, money is always available to ensure that the owners and directors of the team cavort in the lap of luxury. At least one darn-good hockey player could have been acquired for the amount of money poured into building the director's lounge at the Air Canada Centre — with its plush wood paneling and antique-style furniture. And who knows how much it costs for the opulent food-and-booze fests that follow each game.

Without question, it is silly for anyone to assume the Maple Leafs are the public trust they should be (and once were). In fact, the Leafs are no longer a sole entity — just a large corporate asset, operated on a traditional profit/loss basis, providing ego-gratification for the millionaires who guard the company's every dime. The Ontario Teacher's Pension Plan Board has only one concern: return on investment. Flag-waving is immaterial.

This is not to suggest that any of the people who run the Maple Leafs are bad or evil. Or that they don't get a big charge from the team having success, as it did in 1998–99. From an individual standpoint, I've gotten to know Brian Bellmore and Larry Tanenbaum, both of whom are cordial and personable. Stavro, on the other hand, is an enigma because he uniformly shuns the spotlight, refusing practically all interview requests. That's his prerogative, of course, but he winds up looking bad when the team is faring poorly. Hockey fans in Toronto expect some accountability for their copious dollars spent, and Stavro has been an abysmal failure in that regard. Those who know him, however, say that he's a pleasant and kind-hearted man.

In fairness, it must also be pointed out that Maple Leaf ownership has been extremely generous in looking after its most important assets. Pat Quinn was the highest-paid coach in the NHL in the 1998–99 season; Curtis Joseph, the third-wealthiest goaltender, behind only Patrick Roy and Dominik Hasek. And entering the 1999–2000 season, Mats Sundin's salary of $7 million (U.S.) was the ninth-highest in the NHL, and seventh-highest among skaters (behind Jaromir Jagr, Paul Kariya, Peter Forsberg, Theo Fleury, Eric Lindros and Pavel Bure). It can be argued, however, that a team not willing to appease its chief components would be a laughing stock. The Leafs are far from that . . . right now.

But concerns of this nature were rampant prior to the 1999–2000 season, when the Leafs assumed what appeared to be an intractable negotiating stance with two of their most important players. Defencemen Bryan Berard and Dimitri Yushkevich — both restricted free agents — were deemed too expensive and did not attend training camp. This occurred after the 10.5 percent ticket increase had been imposed and the subscribers' cash was safely in the bank earning interest. Only after asking, once again, for more of the public's money, the Leafs chose not to spend any more of their own.

This strategy served to obliterate the cozy feelings of warmth that had developed for the team during the wonderful '98–99 campaign. Phone-in callers to The Fan-590 were almost unanimously appalled by the club's pomposity and thrift, at a time when favorable momentum should have been flourishing. These emotions were augmented by the virtual unwillingness of anyone in the Maple Leaf organization to take responsibility for its actions.

A statement by Tanenbaum early in September flew in the face of all conventional reasoning. During an interview I conducted at the Leafs' training site in Barrie, Ontario, the part-owner told me that the club's $34-million budget — frozen solid from the previous season — was actually requested by, rather than imposed on management. That Dryden and Quinn had appealed for ownership *not* to expand the payroll. This was remarkably difficult to comprehend. Unless, of course, ownership was threatening to decrease the budget (not a preposterous notion) and had to be talked into maintaining the status quo. If that was the case, then, yes, management had asked for $34 million.

But what annoys and confuses all Maple Leaf observers (fans and media) is the hypocrisy that arises in these situations. In his next sentence, Tanenbaum — obviously no fool when it comes to business — insisted that ownership's goal is to "win the Stanley Cup — not only this year, but for many seasons to come." How? I wondered. By alienating the club's premier young defenceman over less than half-a-million dollars? And by going to war with the team's emotional leader — Yushkevich (even though his agent, Mark Gandler, was staging a determined campaign for blockhead of the year)? Stanley Cup contenders don't suck in the fans, then threaten to replace two vital components with castoffs and retreads from the free agent pool. It's irresponsible and foolish behavior.

It did not prevent management, however, from further entrenching itself once training camp was underway. To no one's surprise, Quinn, who frequently took hardline approaches during his years in Vancouver (and who emulates his stated hero, Punch Imlach, a little too closely), chose to play hardball. He ordered a cumulative $50,000 reduction of the club's one-year contract offers to Berard and Yushkevich for each week of the pre-season in which the players remained absent. Beneath the surface, Quinn's ploy meant nothing, as all sides were seeking longer-term deals. But it created a further emotional frenzy among fans and media, who were rightly pondering what the club was trying to prove.

Quinn also went in circles. About Berard, he rhetorically wondered why the club should commit $1.7 million a season to "someone who has an obvious upside, but is maybe our sixth or seventh defenceman right now." Regarding Yushkevich, he then said, "Sure, he had a good season and playoff for us [in '99], but his previous three or four years weren't anything special." In other words, consider Berard only for what he can *now* supply, and disregard his future. But don't pay any attention when we dredge up Yushkevich's past. The Maple Leafs couldn't have it both ways, and they looked silly attempting to do so.

The club did have a more legitimate case against Yushkevich, for it was Gandler who initially requested an unreasonable stipend of close to $3 million annually. This was the same Gandler who drew the ire and disrespect of the hockey establishment by locking arms with client Alexei Yashin of the Ottawa Senators when Yashin walked away from the final year of a signed contract. It was also Gandler whom another client — Pittsburgh defenceman Darius Kasparitus — dumped on his ass after futile attempts to settle differences with the Penguins. Three days before the regular season, Kasparitus told Gandler to take a hike and called Pens' GM Craig Patrick himself. The two men worked out a contract in less than an hour.

Tanenbaum and Dryden both tried vainly to suggest that the hockey club's $34-million budget was not quite so rigidly cast. At the same time they were making that claim, Quinn was all but confirming that if the Maple Leafs wanted to spend $34,000,001, they'd have to sell off a roll of tape to compensate for going over. Many believed that the club was simply "doing its part" in the league-wide covenant to retard the salary upsurge.

The voice most frequently heard through all of this in the Leaf hierarchy was Bill Watters. If you look up the word "survivor" in any dictionary, chances are you'll see his accompanying photo. Why? Because Watters passionately carries out chores that no one else in the organization has any desire to. A tireless worker, he will spend endless hours on the phone bartering with player-agents in his role as the club's chief contract negotiator. In between these conversations, he somehow finds time to return *all* messages from reporters, and often appears on radio and television to champion his bosses' motives.

If you know Bill, it's difficult to figure that even *he* believes half of what comes out of his mouth, but his fervid loyalty can only be admired. That, and his vast prior experience on the opposite side of the ledger (as an agent) has enabled him to remain vital and appreciated by the Dryden regime, when most others hired by Cliff Fletcher have long since been discarded.

Tanenbaum raised more eyebrows at training camp when he made an honest, yet shocking, admission to me: "No matter what I, or anyone else says, it'll be impossible for [ownership] to refute the notion that we don't want to spend money on players." In making this statement, was Tanenbaum also acknowledging that ownership doesn't particularly *care* what the public thinks? And that he and his Maple Leaf partners have established a firm reputation from which there is no retreat? Justifiable questions, to be sure.

In the end, and to the unforeseen delight of Maple Leaf fans, common sense entered the picture. The Leafs compiled a 5-4-0 record in nine exhibition games during the '99 pre-season, but looked frightfully vulnerable defensively. As well, a pop-gun powerplay continued to fizzle. Watters and Tom Laidlaw — Berard's agent — are both affable, intelligent businessmen, and knew from the outset that neither side had anything to gain by prolonged inflexibility. At least once during the negotiation process, the two emissaries had come close to an agreement, only to back off at the last moment. They had never been more than $350,000 apart in their discussions, and both men ultimately came to the conclusion that they were wasting each other's energy. As well, it had never made particular sense for Berard to remain headstrong over such a paltry cash variance so early in his playing career.

With the start of the regular season just four days away, pressure had come to bear on both parties. Even *with* Berard and Yushkevich, the Leafs had been a mediocre defensive team in 1998–99 — unceasingly rescued by Curtis Joseph. And the club's lofty rank was astounding, considering its incapacity while playing with the man advantage. Economical off-season recruits Terran Sandwith and Greg Andrusak had battled nobly for spots during training camp, but neither could be counted on as an adequate substitute. And the Leafs knew that, despite their communal posturing.

Berard had spent all of September working out with a personal trainer (or so he claimed), and likely did not mourn the rigors of camp. Only when foregone pay-checks began to loom did he yield to the futility of his stance. On September 29, after more than a month of gamesmanship, Laidlaw and Watters shook hands on a two-year deal for Berard, worth a base payment of $3.3 million. While Quinn had bickered over paying the defenceman $1.7 million a season, the two sides settled on a split of $1.5 and $1.8 million over the length of the contract. Which means the Leafs had merely been dividing hairs with Laidlaw all along.

Quinn then shrewdly put pressure on Yushkevich and Gandler to end their intransigence by making a smart trade on the eve of the regular season. He acquired mammoth defenceman Cory Cross from Tampa Bay for winger Fredrik Modin, a young but stagnant player who the Leafs had clearly given abundant opportunity to blossom. Cross was no Brian Leetch, but he did have solid NHL credentials and a chance to flourish in a more stable hockey environment. His addition hardly offset the need for Yushkevich, but it beefed up the Toronto blueline and proved to Gandler that Quinn was quite capable of venturing elsewhere to fill the void.

Ultimately, Yushkevich re-assumed his old spot, putting a predictable end to the contract shenanigans. On October 8, he re-joined the team after agreeing to a three-year, $5.8-million pact — the same deal over which he and Gandler had foolishly threatened to bolt to Europe just the previous week. Only hours after welcoming back Yushkevich, the Leafs executed a straight salary dump that they tried to disguise as a roster move. They gave veteran defenceman Sylvain Cote to the Chicago Blackhawks for a second-round draft choice in 2001, a peculiar move for a team that — according to Tanenbaum — is looking to "win the Stanley Cup, not only this year but for years to come."

To make room for Yushkevich, the Leafs simply unloaded Cote's $1.5 million stipend, and they created yet another controversy while doing so. There were two distinct sides to this story, with no gray area whatsoever. According to Cote, he had been seeking — through his agent, Bob Sauve — to discuss a contract extension beyond the 1999–2000 season, after which he was slated to become an unrestricted free agent. Cote claimed that Bill Watters had failed to get in touch with Sauve while trade discussions with the Blackhawks were being finalized. The Leafs countered that they had offered Sauve the opportunity to negotiate an extended agreement, but the agent had said he'd get back to them later in the week. And that Sauve's dawdling cost his client a chance to stay in Toronto.

"I can say that's a pure lie," Cote told reporters moments after the deal. "My agent tried to contact Bill Watters, but he was too busy with the trade."

Terming the Leafs liars was a serious accusation by Cote, and the team shrugged it off as a comment made under emotional circumstances. Indeed, Cote had been taken aback by the trade, and had to walk away from an initial media scrum to regain his composure. But the Maple Leafs, again, seemed less than convincing in their argument. The club was in Ottawa for an early-season game the day after the trade. During the morning skate at the Corel Centre, I coerced Watters into a short interview on the conflict, but only after some serious arm-twisting. Normally willing to discuss any topic of contention, Bill was extremely hesitant to address the Cote accusation, perhaps because he truly liked the veteran blueliner and realized Leaf management had been forced to make the deal thanks to an uncompromising budget.

He could have also been uncomfortable with embellishing a falsehood. One Leaf player told me the club had "lied to Sylvain's face." Of course, there was no hard evidence of that, but it remained open to debate.

At the same time the hockey club was making examples of Yushkevich and Berard, Maple Leaf Sports and Entertainment Ltd. chose to announce it was putting Maple Leaf Gardens up for sale; or, more accurately, on the auction block. Rather than taking responsibility for the hockey shrine it inherited, Leaf ownership was throwing it open to potential shoppers — with no avowal that the cherished edifice would remain standing.

"We tried to make it work and couldn't; let's see if someone else can," declared a suddenly apathetic Dryden.

This, of course, did not come as a shock to anyone with business acumen. MLS & E is sponging every possible nickel from its ticket buyers to help pay off the Air Canada Centre, and the Gardens — for all its historic charm — could not possibly remain economically viable without the hockey team (and peripheral events like concerts, circuses, wrestling shows, etc.). To peddle the building and its valuable property — then pour millions of dollars into the Air Canada Centre debt — makes explicit sense. But the MLS & E announcement came less than two years after the following statement by chairman Stavro: "We'd like to keep [the Gardens] the way it is, the way it was built. We definitely will not tear that building down . . . We're not there for high-rise apartments. That's why we want to keep it. There's too much history there. We love that. All the owners are deeply moved by that."

Such heartfelt sentiments.

Richard Peddie explained that the company had fallen short, despite an "aggressive campaign" to attract sporting and concert events to the Gardens. Another unlikelihood. How aggressive could the company possibly have been while, simultaneously, knocking itself out to fill the Air Canada Centre each night? Why not just come out and say, "Lookit, there's no way we can viably operate two arenas and try to keep a line on ticket prices. The Gardens is a wonderful place, with eternal memories, but we require its potential revenue to offset our financial burden at the Air Canada Centre. We'll do everything we can to help discover an investor who might envision retaining the building."

That's language Joe Public can understand. And empathize with. Instead, we have Peddie declaring, "It's premature to say what's going to happen. We're open to any ideas." Passing the buck, in other words.

Maple Leaf fans may also look at the Toronto Raptors' payroll with some skepticism. While the Leafs and Raptors justly operate on separate budgets (as do the subsidiaries of all companies), and while NBA clubs procure greater monetary rewards from TV money, it was nonetheless intriguing to witness the contrast in financial resolve between the teams in the summer of 1999. Just one month after the Leafs claimed they could not afford a 31-year-old defenceman (Lefebvre) still close to his prime, Maple Leaf Sports and Entertainment Ltd. somehow came up with $18 million (U.S.) for the Raptors to re-sign 35-year-old power-forward Charles Oakley.

It somewhat pains me to make this gauche comparison, because Oakley — in his first season with the Raptors — quickly became one of my favorite Toronto athletes of all time. His veteran influence, on and off the court, was essential to the stirring improvement of the basketball team during the lockout-shortened season of 1998–99, and the Raptors needed him back. But his signing did reveal some inconsistency based on the company's approach to the hockey club.

As such, it'll be interesting to see if the 1999–2000 Maple Leaf budget is cast in stone, or if new GM Quinn can somehow convince his superiors to loosen the purse-strings as the season progresses — if the club continues to perform well. Of course, that prospect was hindered by the choice to do absolutely nothing in the summertime, so it may become a moot point. While Stavro has often been accused of imprudent scrimping, the Tanenbaum-Peddie combo was actually most responsible for freezing the current salary allotment at $34 million. Many observers believe that Stavro — now well into his 70s and a life-long Maple Leaf fan — is aching to win a Stanley Cup, and the fact he still has more than enough authority to influence a budget expansion may present Quinn with a reasonable opportunity at some point.

In most years — dating back to the Ballard era (1972–90) — the cheap route has been the preferred mode of business. A colossal salary purge in 1996 effectively cost the Maple Leafs any reasonable shot at a playoff spot — and its corresponding revenues — for two consecutive springs. The payroll reduction was ordered by Stavro, who some believe had more than just expenditure savings as a motive.

The purge actually began with the March 1996 deal that brought Wendel Clark and Mathieu Schneider to Toronto from the Islanders. It put the hockey club over its budget allocation for that particular year, and rather than assuming a slightly higher financial load, Stavro ordered Cliff Fletcher to hack $5 million from the payroll. Before agreeing to add Clark and Schneider, Fletcher had to part with Dave Andreychuk, who was dealt to New Jersey the very same day for a second-round draft choice in '96 (Leafs took mammoth defenceman Marek Posmyk with the pick). Andreychuk was past his prime years of the early '90s, but had still scored 20 goals.

Clark's 24 goals for the Islanders merely off-set Andreychuk's departure, making it a highly suspect maneuver.

The budget chop continued in mid-June, as Fletcher dealt long-time Maple Leaf defenceman Todd Gill to San Jose for journeyman forward Jamie Baker. At the '96 entry draft in St. Louis a week later, Fletcher traded veteran center Dave Gagner to Calgary for a third-round draft choice, and then nearly caused an international incident by peddling hall of fame candidate Mike Gartner to Phoenix for a fourth-rounder.

Having been acquired by the Leafs from New York at the trade deadline in March 1994 (thus missing out on the Rangers' Stanley Cup run), Gartner worked out a three-year deal with Fletcher that included a verbal no-trade provision. At the time, contractual no-trade clauses were prohibited, as they were not yet part of the collective bargaining agreement. At 35 years of age, and with 617 goals to his credit after the '93–94 season, Gartner wanted to finish his career in a Toronto uniform, and he and Fletcher shook hands on that promise.

Under immense strain a couple of years later to meet Stavro's budgetary guide-line, Fletcher perused his roster and determined that the aging Gartner had to go, gentleman's agreement or not. Gartner was on vacation when he got word of the deal and he nearly keeled over. Normally good-natured and easygoing, Gartner blew a gasket and convened a press conference after returning, letting the world know that Fletcher had betrayed him. Fletcher did not flatly deny Gartner's claim, but he managed to shrug it off.

"Cliff later admitted to me that he was forced to break our agreement," Gartner explains. "It's water under the bridge now, but I was certainly upset when it happened."

The salary freeze was center-stage again in the summer of '96. Stavro has often been assailed for scuttling an arrangement in July of that year that would have brought Wayne Gretzky to the Maple Leafs as an unrestricted free agent. But solely blaming the Leaf chairman is unjust. The story most often told is that Stavro and the MLG board refused to approve a verbal agreement that Fletcher had made with Gretzky's agent, Michael Barnett. But insiders claim there was minimal support in Fletcher's hockey department for the Gretzky acquisition, and that Barnett chose to prey on the fragile emotions of Leaf fans by telling several reporters that Toronto ownership had pulled the plug on a done deal.

"Nothing could be further from the truth," said a former Leaf employee. "Stavro took the hit on that one and didn't really deserve to. It was much more a case of Barnett doing his spin-doctoring. Cliff had re-acquired Wendel against the advice and wishes of most of the people around him; it seemed to be more of a publicity stunt than anything else. And signing Gretzky was pretty much the same thing. The budget was tight, the team was in need of major re-tooling, and it didn't seem at all prudent to spend millions of dollars on a player who was nearing the end of his career — as great a player as Gretzky was."

There are many who will swear that Stavro's budget chop was made so that Fletcher would eventually slice his own throat. The first half of '96 was a time of immense transition and turmoil for the Maple Leaf GM. Sailing along at eight games above the .500 mark early in the new year, his club suddenly and unexpectedly fell entirely to pieces. Between January 11 and March 3, the Leafs were able to win only three of 22 games (3-16-3), and Fletcher fired coach Pat Burns at the Westin Hotel in Denver on March 4, the morning after a dreadful 4-0 loss to the Colorado Avalanche.

Fletcher's personal life was in upheaval. In January, he had separated from his wife Donna (known to everyone as Boots) after more than 30 years of marriage. He was dating an Air Canada flight attendant, Linda Christopher, a woman more than a decade younger than Boots. Physically and emotionally, he appeared to undergo a metamorphosis, not necessarily for the worst. Fletcher dropped a sizable amount of weight, began to coif his familiar white hair in a more stylish manner, and he dressed less conservatively. He seemed, at times, like a giddy teenager gripped in the euphoria of a first love.

Professionally, however, he was in a shambles. Having brought the Maple Leafs almost instant credibility and success upon his hiring in June 1991, the former Calgary Flames GM had gone into a death spiral. Shrewd acquisitions of players like Doug Gilmour, Dave Andreychuk, Glenn Anderson, Mark Osborne, Bill Berg, and Sylvain Lefebvre enabled the Maple Leafs to mold into Stanley Cup contenders in 1993 and '94 — far sooner than anyone, including Fletcher, could have imagined. When the club's fortunes began to regress in the 1994 Stanley Cup semifinals (Vancouver trounced Toronto in five), and continued during the lockout-shortened season of 1995 (largely due to an overplayed Gilmour running out of gas), Fletcher desperately strove to regain its standing with a rash of deals, most of which had no favorable impact.

Sundin was obviously a gem, but the deal with Quebec cost the club Lefebvre, its best defenceman. Mike Ridley, a solid, 70-point-a-year centerman, came over from Washington but his enigmatic moods alienated many of his Maple Leaf teammates. Fletcher unloaded him to Vancouver at the '95 draft for plodding winger Sergio Momesso, who couldn't find the net with radar once he pulled on a Toronto uniform. Mike Craig had been signed as a restricted free agent from Dallas in the summer of '94, and Fletcher and Bob Gainey could not agree on compensation. The matter went to an arbitrator and Toronto lost. The Stars were awarded Peter Zezel (the Maple Leafs' best face-off man) and young defenceman Grant Marshall. Craig was an unmitigated flop, scoring 20 goals in 172 games.

Fletcher dealt a youngster named Dixon Ward to Los Angeles as part of a multi-player minor-league transaction. He yielded numerous middle-round draft choices and made trades for players who had little or nothing to offer: Momesso, Craig, Warren Rychel, Paul DiPietro, Terry Yake, Rich Sutter, Grant Jennings, Peter White, Ken Belanger, Wayne Presley. Invaluable first-round selections were relinquished in deals for Clark, Schneider and Dimitri Yushkevich (though the latter move would eventually show some merit).

Even the apparently sagacious acquisition of Kirk Muller and Dave Gagner failed to prosper. Muller had lost a huge step, and Gagner's salary was ditched after he accumulated a respectable 22 points in 28 late-season games for the '95–96 Maple Leafs.

When asked about his strategy of dealing draft picks late in the 1996–97 season, Fletcher uttered the phrase that will live with him in infamy:

"Draft shmaft!" he replied to a stunned room of reporters.

All of this combined with the prodigious slump of January-March 1996 (and his tumultuous family situation) to send Fletcher close to the edge. His nerves were visibly shot — never more apparent than during the press gathering in which he officially fired Burns. It was a move he savagely attempted to avoid, but one that was finally made upon Burns's own despairing confession that something had to be done. As he announced Burns's dismissal in the media lounge at Maple Leaf Gardens, Fletcher's voice and hands trembled noticeably; he seemed pale and drawn — the accelerating stresses in his life so painfully evident.

One failed season later, he was gone — replaced by Dryden. There are some insiders who believe it was planned that way. While Fletcher had built a stunningly prosperous team in his early Maple Leaf years, it served merely to placate Stavro on an interim basis, as he (along with Gardens treasurer Donald Crump) tried to block the hiring of Fletcher in the first place. After a rancorous process that followed the death (in April 1990) of Ballard, long-time Gardens director Don Giffin had risen to the post of board chairman and CEO. It was Giffin who inherited the chore of finding a chief operating officer for the company (and the hockey club). A search committee of Giffin along with fellow Gardens directors Ted Rogers and Thor Eaton set its designs on hiring someone with "a high hockey profile and equally solid business skills."

When it became known that Fletcher was the leading candidate, Stavro and Crump were piqued. They considered him purely a hockey man; he did not fit their profile of a corporate associate. Without informing Giffin, Stavro and Crump approached Lyman MacInnis, a senior executive at Labatt's and a board member of

Hockey Canada. MacInnis had worked with Alan Eagleson in the early days of the NHL Players Association and though he'd only been with the brewery a short while, he quickly grew interested in the Gardens job — to the point of considering John Muckler as GM of the Maple Leafs.

But Giffin had offered the COO's job to Fletcher and when the names of Fletcher and MacInnis went before the full board on June 4, 1991, Fletcher easily prevailed. He was named chief operating officer, president and general manager — drawing a five-year, $4-million contract, with a $1.5-million buyout clause. The deal sickened both Stavro and Crump, who had voted against it, and Fletcher began his Gardens tenure on July 1 amid the usual turmoil.

Stavro pressed to have MacInnis join Fletcher and assume the business operation of the Gardens, but Fletcher already had a contract and MacInnis had no desire to share the load. It wasn't until early October of 1991 that peace began to prevail, after several private meetings between Stavro and Fletcher. Pure joy was experienced in the spring of '93, when the Fletcher-made Leafs advanced to within five minutes of the Stanley Cup finals, losing to Wayne Gretzky and the Los Angeles Kings in a Game 7 semifinal showdown at the Gardens.

But when times eventually turned tough, Stavro's support of Fletcher dissipated like air escaping from a balloon. The notorious 1996 budget cut was seen by many as Stavro revving the wheels that would ultimately trample the GM he had so fervently opposed. In mid-February of 1997, the Gardens board met and voted to replace Fletcher for the following season — a story that was broken by columnist Marty York in the *Globe and Mail*. Unbeknownst to anyone outside the board, Dryden had become the apple of its eye, particularly in light of his long-time friendship with director Brian Bellmore. It took a second season of chaos and tumult to seal Fletcher's fate. The club missed the playoffs under Mike Murphy (his choice as head coach); Fletcher's nerves took another hit as he had to trade favorite son Doug Gilmour and deal with the Gardens sex scandal, and on May 24, 1997, he was officially fired. Displaying his renowned class and dignity, Fletcher showed up at the press conference that signaled his demise and faced the heat, straight on.

Less than a week later, Dryden was coronated president of the hockey club and it took him nearly three months to anoint himself GM, hire Mike Smith as his associate, and put the wheels in motion towards the acrimonious divorce that would rock the Maple Leaf Sports and Entertainment Ltd. empire.

Toronto winger Gary Valk is watched closely by Rangers counterpart John MacLean during New York's final visit to Maple Leaf Gardens, December 19, 1998. Valk would be a playoff hero for the Leafs, scoring the overtime series winner against Pittsburgh in the Eastern Conference semifinal.

Mike Smith (left), the Maple Leafs' associate general manager during the 1997-98 and 1998-99 seasons, watches the club practice. Smith was fired by Leaf president Ken Dryden, after an acrimonious relationship.

Goalie Curtis Joseph smothers a scoring opportunity by Carolina's Keith Primeau during the first-ever weeknight game at the Air Canada Centre, February 24, 1999. Defenceman Bryan Berard (34) slides by net.

Maple Leaf captain Mats Sundin:
unqualified skill and finesse; will the intangibles ever emerge?

A foreboding picture: Maple Leaf center Alyn McCauley, with loosely fitting helmet, collides with former Leaf Dave Andreychuk of New Jersey at Air Canada Centre, March 3, 1999. Moments later, McCauley would suffer a season-ending concussion when slammed to the glass by Devils defenceman Sheldon Souray.

Maple Leaf chairman Steve Stavro (left) shares a smile with team president Ken Dryden. No two men are more anxious to see the Leafs win a Stanley Cup. Do they have the know-how and wherewithal to bring it about?

Cantankerous, moody, vindictive ... and a damned good coach. Pat Quinn puts his charges through a practice at the Air Canada Centre. The GM role landed in his lap during the summer of 1999.

Mats Sundin in perfect scoring position. Boston goalie Byron Dafoe goes down to try and thwart the Maple Leaf captain.

The Great One at work during what would turn out to be No. 99's final NHL season

The addition of goalie Curtis "Cujo" Joseph played an important part
in the Leafs' dramatic turnaround during the 1998-99 season.

Mats Sundin sports the commemorative uniform worn by the
Maple Leafs on ten occasions during 1998-99 season to
mark the team's final year at Maple Leaf Gardens. Its style
is identical to the road uniform of 1964 to 1967.

* * *

As Smith persisted in venting his emotions over his relationship with Dryden and their ultimate parting of the ways, it became imperative that I at least offer the Maple Leaf president any opportunity he wished for a rebuttal. While Smith evidently believed strongly in his convictions, he had been petulant and insubordinate during his tenure with Dryden and throughout their period of separation. Employees simply cannot ignore their superiors — no matter what the level of antipathy — and expect to retain their positions.

"I was not insubordinate," Smith vehemently counters. "Ken was always made aware of any decision I was considering. But I had the authority to make the final call on hockey matters. It was an agreement that was made initially, and one that was clarified at the time Pat Quinn was hired as head coach. There were four of us in the room during that negotiation — me, Ken, Pat, and Dick Babush. And all of us know exactly what that agreement was — that I maintain control over personnel decisions, and that Pat reports to me. From the beginning, it was a given that I keep Ken informed of possible moves. And I did."

Somewhat puzzling about that agreement — as contentious as it became — was that it lacked written validation. According to Smith, it was simply a verbal covenant. "It didn't have to be in writing," he insists. "Any worthy employee in my position would have the same authority. But Ken tried to change the whole thing right from the start."

Smith contends that had he not "ignored" Dryden, the 1998–99 Maple Leafs would never have taken such enormous strides. Sources claim that Dryden apparently fought for the acquisition of veteran Guy Carbonneau (from Dallas) at the trade deadline, rather than the deal that brought Yanic Perreault to the Maple Leafs from Los Angeles. Also disregarded — according to Smith — were occasional attempts by Dryden to influence the lineups on a given night, though he'd be far from alone in contemplating tactics of that nature. GMs are notorious for sticking their noses in on game strategies.

As alluded to in Rosie DiManno's *Star* column of June 26, an irate Smith tempted Dryden to fire him when Dryden opposed the acquisition of Alexander Karpovtsev. The Leaf president backed down. When Smith told Dryden he would trade minor-league defenceman Jeff Ware at the first offer of any value, he claims Dryden again voiced opposition.

But more than anything else, Smith maintains that his relationship with Dryden took an irreparable turn once the Maple Leafs began to have success.

"Ken was always changing his role. As soon as the club started to show improvement, it was my sense that Ken wanted to take credit for it. He wanted to be portrayed as 'The Man' and rub shoulders at the GM's level. Of course, the opposite was never true. When the media ripped me for not being able to pull the trigger during the Felix Potvin trade talks, I don't remember Ken coming to my defence and saying anything supportive."

Smith's self-righteous independence destroyed any expectancy for his partnership with Dryden to succeed. Occasionally, it even impacted on Quinn, who Smith respected. Several times during the season, players were recalled from the Leafs' minor-league system without Smith informing anyone — the most prominent example being Kevyn Adams's arrival during the playoffs. Not until he spotted Adams on the ice for a practice did Quinn realize he had been summoned from St. John's.

Beyond their earliest days together, Smith never felt a shred of goodwill towards Hedberg. His loathing for the Swede intensified even before he and Dryden began to knock heads. Smith simply believed that Hedberg's area of responsibilities (overseeing the organization's amateur scouting and player development programs) fell under his umbrella of authority, and that Hedberg should report directly to him. After all, Smith was in charge of the team budget and any spending Hedberg did would have to be coordinated. Dryden, however, structured the power pyramid so that Hedberg (*assistant* GM in name) report to *him* (which Hedberg did), even though Smith controlled the finances. It was a procedure that doomed yet another relationship in the organization.

Smith basically wrote Hedberg out of his life — a potentially calamitous maneuver given their significance to the hockey club. Imagine a team in which the hockey operations director has no communication with the person in charge of developing players. Several Leaf employees claim that Smith incessantly bad-mouthed Hedberg, while the affable Swede merely went about his chores without getting involved in any strife. Hedberg knew he had the support of Dryden, but he was fully in tune to the acerbic feelings Smith had towards him. The repugnance quickly became mutual.

It therefore requires no reasoning to understand why Hedberg informed Dryden he would resign if Smith were named GM, and Hedberg suddenly had to report to a man who both despised him and would have the authority to alter his scope of influence and responsibility.

In the end, Hedberg saw one roadblock disappear but another quickly materialize. When Quinn became GM (closing a door that Hedberg aspired to one day enter), it became apparent that Nick Beverley's influence on the hockey club would deepen. Beverley and Quinn were long-time pals, having worked together in the Los Angeles organization from 1984 and '87. Beverley was later GM of the Kings, who went to the Stanley Cup finals under his direction in 1993. When L.A. plummeted 22 points in the standings the following year and failed to make the playoffs, he was fired.

Cliff Fletcher hired Beverley as director of scouting and player personnel on September 1, 1994, giving the former NHL defenceman a full biography outline and photograph in the club's media guide the following year. Most Leaf fans best remember Beverley for assuming the interim coaching reins late in the 1995–96 season after Pat Burns was fired. He guided the club to a 9-6-2 record, and during a first-round playoff loss to St. Louis gained immortality by calling his players a bunch of "nimrods."

Beverley and Bill Watters survived the Fletcher firing and the onset of the Dryden-Smith regime a year later. But Beverley saw his overall responsibilities diminish, and his bio disappear from the media guide. In his unassuming, often self-deprecating manner, however, he quietly became an invaluable aide to Smith in the role of pro scouting director. Smith wasn't in the habit of liberally dispensing accolades, but he rarely concealed how vital Beverley was (along with Joe Yannetti) in the club's evaluation of personnel at the NHL level.

Two elements combined to spell Hedberg's demise with the Maple Leafs. As mentioned, Quinn replaced Smith in the GM's chair and Beverley received an offer to join the Tampa Bay Lightning in a prominent player-development role. He did not, however, wish to make a sideways move and he informed Quinn of his desire to assume more responsibility in Toronto. Looking to streamline the Leafs' management "committee," Quinn offered Beverley the soon-to-be-named position of director of player personnel, including amateur and professional scouting — surely realizing that Hedberg would resign. Quinn gave Hedberg the choice of remaining with the organization as head amateur scout, reporting to Beverley. It therefore came as no surprise when Hedberg announced — on August 16, 1999 — that he was leaving the Maple Leafs, though he did so with notable class and dignity.

* * *

During the period in which Dryden and Smith were said to be negotiating a new contract, Smith flippantly maintained his demand for full authority, while mentioning in a saucy, unmannerly way that he could take the job or leave it. There was always the family antique shop in Martha's Vineyard to attend to. He was calling Dryden's bluff in no uncertain manner. When a reporter like myself would question Smith about an apparent mystery in the negotiations — such as a promised meeting with Dryden that never materialized — Smith would play along with the bafflement and cast Dryden in a darker light. It made for good copy but was clearly objectionable conduct by an employee.

Dryden maintained a peculiar silence through it all, allowing Smith to degrade him in any manner he preferred. But there was no way on earth I, or anyone else, could write a chapter like this without attempting to obtain his version of the events. I passed on my request to Ann Clark, Dryden's secretary, and did not hear back from the Leaf president. Therefore, I approached him in person after the Quinn media conference and laid out my request. He quickly rebuffed the opportunity for a straight rebuttal, claiming that a pissing match with the departed Smith was not his desired platform. But he did welcome the chance to summarize his thoughts on the matter, and suggested I call Clark to set up a meeting.

Dryden and I sat for more than two hours in his office at the Air Canada Centre on the afternoon of July 19, 1999. He insisted that his particular comments were off the record and would not permit me to record the meeting. But the essence of his remarks were very much for publication. During our chat, I noticed a side of the Leaf president I'd had glimpses of before, but no prolonged exposure to: a passion and vehemence that the public Dryden hardly ever projects. And some ardent, sincere anguish over the manner in which he'd been portrayed during his two years on the job.

Dryden simply believed that by appointing himself general manager of the Maple Leafs in the summer of 1997 he'd be removing the burden of failure from his executive tandem of Smith and Hedberg. He knew there was no possible way for the bad Leaf team he'd inherited to make any noticeable strides in his first season at the helm. And after his GM overtures were rejected by Bob Gainey and David Poile, he clearly felt — rightly or wrongly — that there was no single person available to him who could function with full autonomy.

Smith had been out of the game for six years and NHL teams were clearly not beating down the door to employ him. And Hedberg, though he had (at the time) long-term Maple Leaf aspirations, knew he was not equipped to handle the GM's portfolio so soon after moving from his native Sweden to North America. But Dryden saw great potential in the skills of both men and was eager to determine how they would grow during a two-year apprenticeship as his chief lieutenants. Ultimately, he believed he would shoulder the burden of responsibility for the team's fortunes, or lack thereof, while immersing himself in the full scope of his presidential and managerial duties.

It's clear that in Smith's case, these advances were interpreted to be infringements on his territory, and a wall immediately rose between himself and his hands-on boss. Dryden merely felt that he was doing his job — helping to "find a way," as he so often describes it — but Smith rebuffed his attempts. When it became clear that a pivotal confrontation was on the horizon, both men sought advocacy from members of the board of directors, and discovered a fault line nearly as volatile as their own. The resultant tremor was nearly cataclysmic.

Dryden fervently takes exception to Smith's claim that his offer to become GM did not embody full authority and final say on all hockey matters. Yes, he was requiring that Smith continue to keep him abreast of affairs, but he made it clear to me that even if he objected to a potential move, Smith would make the ultimate call, and be judged on its merits. Smith's response was a two-syllable word, the first of which was "bull."

"Before doing anything of significance, I would have to get both Ken's and the board's approval," he insists. "That pertained to contracts or any player movements. All I aimed to do with my counter-offer was remove that provision. Everyone made a big deal over my request to become an alternate governor, but much more important was that I gain the type of autonomy required by any GM to properly do his job. Ken was never prepared to give that up. Not even close."

Not to Smith, anyway.

Initially, Dryden was terribly confused and deeply wounded by Quinn's expressions of disbelief over Smith's banishment. He knew that he'd conversed with his coach on at least two occasions prior to taking his decision to the board, and had undoubtedly conveyed to Quinn the perilous nature of the negotiations. When Quinn made it known, with conviction, that he'd been told to anticipate a settlement between Dryden and Smith — one that surprisingly did not occur — it was construed as some sort of cover-up by Dryden, and was generally reported that way. Knowing what he had told Quinn, Dryden was thoroughly perplexed over the coach's reaction, until it was related to him that someone on the board had obviously misrepresented the negotiations. Then, according to Dryden, the misunderstanding was clarified.

But nothing Dryden related to me during our meeting could match the pure abhorrence he felt towards members of the media. His emotions were raw and unrefined. While he insisted he does not listen to radio commentaries or read newspaper columns, the essence of these summations "filter through," and he's in a categorical state of incomprehension over their intent. They have hurt him, personally, to depths he never knew. In many ways, he's like a lot of us — incapable of conceiving why others choose to randomly act with indignity and spitefulness. He believes these qualities result from blatant myopia — the inability and unwillingness to take the time to consider the logic and purpose behind decisions that are made.

Being portrayed as some sort of babbling lout grieves him to a great degree. For a brief moment during our chat, tears began to well up in his eyes, and his undiluted anguish became painfully evident. He is clearly a man whose depth of curiosity is greater than most, and his painstaking manner of communicating what he thinks can often be misinterpreted. There is a cultivating, benevolent side to Dryden that he senses is too frequently overlooked. He is also — so many of us forget — the president of a hockey team that finished with 97 points and among the top half-dozen teams in the overall NHL standings in the 1998–99 season. Perhaps those who mock and criticize him should pause and consider the predicament the Maple Leafs were in when his regime — unorthodox as it may have been — came aboard in 1997.

Smith doesn't buy any of this. He believes Dryden has been exposed as something of a fraud, based on Quinn's impulsive reaction to his firing, and the media's subsequent remonstration against Dryden (i.e., David Shoalts's *Globe and Mail* column). And that Dryden's emotions do not reflect a justifiable disdain for the media, but rather his own personal chagrin and loss of reputation.

The scope of dissension between Dryden and Smith was so remarkably evident during the most exhilarating moments of the Maple Leafs' 1999 playoff run. Smith says the two men never even exchanged a smile in either Philadelphia or Pittsburgh on the nights the club won its two post-season series. Clearly, these were men whose professional paths were never designed to cross as they did.

My own feelings about the Dryden-Smith feud and eventual split-up are deeply mixed, because I genuinely like both men. Prior to our commiseration, Dryden may have found that difficult to believe, as I've often been critical of his sluggishness in making decisions. In dragging his feet on most Leaf issues — claiming there is always a "process" to carry out — he seems to be grasping for answers rather than carefully considering practical options. On a personal level, I've often felt that Dryden considers me nothing more than an inconsequential pest. He clearly loathes the issues I question him on — calling them predictable and mundane. "*You* know what you're going to ask, and *I* know what you're going to ask," he often remarks in a disdainful manner.

Prior to the 1998–99 season, Dryden arranged for informal gatherings with the various media outlets that cover the Maple Leafs. Given my nature, I was a trifle suspicious of his objectives — possibly because they were never clarified beforehand. And, it's not often that a company president brings along two members of his publicity department for a self-arranged meeting (Dryden had both Pat Park and John Lashway at his side). As it turned out (at least, in the meeting he held at The Fan-590), Dryden merely wanted to initiate a "bull" session, and answer any questions I or my radio-station colleagues may have had. I'm told that some of his other sessions — particularly the one at the *Toronto Sun* — became confrontational (big surprise with Strachan present), but ours was primarily congenial. Several of my co-workers' eyes were practically bulging out of their sockets from merely being in the same boardroom as Dryden; one of them even brought along a copy of *The Game* to have autographed. So, if Dryden's purpose was to address the communication chasm between him and me, it proved to be an impractical environment.

I sat quietly through the two-hour meeting, while Dryden tried several times to draw me into the conversation. He wasn't saying anything I hadn't heard before, and I actually enjoyed observing my star-struck colleagues. When Dryden finally turned to me and inquired about our "awkward" relationship, I responded that we had not spoken enough times, or at sufficient length, to fashion any sort of "relationship." Dryden alluded to my so-called ambushing of him at the Gardens during the Mike Murphy affair, and I offered no apology. "It was the first time in four weeks that I attempted to speak with you," I told him. "For someone who covers the team on a full-time basis, I didn't feel that was an unreasonable request."

At other times, Dryden and I have engaged in pleasant and harmonious conversation, and those are the moments that stand out for me. Blessed with a vivid memory and an intrinsic ability as a wordsmith, Dryden can be a captivating speaker and I thoroughly enjoy the rare moments of casual time that I spend in his company. Perhaps his disinclination towards me stems from my various attempts — prior to his Leaf days — at badgering him for an interview. His initial response would almost always be to decline these overtures, but with a bit of arm-twisting, I did prevail on several occasions and never regretted my efforts.

When it was announced in April 1991 that a new arena would be erected to replace the fabled Montreal Forum, Dryden provided me (and our sportsradio audience) with a superb, heartfelt reflection on the building that housed so many of his finest hockey moments. When writing my second-last book, *Maple Leaf Moments,* in 1994, I called Dryden for his perspective on Mike Palmateer — the brash Maple Leaf netminder of the late 1970s. More specifically on a game back in November of the 1976–77 season, when Palmateer — in the first two weeks of his NHL career — turned in a startling performance against Dryden's Canadiens: a 1-0 blanking of the Montreal team that would lose only eight of its eighty games, and ultimately capture its second of four consecutive Stanley Cups.

"It wasn't just that Mike was making the saves, as much as the way he was making them," Dryden recalled for the book. "There he was, a rookie, playing against a team that hardly ever lost, and he was winning every challenge . . . charging out of his net to confront our best shooters. I remember thinking, 'How dare you come into the league and not just play so well against us, but with that in-your-face style.' It really was a terrific performance."

In the autumn of 1997 — Dryden's first in command of the Leafs — the club held its training camp in Kitchener, Ontario. A large room on the second level of the Kitchener Auditorium was set aside for the media, and there was abundant space to sit around, have a Coke, and shoot the breeze between workouts. Early one afternoon, Dryden came in and sat down at one of the large, round tables. Slowly but surely, a growing mass of media gravitated towards him, and we sat there for a full 90 minutes — captivated by Dryden's stories from the 1972 Canada-Russia series. It was an absolutely delightful gathering, one that we had to reluctantly disband for the purposes of our work.

I have known Mike Smith much longer than Dryden. He was assistant GM of the Winnipeg Jets when I did editorial work for the club's program back in the mid-1980s. For three or four consecutive years, I'd travel to Winnipeg during the Jets' training camp (one year it was held in Sherbrooke, Quebec), and spend two weeks compiling notes and interviews for the magazine. Smith had a profound interest in writing (he's authored several books himself), and our common ground led to a number of prolonged chats.

He has a tougher outer shell than Dryden, but it can be easily penetrated when he's provoked. As you've witnessed on previous pages, just mention the name John Ferguson and away he'll go. I remember sitting with Mike in the Oakland Coliseum-Arena during an exhibition game prior to the 1988–89 NHL season. Promoters had brought the Jets, Detroit Red Wings and Los Angeles Kings (with newly acquired Wayne Gretzky) to northern California for a series of friendlies. Games were played in Oakland, San Francisco's Cow Palace, and the Arco Arena in Sacramento.

During the first period of a Jets-Detroit game in Oakland, I sat next to Smith in a makeshift press box in the second level of seats. This was the arena where the California Seals played their home games from 1967 to 1976. I had always been fascinated by the stories I'd read from those early expansion days in the NHL, and how the Seals failed so miserably to draw crowds to their modern building. I finally had the opportunity to see a hockey game there and was curiously looking about the place while Smith treated me to a full 20-minute dissertation on his troubles with Ferguson, who was fired by the Jets a month later.

There were times during the 1998–99 Maple Leaf season when I felt great sorrow for Smith and his family situation. How he was able to juggle his job and maintain focus while his wife battled incurable cancer was beyond my grasp. He did a wonderful job shaping the Maple Leafs' on-ice success, and all things being equal (which they weren't), most certainly deserved a new contract. He is a man who commands greater respect around the NHL than his personality often suggests, and he could be missed by the Leafs. The malice and animosity he and Dryden manufactured for one another clearly will not be.

* * *

The summer of '99 proved to have no mellowing effect on Pat Quinn. In fact, the recently appointed GM came to training camp in September fully loaded for bear. When his very first media scrum at the Air Canada Centre (on the morning of the Leaf medicals) began to extend longer than he had planned, Quinn sighed heavily and snapped, "Jesus Christ, what is this, *Gone With The Wind Two*?!!" That eruption was merely a preview of what became known as "McCauleygate." The events of Thursday, September 23, proved that Quinn's scorn for the media was at an all-time high. With no apparent limit.

Just one day earlier, in his post-practice session with the media, the Leaf GM/coach had been direct and purposeful in his comments about Alyn McCauley. The young Maple Leaf centerman, sidelined since the previous March with lingering post-concussion symptoms, had been medically cleared by the Leaf doctors to participate in full training-camp drills and scrimmages. However, Quinn refused to play him in exhibition games until one final opinion was obtained — from Dr. James Kelly, the famed Chicago neurologist who had stood between the Leafs and Florida in the scuttled Potvin-Niedermeyer deal a year earlier.

McCauley visited Kelly on September 22 — the same afternoon Quinn stood before a flock of reporters and said, "We expect this to be merely a confirmation of what he already has [*medical clearance from the Leaf doctors*]. In fact, I have confidently penciled him in to play in tomorrow's pre-season game [against the Vancouver Canucks]." These remarks clearly reflected the information about McCauley emanating from the Maple Leaf camp, and were not questioned by reporters. The long period of recovery was over for the injury-plagued forward, who would appear in the lineup 24 hours hence.

But strange things began to happen later that day. Normally accessible to members of the media, McCauley suddenly went incommunicado, as did his representative, Don Meehan, one of the most recognizable and widely quoted agents in the hockey business. Though McCauley had returned from Chicago on Wednesday afternoon, neither he nor Meehan was answering his telephone. Reporters were fervently trying to confirm Quinn's analysis from earlier in the day, and merely wanted to hear McCauley (or Meehan) say that he was indeed fine, and would be in the lineup against Vancouver.

Of course, when the situation grew desperate for the writers working on deadline, the Leafs had nothing further to offer. That came as no surprise. But the fact that McCauley and Meehan were running created immense suspicion. Around 10:30 Wednesday night — after exhausting all reasonable options — Paul Hunter of the *Star* (with more than a slight nudge from his colleague, Damien Cox) took it upon himself to visit McCauley's mid-town residence. He knocked on the door, and was greeted by a less-than-amused Meehan, who curtly asked him to retreat without offering a smidgen of insight about his client.

It may or may not have been an appropriate move by Hunter, but he was simply reacting to the dilemma facing all reporters who cover Quinn's Maple Leafs — a sheer lack of respect and consideration for the job at hand. Naturally, when Quinn got word of Hunter's impromptu sojourn, he dug in his heels even further than usual, and made the following day an exercise in futility that, once again, reflected poorly on the Maple Leaf organization.

It all began with McCauley's unexpected absence from the morning skate at the Air Canada Centre. According to the most recent communiqué from the coach, McCauley was "penciled in" to play against Vancouver, and his name was in fact on the lineup sheet that morning in the press room. NHL GMs were meeting in Toronto throughout the day, giving Quinn a convenient excuse to sidestep the media wondering about McCauley's whereabouts. During the GM's lunch break, Quinn was tracked down and questioned on the circumstance by hockey writer Alan Adams of the *National Post*. "Go ask Hunter, he's got all the answers," the coach snapped, still angered over the previous night's events.

That's all anyone would hear from Quinn until after the hockey game. It once again left his staff in the lurch. Pat Park and Anthony Alfred had no idea how to respond to the avalanche of queries from reporters justifiably confused by the situation. Athletic therapist Chris Broadhurst was typically accommodating, but would not divulge any secrets. The entire day passed by without so much as a peep from the hockey club on the well-being of McCauley. Radio and television outlets hoping to update Leaf fans on the story during their late-afternoon and supper-hour sportscasts were out of luck. All of the silence gave rise to speculation that something about McCauley's health was terribly amiss, casting an even dimmer light on the club for its mishandling of the affair.

A long media vigil outside the Maple Leaf dressing room prior to the game was more wasted time, and reporters filed up to the press box with no further lead on the story. That's when the team finally chose to release a lame and feeble statement, in written form. Quoting Quinn, it read: "Tests have been carried out over the past two days and the results at this stage are inconclusive. Further testing is required and that will take place over the next few days."

What the hell did all of *that* mean?

According to Dryden, who found himself surrounded by reporters in the first intermission, the terse statement spoke for itself — an odd declaration from a man whose mere preamble to such matters would normally be five times more detailed. In fact, the statement said absolutely nothing. How could results of any further tests be inconclusive after Leaf doctors — a month earlier — had given McCauley the green light to fully partake in the rigors of training camp? And if further tests were required, then why? The inane statement answered none of the key questions. It was a puny effort after a long day of bewilderment.

And Quinn did nothing for his image after the game when he ducked the issue of why there had been no communication from the hockey club.

"I was busy in meetings until 4:30," he said, weakly.

"Too busy to release one measly paragraph on the issue?" I pressed.

"I was meeting with the GMs."

It came out later in his post-game briefing that Dr. Kelly in Chicago had evidently presented McCauley with further reasons to proceed cautiously — a tack that rubbed Maple Leaf doctors the wrong way. Like McCauley himself, the team felt the young centerman was ready to play. Evasiveness rose to an all-time high, with the Leafs and Don Meehan tip-toeing around the issue like a Russian ballet ensemble. Why did McCauley need further tests? What kind of tests were they? Why hadn't he undergone them a month earlier? What had Kelly said to McCauley that the Maple Leaf doctors possibly overlooked? Did anyone advise him flatly to retire? These were all questions that begged for answers, but none were forthcoming. Quinn was having a field day with the dastardly media.

Skip forward two days, to a quiet Saturday morning at the Air Canada Centre. Meehan sat alone high up in the northeast stands as the Leafs — sans his client — practiced down below. Only three reporters, including myself, were in the building, and we all joined Meehan at his perch. The agent was suddenly far more forthcoming than anyone had previously been about McCauley. All of the testing had been completed, Meehan confirmed, and the young Maple Leaf would now conduct one further conference call with doctors to determine his fate.

"I can assure you that the final decision rests with Alyn," Meehan said. "He's now armed with all the necessary information to make that decision, and I can see it happening within the next couple of days. Alyn will skate by himself after today's practice."

That solo session endured for almost an hour, with the small media cluster observing McCauley like scientists looking at mice. As per his agent, the player was infinitely more direct when he spoke with us afterwards.

"I'm going to talk with the doctors one more time and make a final decision on Tuesday," he said. "I feel just fine, but I obviously have to weigh some potential concerns. Hockey is just part of my life; there are other things I want to accomplish, and do I feel like risking all of that to keep playing? I don't know right now. I'll decide Tuesday."

Nobody realized that McCauley was actually a hair's width away from making that decision. One further confab with his wife of two months, Nicole, was all it took. At no time had he seriously pondered throwing away his entire career at age 22, and he called Quinn Saturday night to inform him that he was going to return. He then called Meehan, who had flown to Philadelphia on business, and told his agent the same thing. Now, most GMs with even a snippet of prescience would have understood that this was generally cheerful news, and should be shared with the devoted hockey fans of Toronto. Not Quinn.

Instead, the mystery intensified with McCauley's sudden presence among his teammates at Sunday morning's practice. After consulting with Dr. Kelly, he had been removed from mainstream activities — evidenced by his solo skate the previous day. No further action would be taken by McCauley at a team level until his final conference call with doctors on Monday. Why, then, was he now on the ice with the rest of his 'mates? The answer became obvious soon after the practice when McCauley casually mentioned that he had chosen, the previous afternoon, to continue playing. Fairly gargantuan news, considering all the confusion and chaos of the previous week. Being a Sunday, there was a lighter-than-usual media load, and those present merely stumbled across the story. Those absent, including network TV affiliates like TSN and Headline Sports, were out of luck.

What would it have taken for the generally competent Maple Leaf publicity staff to photocopy a one-paragraph release announcing McCauley's return, and fire it off by FAX to all of the Toronto media outlets? The answer is simple: Quinn's blessing and cooperation.

But the Leaf GM/coach — myopic beyond comprehension only when it comes to the media — would have never considered such a gesture. With his notable lead, the hamstrung Maple Leafs remain miles behind all other clubs in media relations. Toronto should be the focal point of such matters, considering the prominence of hockey in the city and the unwavering devotion of Maple Leaf fans. But it can't happen when the boss is perpetually gunning for the undesired messengers.

Chapter 2

The Great One Bids Farewell

With the 1999 Stanley Cup playoffs on the horizon, an event of unparalleled magnitude gripped the entire hockey world. The finest and most noteworthy competitor the game had ever seen chose to retire after 21 glorious seasons. The celebration of his last dance will forever be the stuff of legend.

Sunday, April 18, 1999
New York

There were 20,000 people shoehorned into Madison Square Garden this afternoon for one of the truly historic occasions in the annals of professional hockey.

I was lucky enough to be among them.

Wayne Gretzky, chosen last year as the game's greatest all-time performer by a distinguished poll in *The Hockey News,* played his final game in the NHL. His New York Rangers were defeated, 2-1, by the Pittsburgh Penguins — party-pooper Jaromir Jagr scoring in overtime — but hardly anyone seemed to notice, or care. It was a day for Gretzky. A day for friends of the ice game to laugh and cry. A day to celebrate the noblest hockey career ever. A moment in time.

But distractions? There were a few.

I was surely the only numbskull paying as much homage to the out-of-town scoreboard as the majesty unfolding on the ice. While a genuine legend played his final hockey game, I spent the afternoon cocking my neck towards the southwest corner of the Garden, where, beneath the upper concourse, an electronic board up-dated the three other matinees on this last day of the 1998–99 regular season.

My eyes were affixed on the Boston at Philadelphia match-up, as it would determine Toronto's opponent in the first round of the Stanley Cup playoffs. And, just as importantly, my travel destination for four days next week. A win at home by the Flyers, and the Maple Leafs would face Philadelphia, sans Eric Lindros. A Boston victory or tie would forge a Leafs-Bruins series, and a showdown with former Toronto coach Pat Burns. Both possibilities were intriguing.

But back to Gretzky. No. 99 decided to call it quits in '99 two days ago. Actually, he confirmed what most of the hockey world already figured. Earlier in the week, the *New York Post* — citing "unimpeachable" sources — broke the biggest hockey story of the year: that Gretzky would hang up his celebrated skates at the end of his 21st professional season. The Rangers were not among the NHL playoff qualifiers, prompting (the *Post* said) a dramatic announcement by week's end.

Sensing the occasion, a Stanley Cup final-like swarm of hockey reporters and columnists descended upon Kanata, Ontario, this past Thursday for what figured to be Gretzky's final road game, and final game in his native country. The sell-out audience in the Corel Centre stood and wildly cheered Gretzky during his late shifts against the Ottawa Senators, then remained on their feet, chanting, once the teams had left the ice. Like an idolized rock performer, Gretzky returned for the requisite encore — bowing and waving to the crowd from the Ranger bench.

During a dramatic and lengthy post-game news conference — televised nationally by three Canadian networks — Gretzky did everything but confirm he'd retire after the upcoming Ranger finale against Pittsburgh.

"Let's just say it'll take a miracle for me to change my mind," he smiled.

That miracle did not occur in the overnight and early hours of the following day, and Gretzky stood — on Friday afternoon — before a spellbound media throng in New York. Somehow maintaining his decorum, he bade an emotional farewell to the game he had shaped in a generation of unprecedented splendor. Sunday afternoon, he insisted, would be his NHL swan song.

It was an occasion not to be missed. Therefore, after covering the Maple Leafs' regular-season finale in Montreal last night, I hopped on a plane to New York early this morning. While checking in at the LaGuardia Airport Marriott, I ran into Bill McCreary — one of the NHL's senior referees — who'd been chosen, at the last moment, to work Gretzky's farewell encounter. Though McCreary wouldn't say, it appeared that he and younger referee Dave Jackson had swapped assignments — the league sending Jackson to Montreal for last night's Leafs-Canadiens tilt once the New York-Pittsburgh game took on legendary significance.

This is habitual for the NHL, which reserves its most important occasions for its longest-serving officials. McCreary, for instance, had worked the final NHL game at Maple Leaf Gardens in February while his veteran colleague, Terry Gregson, refereed the inaugural Air Canada Centre match the following weekend. Today, here in New York, the honor and appreciation of that loyalty was written all over McCreary's face, and he invited me to drive into Manhattan with him.

As we approached Madison Square Garden two hours later, the magnitude of today's event was unmistakable. There were swarms of hockey fans on the 7th Avenue side of the building — literally hundreds of them wearing the familiar blue and white Rangers jersey with No. 99 and "Gretzky" emblazoned on the back. Many were looking for tickets to the game, and many less were selling them. Hockey collector and souvenir hunter that I am, I was angling to get my hands on a couple of programs for this afternoon's game, but several hundred people were already lined up to purchase the coveted magazines at a kiosk outside the Garden's main entrance. The media gate was on the 8th Avenue side, but McCreary said, "C'mon with me."

He whisked me through the officials' and employees' entrance and along a corridor leading to a bank of escalators. The arena had not yet opened to ticket holders and the souvenir kiosks inside the Garden were still setting up their displays. Stacks of programs were available at these unpopulated locations and I was both thrilled and relieved to buy several of them and stick them into my equipment bag.

As I mentioned, this occasion very quickly attracted a media throng similar to that of an All-Star game or Stanley Cup final. The Rangers' P.R. department did yeoman's work accommodating roughly 300 credential requests in just more than 48 hours. Unlike an All-Star or Stanley Cup event, however, there was insufficient time to plan for an auxiliary press location. During the Cup final, the league reserves several rows of arena seating for the overflow army of media. Temporary tables are constructed, telephone lines are installed, and television sets hang from makeshift scaffolding. No such system was in place for today's game and, therefore, almost two-thirds of reporters welcomed into the building did not have an assigned seat . . . myself included. A large area of the Garden substratum had been cordoned off as a post-game interview area, with rows of tables, TVs, telephones and electrical outlets. This was the auxiliary press box.

But I didn't come here today to watch Gretzky's momentous last game on television in a wired-up basement. I could've done that with infinitely more comfort on my easy chair at home in Thornhill, Ontario. The attraction of this event — and its reporting value for radio — wasn't so much the game, but the atmosphere in the arena, and the resonance of the sold-out audience. The "sound" of today's experience would be its compelling feature, and makeshift catacombs aren't particularly noisy. As such, I set out on my own auxiliary mission and wound up being extraordinarily lucky.

The press box set-up at Madison Square Garden is rather unique. Mainstream members of the local media — newspaper reporters who cover the Rangers all season — as well as scribes traveling with the visiting team, are located in a small annex of the building's southeast corner, immediately above the Zamboni entrance. It's the only press location in the NHL situated at ice level. The vast majority of reporters view games from an elongated position on the south side of the arena, known as the Upper 33rd St. press box. Two-thirds of the way up from the ice, it presents a decent view of the action, and that's where I headed today, two hours before game time, hoping that at least one of my media colleagues would not show up. Fat chance.

But, I lucked out. The press box attendant — a man named Sal — permitted me to take an unoccupied seat in front of the box, and promised that if the seat owner showed up, he'd move me around. Incredibly, that particular ticket holder had something else to do this afternoon, and I wound up viewing the entire day's events from a padded seat almost directly at center ice.

And what a day it was. The Rangers wore their old-style blue uniforms, as they did for home games in the 1950s and '60s. The Penguins, clad in their white uniforms with the yellow and black trim (their usual home duds), were very much part of the event as the Rangers' opposition, yet they seemed as much spectator as participant. When Gretzky appeared for a brief but extremely tasteful pre-game ceremony, the Pittsburgh players stood watching at their bench, and several of them — including Jagr — actually hugged the Great One when he skated by. Before a game!!

The ceremony, emceed by Rangers' broadcaster John Davidson, lasted all of 15 minutes. Introduced to the audience was Mark Messier, anointed by Gretzky as the best player he ever played with, and Mario Lemieux — the best he'd ever played against. Both came out to the ceremony carpet and embraced Gretzky. Messier, wearing his Darth Vader sunglasses, generated perhaps the loudest ovation of the entire day. Gretzky's family, along with the coach from his glory years in Edmonton, Glen Sather, were also on hand.

NHL commissioner Gary Bettman made it known that Gretzky's No. 99 would never again be worn in the league, marking the first and only time a player has been so honored. Gretzky's Ranger teammates presented him with the largest TV you'll ever see (a 72-inch screen!), and the Great One made a very brief address, not wishing to delay proceedings any longer for the visiting Penguins. Class to the very end.

The game itself was a footnote, and one that couldn't end soon enough for Bill McCreary. As we rode into Manhattan today, I asked him what he'd do if Gretzky were to accidentally clip a Pittsburgh player with his stick and draw blood — the requisite for a game misconduct. McCreary could only shiver. "Let's hope it's a nice touchy-feely game and we get it over with quickly," prayed the referee.

He needn't have worried. Only three penalties were handed out — two of them to Jagr — and the game whizzed by in just more than two-and-a-half hours. Other than the fast-moving clock, there was little for Ranger fans to cheer about until the final minute of the second period, when Gretzky recorded his 2,857th and last point in the NHL. He and defenceman Mathieu Schneider fed Brian Leetch for a goal that offset one earlier in the period by the Penguins' Alexei Kovalev (once Gretzky's line-mate in New York).

As the third period developed, it presented everyone in the Garden with a dilemma. The score remained deadlocked at 1-1, and overtime became a distinct possibility. Therefore, no one was sure when Gretzky would take his final shift in the NHL — an occasion the fans were hoping to recognize with long and loud applause. But, they were not to be deterred. Anytime Gretzky appeared in the final 10 minutes of regulation — obviously, in the event of a late goal — the decibels rose considerably. The Great One paused several times — including once just before taking a face-off — and acknowledged the standing ovations with a quick wave. As a gift to his teammates and various charities, and a promise to the Hockey Hall of Fame, Gretzky used 51 different sticks during the afternoon.

To the delight of absolutely no one, the game did go into extra time and Jagr saw fit to end it at the 1:22 mark, slapping a rebound past Mike Richter. He then skated over to Gretzky, put his arms around him, and apologized. Gretzky began to warm to the crowd, which instantly shook off its disappointment over the meaningless Ranger defeat.

And the ensuing 15 minutes were pure, unrehearsed magic. The Garden P.A. announcer, perhaps wanting to hear himself say the name one last time, droned, "Ladies and gentlemen . . . Wayne Gretzky," at which time the moment's hero began a sequence of deliberate and triumphant laps around the ice. The Pittsburgh players remained on the scene, banging their stick-blades the way hockey players do when they're cheering.

Gretzky soaked it all in — waving continuously to the fans; recognizing familiar faces in the crowd and pointing at them with a wink. He paused on every lap to embrace one person or another at the Ranger bench, and broke down emotionally when his close friend and former New York teammate Ulf Samuelsson unexpectedly came upon the scene.

Not wanting to skip a moment of this remarkable drama, I left and excused my way down to the first rows of seats near the Zamboni entrance. Gretzky skated right by, not 10 feet in front of me, five or six times. The look on his face was one of surrealism. Walter Gretzky, the Great One's famous dad, was escorted past me by security personnel so he could join in on his son's farewell. The video screen above center ice showed Janet Gretzky, Wayne's wife, standing on the opposite side of the arena, completely unable to mask her emotions.

Every time No. 99 appeared ready to exit via the Ranger bench, the tumult from the stands erupted once again, and out he came for yet another lap. And he seemed to be delighting in every moment of it — not wanting to let go; not wanting to leave.

Nor did I.

But y'know, I've gotten far too carried away with this Gretzky stuff. I mean, isn't this a book about the Toronto Maple Leafs? That out-of-town board I alluded to much earlier showed a final score of Philadelphia 3, Boston 1. It's the Leafs and Flyers in the playoffs for the first time since 1977. Let's get it on.

Chapter 3

Pursuing the Dream:
The Stanley Cup Playoff Ride of '99

When expectations for the 1998–99 regular season were monumentally surpassed, the Maple Leafs raised their own bar for the playoffs.

Only four teams in the NHL finished the regular schedule with more than the Leafs' 97 points, and no team scored more goals than Toronto's 268. And while defensive hockey frequently prevails in the post-season, the Maple Leafs and their fans were confident that Curtis Joseph — who had been so brilliant with Edmonton the previous two springs — would maintain that trend and be the equalizing factor.

Furthermore, the Leafs positioned themselves for home-ice advantage in the opening round, and everyone was anxious to see if the club had fashioned any sort of edge in its new dwelling at the Air Canada Centre.

The first-round opponent — Philadelphia — finished four points behind Toronto in the Eastern Conference and the Flyers did not have their best player, Eric Lindros. The Big "E" had been in dire straits after suffering a collapsed lung in Nashville, April 1; he'd be unavailable until at least Round 2.

When it all shook down, the Leafs played seventeen games in three playoff series over forty days, between April 22 and May 31. Fans of the blue and white surely have cherished memories of the six-game victories over Philadelphia and Pittsburgh — Toronto's first post-season conquests in five years.

In the form of a daily journal, here are my recollections of those two playoff rounds, with an added postscript on the Eastern Conference final defeat against Buffalo.

Monday, April 19, 1999
Barrie, Ontario
As Maple Leaf president Ken Dryden sat watching his club practice today from a corner of the Barrie Molson Centre, I couldn't help but reflect on the years in which he played goal so brilliantly for the Montreal Canadiens.

The Leafs are about to face the Philadelphia Flyers in the playoffs for the first time since April 1977 — a time of Dryden's career that saw him in his prime. During that spring 22 years ago, the rangy netminder backstopped the Habs to their second of four consecutive Stanley Cups, and this entire Leafs-Philly thing has me — and others — waxing nostalgic.

The Leafs and Flyers met in the post-season three consecutive years in the mid-'70s — Philadelphia winning all three series. For a Maple Leaf fan, that era represented the lone bright spot in Harold Ballard's ownership tenure; the young and brash Toronto side featuring star players like Darryl Sittler, Borje Salming, Lanny McDonald, Ian Turnbull, Mike Palmateer and Dave (Tiger) Williams. The Flyers were in the midst of their Broad Street Bullies era, dismantling opponents with a lethal combination of finesse and brawn. Those teams are now legendary for belligerent characters like Dave (Hammer) Schultz, Bob (Hound Dog) Kelly, Don (Big Bird) Saleski, and Andre (Moose) Dupont. But it was the players without the thespian nicknames who were the actual keys to a pair of Stanley Cups, including Bobby Clarke, Bernie Parent, Bill Barber, and Reggie Leach.

The three Toronto-Philadelphia series have been well documented in the past generation, and remain quite vivid for those old enough (like me) to recall witnessing parts of them in person. In '75, the Leafs had shocked Los Angeles in a best-of-three preliminary round to advance against the Flyers. The Kings set a club record that year, which still exists, with 105 points in the regular season — 27 more than the Maple Leafs. But an unheralded goalie named Gord McRae held Marcel Dionne, Mike Murphy, Gene Carr and Co. to just a goal in the deciding third match at the L.A. Forum, and Toronto advanced against Philly.

The best-of-seven quarterfinal was no contest, as the Flyers manhandled a passive Leaf squad in a four-game sweep. I remember sitting high up in the east greys at Maple Leaf Gardens when Moose Dupont blew a slapper from the point past McRae in overtime, clinching the series for Philadelphia, which went on to defeat Buffalo for its second Cup title in a row.

By the following spring, the Leafs had become a more aggressive team, with the establishment of players like Tiger Williams and Pat Boutette, and the late-season addition of a bruiser named Kurt Walker. During the course of the 1975–76 season, a top-notch forward unit had evolved in Sittler, McDonald, and Errol Thompson, combining for 121 goals. There was the strong checking line of Jack Valiquette, Boutette, and Williams, and a goalie (Wayne Thomas) enjoying a career year. A three-game conquest of Pittsburgh in the preliminary round set up the second Maple Leafs-Flyers quarterfinal, and this one was hotly contested — evolving into an all-out war that Leaf fans still talk about.

The Flyers prevailed in a seven-game marathon — neither club winning a single game on the road. When Philadelphia stormed to a pair of victories in Games 1 and 2 at the Spectrum, a recurrence of the previous year's annihilation appeared to be in the offing. But the Leafs bounced back at home to square the series with back-to-back wins — Game 3 featuring a riotous eruption that will forever be a part of Maple Leaf lore.

Knowing they had to somehow respond to the Flyers' hostility, the Leafs set the tone for a 3½-hour bloodbath when Kurt Walker jabbed the blade of his stick at Dave Schultz early in the game. The Philadelphia players took the bait and referee Dave Newell banished them in a steady parade to the penalty box. Philly played 24 of the first 40 minutes with less than five skaters.

It was terribly hot in Maple Leaf Gardens that night. I was sitting at the top of the south mezzanine blues, in the season tickets my father had purchased for the 1975–76 campaign. The Gardens wasn't air conditioned, and the heat rose in the building as the penalty-filled affair dragged on, and the atmosphere on the ice steadily eroded. Newell tried mightily to preserve order, but everyone in the arena could sense an outbreak of epic proportions.

Late in the second period, it happened . . . twice. First, Don Saleski took yet another Philadelphia penalty, and as he was sitting in the box, a spectator in the gold seats reached into his drink and tossed a chunk of ice at him. The incensed forward stood up, raised his stick, and turned around to confront the fan. As he motioned to strike back, Metro police-constable Art Malloy — who had patrolled that section of the Gardens for many years — instinctively grabbed Saleski's stick, and a tug-of-war ensued, the player attempting to wrest control of his lumber.

Perceiving their teammate to be under some form of duress, the Philadelphia players swarmed the area in front of the penalty box. Defenceman Joe Watson — an original Flyer from the 1967 expansion team — swung his stick over the glass and wound up hitting Malloy on the shoulder, a definite no-no. Several minutes of near-pandemonium erupted before calm was restored. But that was merely the undercard; the night's main event would follow, moments later.

Figuring that any success the Leafs might have would hinge on Borje Salming's ability to lead the attack, Philadelphia coach Fred Shero instructed his charges to harass the Swedish defenceman in any conceivable manner. In only his third NHL season, Salming had not yet developed the fortitude to answer opponents' improprieties (he'd soon become as good a stick man as any in the league). Cries of "Chicken Swede" would reverberate through the Spectrum when Salming and fellow countryman Inge Hammarstrom came to town with the Maple Leafs.

Despite his reluctance to engage in combat, Salming had developed into Toronto's defensive wheelhorse. He was in immaculate physical condition, with unparalleled stamina. If given room to maneuver, he could lead offensive forays all night long without tiring. Realizing this, the Flyers repeatedly assailed him in Game

3 of the '76 playoff series. They mindlessly hacked at him with their sticks and ran him roughly into the boards at every opportunity.

Late in the second period — moments after the Saleski incident, and with the building still electrically charged — the Hound Dog, Bob Kelly, took a run at Salming beside the Maple Leaf net. This time, Salming summoned the effrontery to push back, and the Philadelphia players responded like a pack of dogs. A wild melee erupted in the corner, and Salming emerged in the grasp of Flyers rookie Mel Bridgman, who laid a merciless bludgeoning on the pestered Swede. The Leafs came out victorious from the battle, 5-4, to get back into the series.

The following day, to the astonishment of the Flyers, Ontario's attorney general, Roy McMurtry, levied criminal charges against Saleski and Watson for the penalty box incident, and Bridgman for his assault on Salming. It marked McMurtry's second foray into NHL matters; the previous November, he had charged Detroit forward Dan Maloney with assault causing bodily harm after Maloney pole-axed Leaf defenceman Brian Glennie, lifted him by the back of his sweater, and repeatedly bounced him off the ice like a sack of potatoes. Saleski and Watson were each charged with possession and use of an offensive weapon (their sticks), while Bridgman received an assault rap.

In Game 4 the next night, Salming — black and blue from his assailing in the previous match — gained some delightful revenge. In the second period, he broke up the middle of the ice and received a perfect feed from Sittler. He skated in alone on Bernie Parent and whipped a high shot past the Flyers' goalie. The scoring play happened at the south end of the building — directly below my vantage point — and the Gardens detonated. In all my years watching hockey on Carlton Street, nothing ever came close to matching the unconstrained outburst of sheer tumult when Salming scored that goal. It was the Maple Leaf defenceman's 25th birthday, and the fans wildly exalted him for a full three minutes. Toronto won, 4-3, to square the series at two games apiece.

Following a one-sided triumph by the Flyers at the Spectrum, the Maple Leafs returned home, facing elimination, and history was made in Game 6. Less than three months after single-handedly destroying the Boston Bruins with an unheard-of 10 scoring points in one game (six goals, four assists), Darryl Sittler stole another page from the NHL record book. He tied a league playoff mark by firing five goals past Parent in the Leafs' 8-5 series-evening victory.

Philadelphia then prevailed in the deciding seventh match at home, after an early scare when Jack Valiquette opened the scoring for Toronto less than two minutes into the game.

The third consecutive playoff meeting between the Leafs and Flyers — in the 1977 Stanley Cup quarterfinals — was easily the most gut-wrenching for fans of the blue and white, and it wound up costing coach Leonard (Red) Kelly his job.

The series again began at the Spectrum, but this time, the Maple Leafs won the first two games on enemy ice and should have swept Philly in four straight. In Game 3, at Toronto, the Leafs held a 3-2 lead in the final minute of play. Sittler won a big defensive-zone face-off from Bobby Clarke, and Salming attempted to backhand the puck out to center ice.

But he failed to lift it high enough. Flyers sniper Rick MacLeish was able to knock it down with his glove, skate in a couple of strides, and plant a screen-shot past Mike Palmateer with 38 seconds to play in regulation time. It took only 2:55 of over-time for MacLeish to score again on the disgruntled Maple Leafs and get Philadelphia back into the series.

That loss, however, was practically a joy for Toronto compared to its inconceiv-able fold-up in Game 4 two nights later. The Leafs swarmed all over the hapless Flyers and bolted to a 5-2 lead by the midway mark of the third period — thanks largely to a four-goal effort from Lanny McDonald. Gary Dornhoefer and Ross Lonsberry of Philadelphia were both excused from the match for blowing up at ref-eree Bruce Hood.

But Mel Bridgman scored a shorthanded goal for the Flyers as they were killing off Lonsberry's unsportsmanlike-conduct penalty, and the roof caved in on the Maple Leafs. Bobby Clarke played one of the finest seven-minute stretches of his career. He fed defenceman Tom Bladon for the goal that made it 5-4 with 1:49 to play, then tied the game himself by lifting a rebound over Palmateer 16 seconds later.

The Gardens was absolutely stunned. Practically everyone expected a quick Philadelphia triumph in overtime, but the Leafs held a slight edge in play before Reggie Leach slapped a puck past Palmateer at 19:10 of the extra period. Toronto went on to drop a pair of one-goal decisions (both in regulation time) and lose the series in six.

All of this forms a romantic backdrop for the latest Toronto-Philadelphia match-up, and many observers believe the Leafs will finally emerge victorious, as Eric Lindros — the Flyers' current-day answer to Bobby Clarke — is unlikely to play this spring. After a game in Nashville against the expansion Predators three weeks ago, Lindros woke up in the middle of the night with nausea, chest pains and shortness of breath. He tried to remedy his symptoms by taking a bath, and when roommate Keith Jones noticed him grimacing in the tub a little after 8 a.m., he called Flyers ath-letic trainer John Worley, who got in touch with Predators doctor Rick Garman.

"Get him to the hospital, right now," Garman told Worley.

Lindros was rushed to the emergency department at Baptist Hospital in Nashville, where he was found to have suffered a collapsed lung — apparently caused by a cross-check during the game the previous night. Doctors inserted a tube to drain the blood filling his chest cavity before re-inflating the lung. While they were able to stabilize his condition, Lindros's life had been in peril, and he is not expected to suit up again until next season.

"I probably shouldn't say this — I don't work for the Flyers — but I would not let him skate or be hit for the rest of the season, including the playoffs," warned Dr. Garman later that day.

Without Lindros, the Flyers should be a softer touch for the Maple Leafs, but coach Pat Quinn wasn't taking anything for granted after today's practice. "Of course any team would miss a player of his stature," Quinn said, "but [Flyers coach] Roger Neilson will have his team prepared; he's faced situations like this before."

Meanwhile, the first volley in what should be a war of words occurred today when Quinn and Neilson went at it, long distance. Standing in a dressing room at the Barrie arena, the Maple Leaf coach warned about the Flyers' tactic of crashing the net and trying to pester Curtis Joseph. "This is no ploy on my part — they do it all the time, I can show you on the videos," Quinn griped.

At the Flyers' practice facility in Voorhees, New Jersey, Neilson was unperturbed when he heard about Quinn's charges. "Pat's an old lawyer," the Flyers' coach told Tim Wharnsby of the *Toronto Sun*. "He's pretty smart using the press. We assume the referees are too smart to fall for that."

Meanwhile, Sergei Berezin, the Leafs' top goalscorer during the regular season with 37, looked like he had a small grapefruit lodged in his right cheek today. Berezin took a careless high-stick in the face from Canadiens defenceman Craig Rivet during the season finale in Montreal Saturday night and he's badly swollen — having difficulty eating solid food. But the training staff fit him with a full faceguard today and he's been cleared to play in Thursday's series opener against the Flyers.

"I thought I was going to die the other night, the pain was so bad," Berezin said. "You work hard to play in the playoffs all season long, then you get hit with a stick like that. I would have felt terrible if I couldn't play."

The Maple Leafs and Flyers met four times during the regular season, with Philadelphia enjoying a 3-1 edge. The Flyers were physically dominant in both games at Toronto, winning 3-0 at Maple Leaf Gardens in December, and 3-1 in March at the Air Canada Centre. The two games in Philly were much closer and more interesting. On Friday afternoon of the American Thanksgiving, the Leafs dominated the entire ice except for the immediate perimeter of their own net, and the Flyers won, 4-3, scoring all of their goals by out-muscling the Maple Leaf defence down low. In January, just prior to the All-Star break, the Leafs were playing their best hockey of the season when they scored a 4-3 win of their own at the First Union Center, ending the Flyers' 15-game unbeaten streak (tied with Dallas for longest of the 1998–99 regular season). Derek King blew a slapshot past John Vanbiesbrouck in the third period for the decisive goal.

The prevailing wisdom in the upcoming playoff series between the teams is that Toronto must avoid being dominated, physically, by the bigger Flyers — something the Leafs were unable to do in their three losses to Philly during the season. But many observers, including me, believe Toronto should have an edge because of Lindros's absence and the anticipated work of Curtis Joseph in goal.

Tuesday, April 20, 1999
Barrie, Ontario
Much of the talk around Leaf camp today centered on captain Mats Sundin, and what he might have in store for the playoffs. The post-season has not been Sundin's time of year, as the big Swede has never advanced past the opening round during his eight-season career in the NHL with Quebec and Toronto. If he were a tennis player, that would be a major blot, but Sundin has practically always been a big wheel on a very small train.

His first playoff experience may forever be his least memorable: the 1993 Adams Division semifinal in which his Nordiques blew a 2-0 series lead to the eventual Cup champions from Montreal. The television image of Quebec coach Pierre Page losing his composure and reaming a young Sundin on the bench remains etched in the minds of all hockey fans who saw it live or on tape. Now older and more accomplished, Sundin will shoulder an immense physical and emotional burden once the Leafs-Flyers series begins. He is expected to be the man who will lift Toronto out of the doldrums of two lost springs.

"I want to establish myself as a player who really steps up at this time of year," the captain mused in a media scrum after practice today. "I want to be known as being a great player when it matters the most."

In his first playoff appearance with the Maple Leafs, Sundin looked to be an unstoppable force. He was brilliant as the Leafs won the first two games of a 1995 Western Conference series right in Chicago. But that Toronto club could not maintain its defensive composure, and the Blackhawks roared back to win the next two games at the Gardens, and the series in seven.

The following spring, Sundin scored three goals, including an overtime winner, but could not lift the Leafs past a St. Louis team that lost its starting goalie, Grant Fuhr, in Game 2 of the opening-round set (you might recall Nick Kypreos "falling" into Fuhr in the goalcrease, causing knee-ligament damage that required surgery). Uncelebrated Jon Casey (who backstopped Minnesota to the 1991 Stanley Cup final) stepped in for Fuhr and rang up a 2.77 goals-against average in the Blues' six-game triumph.

So, Sundin will try for a fourth time to advance past the initial round of playoff action when the Leafs take on the Flyers.

Otherwise, Pat Quinn was at it again today, responding to a charge of gamesmanship from Philadelphia forward Keith Jones about his comments regarding the Flyers' crease tactics. I cautiously asked him for a reply after the workout today in Barrie, and lit a fuse.

"[Jones] is the worst of them all — he taught the other guys how to do it!" the coach thundered. "If the referees aren't going to call that crap, we'll do what we have to. I'm not saying, 'If you run us, we'll run you,' but we intend to win, so if that's what's required . . ."

His silence at the end was ear-splitting.

Wednesday, April 21, 1999
Barrie, Ontario

The Leafs had one final tune-up today at the Molson Centre prior to their series-opener tomorrow night with the Flyers. Pat Quinn spent most of the day pondering who he will play on Sundin's left flank — not an ideal scenario on the eve of the post-season. Fredrik Modin skated on the line with Sundin and Steve Thomas through much of the season, but scored only 16 goals in 67 games. He is a strong forward, willing to crash and bang in the corners, but has rarely shown the scoring touch (at any level) to be considered a front-liner in the NHL.

Why it's taking so long for people in the Leaf organization to figure that out is a mystery. The coaching staff has evidently been mesmerized by Modin's size (6-foot-4, 220 pounds) and his cannon-like shot. The fact he'd have trouble hitting a soccer net most nights seems to have been overlooked. Only once in his three-year tenure with the Leafs has Modin broken out offensively. For reasons that have not been adequately determined (and may never be), the young Swede was unconscious during a stretch of games just prior to the Nagano Olympics last year. Hard slapshots and soft backhands were fooling opposing netminders. Pucks were going in off parts of his anatomy that would cause immense grief if not protected. He had back-to-back two-goal games against Ottawa and Florida just prior to the suspension of play, then another deuce — against the New York Rangers — once the season resumed. In all, he scored eight goals over a six-game span (February 4 to 28), representing precisely half his total for the entire season. It takes no math wizard to compute that he scored the other eight over the span of 68 games — far more indicative of his normal pace.

As mentioned, Modin scored another 16 this past season, with a uniform distribution of goals; there were no hot streaks. Therefore, Quinn is seriously thinking about moving Igor Korolev to the left side on the Sundin-Thomas line. There are a couple of potential drawbacks to that move: a) Korolev has been out of action for almost five weeks, missing the final 16 games of the regular season with a fractured index finger (courtesy of a vicious slash by New Jersey's Bobby Holik in a March 22 game at the Air Canada Centre). And, b) the forward unit he centered when healthy — with Gary Valk and Sergei Berezin — was both stable and effective. But Yanic Perreault, acquired from Los Angeles at the trade deadline, has filled in nicely for Korolev on that line, providing Quinn with some versatility.

"We're looking at that left-wing position, which we've looked at all season long on Mats's line, and wondering who's best to play there," said the coach. "So, that's the dilemma we're facing at this point."

Thursday, April 22, 1999
Toronto
The Leafs began their playoff journey tonight with a disquieting 3-0 loss to Philadelphia at the Air Canada Centre, in the first-ever post-season game played at the new arena. The highest-scoring team during the regular season fizzled on the attack, as John Vanbiesbrouck — both brilliant and lucky — stopped 25 shots for his fifth career playoff shutout.

Adding injury to insult was an apparently severe leg ailment suffered by Igor Korolev in a second-period collision with Flyers defenceman Dan McGillis. In his first game back after the month-long absence, it appears that Korolev may have to sit out another stretch of games, as he was unable to put any weight on the leg in the dressing room after the incident.

There was an exasperating air of restrained pandemonium in the building, as the fans were practically bursting for something to cheer about. But all of that emotion was somehow repressed — especially during a third period in which the Leafs found their legs and swarmed the Philadelphia net. The defining moment of the night occurred just 51 seconds into the final frame, when Mats Sundin was awarded a penalty shot. The call was highly questionable — referee Richard Trottier hastily determining that Flyers defenceman Steve Duchesne had closed his hand on the puck in the goalcrease, even though it appeared Duchesne had merely swatted the puck out of harm's way towards the corner.

Sundin's feeble scoring attempt was a microcosm of his struggles during the entire game. The big Swede skated in and sort of nudged the puck towards the upper left-hand corner of the net. Vanbiesbrouck merely had to raise his left arm a couple of inches to easily block the frail drive. There was a brief moment of absolute quiet after Sundin's visibly weak effort, followed by a collective groan. The Leafs were trailing, 2-0, and could have climbed right back into the game.

"When I saw [Mikael] Renberg whisper something to Vanbiesbrouck just before the penalty shot," said Sundin, "I figured he was telling him to watch for my favorite move on a breakaway, which is faking five-hole [through the legs] and trying to go high on the glove-side with my backhand. That's why I decided to try and fool him with a quick forehand shot, but he got his arm in the way."

Another cry of anguish filled the arena just more than a minute after the failed penalty shot when Steve Sullivan and Derek King broke in, two-on-one. Sullivan passed to King in the left-wing circle and the veteran winger somehow decided not to shoot. Instead, King mindlessly slid the puck back to Sullivan, whose momentum had taken him past the goalline and behind the net! It's something you'd see in a late-night pick-up game, but almost never in the NHL.

The Leaf powerplay was an embarrassment through much of the season, and it misfired again tonight during a two-man advantage for a full two minutes in the opening period. Chris Therien and Keith Jones were each sent off for cross-checking at the 10:46 mark, and the Leafs were able to generate only one bona fide scoring chance. It produced the most spectacular save of the night by Vanbiesbrouck, who snared what appeared to be a certain goal by Steve Thomas. Sundin feathered a pass across the crease and Thomas one-timed the puck towards a gaping net. But Vanbiesbrouck anticipated the play — did the splits — and made it appear as if Thomas fired the puck directly into his yawning mitt.

"He was on his back," said Thomas, afterwards. "I shot it straight in his glove. But Beezer stood on his head tonight. Remember, though, we led the league this year in scoring. There's no goalie we haven't been able to score on. And there's no reason to believe we can't score on [Vanbiesbrouck]. No goalie can keep them *all* out."

Valeri Zelepukin scored the only goal of the first period. The Flyers were accorded a two-man advantage of their own midway through the middle frame and, unlike the Leafs earlier, they capitalized — John LeClair counting from the slot to make it 2-0. After the failed Toronto onslaught in the third, defenceman Eric Desjardins iced the Flyers' win with an empty-net goal.

Friday, April 23, 1999
Toronto

The extent of Igor Korolev's leg injury was painfully evident by his facial expression after today's Maple Leaf practice. Supported by a pair of crutches in the Leaf dressing room — looking dreadfully forlorn — Korolev confirmed that he had suffered a broken left fibula (small bone in the lower leg) in the Game 1 collision with Dan McGillis. His season is over.

"I only have bad luck now, it seems," lamented the Russian forward. "This is the first time I've had this many injuries. I've never missed more than two or three games before, it's very disappointing." About the leg fracture, he said, "It wasn't that bad last night, but I came in today and it was really swollen. I had an X-ray taken and it showed the break."

Practically all the Maple Leafs understand that another home-ice loss to the Flyers tomorrow night will likely thwart any long-term aspirations. "Most people expected us to win in four straight, but that's definitely not going to happen," said Kris King, tongue-in-cheek. "We've discussed a lot about the Flyers the past five days, but you really don't know what to expect until you play a team. Now we know what we have to do to beat them."

Scoring at least one goal is paramount. And getting Sundin untracked will go a long way towards solving Vanbiesbrouck. "He's done fine," Quinn said today, in defence of his captain. "Is he supposed to walk in the footprints of the Lord? That's not reality. We have to get everyone to respond better."

Saturday, April 24, 1999
Toronto

There's a fair amount of relief and contentment in the city tonight, after the Maple Leafs pulled off a miraculous victory to even their series with Philly.

Stymied by the Flyers' smothering blanket in the neutral zone, the Leafs were trailing, 1-0, in the dying moments of regulation time, and it appeared they would move on to Philadelphia for Game 3 still looking for their first goal of the series. Somehow — and it's still quite unbelievable — they scored a pair of fluky goals in the final two minutes and won the game, 2-1.

John Vanbiesbrouck had enjoyed an easy night's work — blocking only 19 Toronto shots — when the roof caved in. The first blot on his performance was a severe one, as Steve Thomas dribbled a bad-angle backhand shot past him with 1:59 remaining on the clock. Thomas managed to veer past a backpedaling Chris Therien and cut in on Vanbiesbrouck, but the Flyer goalie should have made the save. The unexpected tally set off a concussion of noise in the Air Canada Centre, as the home-town fans finally had something to cheer about. They were still on their feet when the evening's ultimate moment occurred.

It would take the minute perusal of a slow-motion replay to show exactly how Mats Sundin's shot eluded Vanbiesbrouck at 19:07 of the third period — just 1:06 after Thomas's marker. Following some diligent spadework by Sergei Berezin, Sundin motored out from behind and to the right of the Philly net, and his quick backhander glanced upwards off the stick of Eric Desjardins. It somehow found a tiny space over Vanbiesbrouck's shoulder and the Leaf captain (like all others in the arena) had to do a quick double-take before exploding into unrestrained celebration. It capped a truly improbable comeback.

"Mentally, we now know we can score on Beezer . . . he's not invincible," said Thomas afterwards in the happy Leaf dressing room. "He's a great goalie — don't get me wrong — but he can be beaten. It's huge pressure off our shoulders to know that we can score on that team. If we had lost again tonight, our chances [of winning the series] wouldn't have been very good."

Thomas is privately concerned that he may not be in the lineup when the series shifts to Philadelphia on Monday. At 7:56 of the second period tonight, the veteran winger slammed his right elbow into the jaw of Eric Desjardins behind the Flyers' net. Desjardins went down in a heap — apparently colder than a mackerel — only to re-appear a few moments later, and play the rest of the game. Neither of the referees, Stephen Walkom or Rob Shick, saw fit to penalize Thomas. In the third period, Toronto's Kris King went off for boarding after bowling over Philly defenceman Adam Burt from behind. Believing they were manhandled, the Flyers screamed bloody murder afterwards.

"Thomas is a tough player but he should know better," said GM Bobby Clarke, hardly a choirboy during his belligerent playing career. "You expect that sort of stuff out of King, he probably doesn't know any better. If Burt doesn't lift his head up at the last moment, King could have killed him, or broken his neck."

The Maple Leaf enforcer was less than overwhelmed by Clarke's words. "What Bobby Clarke says, I don't worry about," King said. "[Burt and I] were both racing for the puck and he turned at the last moment. I was in too close to stop. I tried to put my hand up to help him, but it was too late. I wasn't trying to hurt him. I've looked forward to playing in the playoffs for two years since I signed with the Leafs. I'm not about to do something stupid."

Clarke is loudly campaigning for Thomas to receive a stiff suspension from the NHL. "He deliberately tried to hurt Eric," Clarke said. "It wasn't much different than the Hatcher-Roenick incident. [*Early in the Dallas-Phoenix Western Conference play-off, Derian Hatcher of Dallas viciously boarded Jeremy Roenick, breaking the jaw of the Coyotes player, and receiving a seven-game suspension.*] Hockey is a tough game — I know that as well as anyone. But players shouldn't do stuff like that."

Thomas was less than convincing afterwards when claiming that he had hit Desjardins with his shoulder. "I was just trying to make a hit, and I think it was a clean one," he said, weakly. "I just don't think [Desjardins] was expecting it. You never want to injure a player . . . I've not played that way in my career."

Ultimately, any judgment on a suspension will be made by series supervisor John D'Amico (the former NHL linesman) and the league's disciplinary guru, Colin Campbell.

Sunday, April 25, 1999
Philadelphia

The flight-pattern approach to runway 27 at Philadelphia International Airport is a virtual sports tour unto its own.

At an altitude of roughly 2,500 feet, a passenger seated on the right side of a descending aircraft will notice a trio of athletic facilities, aligned vertically. At the north end of the alignment is giant Veterans Stadium, home of the baseball Phillies and NFL Eagles. In the middle — immensely dwarfed by its neighbors — is the old Philadelphia Spectrum, the sardine can–shaped arena where the Flyers played from their inception in 1967 to 1996. And closest to the aircraft is the new First Union Center — the Flyers' (and NBA 76ers') current home, easily large enough to piggy-back the Spectrum on its roof.

Flying here this morning and seeing the sports complex from the plane reminded me that Philadelphia is one of the premier sports cities in the United States — even though none of its four big-league teams has won a championship since the 76ers (and Julius Erving) beat the Los Angeles Lakers in 1982. Unlike many of their American cousins, Philadelphians do not rank hockey a distant fourth in popularity; in fact, only the football Eagles have a following as strong as the Flyers. And the Eagles are coming off one of the truly dreadful seasons in their long history (a 3-13 record in '98, tied with Indianapolis and Cincinnati for worst in the NFL). Even the American Hockey League Phantoms — a farm team owned by the Flyers — regularly fill more than two-thirds of the Spectrum.

The Flyers developed a cult-like legion of followers during the early and mid-'70s, when they became the first of the NHL's modern-day expansion teams to win the Stanley Cup. The Broad Street Bullies captured the hearts of this city's sports fans during an era in professional hockey almost the polar opposite of today. Terms and strategies like the neutral-zone trap and left-wing lock were unheard-of. Parity throughout the NHL was severely limited, and the best teams beat you either with overwhelming might (like the Flyers), or unmatched skill (like the late-'70s Montreal Canadiens, who followed Philadelphia's consecutive championships with four of their own). Breaking into the top six teams in the league practically guaranteed a run for the Stanley Cup; a precipitous decline existed among the teams ranked seven on downward.

And the orange-clad Flyers were always among the elite six.

The Maple Leafs practiced at home this morning, then arrived here in Philadelphia late this afternoon. The club (and Toronto media) is staying at its regular-season haunt — the Sheraton Society Hill, a quaint, four-story hotel on the eastern fringes of downtown. I was on hand (with several of my colleagues) when the Leaf players walked into the main lobby, suitcases and garment bags in hand. Room keys were laid out on a table and most of the players bolted for the elevators. Steve Thomas and Kris King stayed behind to talk with the media.

Most people expected the NHL to investigate both the Thomas elbow on Desjardins last night and the King hit from behind on Adam Burt. But Pat Quinn met with reporters late this afternoon and said that no review will take place. "Mr. Dryden called the league today and they said that there was nothing under review, nor would any hearing be called," Quinn said. "And that's the way it should be. If Bobby Clarke wants to start sending in tapes, I'll show the league videos of his players running our goaltenders."

Details surfaced today about the snippy little conversation that ensued between Thomas and Desjardins late in the game. Though apparently knocked unconscious, Desjardins missed only five minutes of the match before returning.

"I asked him why he was out on the next shift if he was so badly hurt," Thomas recalled. "He told me I had knocked him out, but he didn't seem all that woozy when he got back from the dressing room."

Quinn put it more bluntly. "He was trying to draw a penalty," the coach said. "Maybe he thought he was in the Italian Soccer League or something."

Meanwhile, Clarke was venting steam again today at the Flyers' practice in Voorhees. "To deliberately go after another player's head and not make any attempt to go after the puck — I think Thomas knows that is wrong," said the Flyers' GM. About King's hit on Burt, Clarke said, "The ref told us he would have given King a major penalty if Adam had laid on the ice longer. Boy, how stupid that is. Adam Burt's tough enough to pick himself up and get to the bench, and the ref is saying,

'Make my job easier.' If the league doesn't want to address the things that went on the other night, it'll be open warfare out there."

Monday, April 26, 1999
Philadelphia

The Flyers' eagerness to exact revenge on Steve Thomas wound up costing them dearly tonight, as the Maple Leafs skated off with a 2-1 victory at the First Union Center to grab a one-game lead in the series. But the final result was completely overshadowed by a disturbing allegation from Philadelphia enforcer Sandy McCarthy afterwards.

First, to the game.

After blanking the Leafs in the series opener, John Vanbiesbrouck has allowed only four goals, but three of them have been dreadfully soft, including both tonight. The Beezer's timing has also been horrid. Karl Dykhuis caused the First Union Center to quake when he whistled a slapshot through a screen and past Curtis Joseph at 16:16 of the opening period. The fans were still on their feet — cheering the public address announcement of his goal — when Toronto winger Mike Johnson instantly turned delight to despair. A mere 10 seconds after the face-off at center ice, Johnson bolted in on the left-wing side and dribbled a weak backhander through Vanbiesbrouck's legs from a terrible angle. I doubt that I've ever witnessed such complete deflation in a hockey crowd. The arena just wilted.

In the dying seconds of the period, Craig Berube of the Flyers took one of the great bonehead penalties of recent times. As several players jostled behind the Philadelphia net, Berube — a one-time Leaf — pushed Thomas over after the whistle had sounded. Referee Paul Stewart sent him off for roughing, leading to an incredibly sweet powerplay goal by Thomas himself, 40 seconds into the middle frame. The Maple Leaf winger unleashed a quick shot from the left-wing face-off circle, beating Vanbiesbrouck high to the stick side. It was a strange goal, as Vanbiesbrouck — completely unscreened — seemed mysteriously frozen. He hardly reacted with more than a flinch as the puck sailed past him.

From that point on, it was Cujo's night. This series had been billed as a battle of sorts between Joseph and Vanbiesbrouck, both of whom were members of last summer's free agent crop. Joseph, by most accounts, wanted to play in Philadelphia, but the Flyers were unwilling to spend lavishly on a goaltender. They ultimately turned to Vanbiesbrouck, who did not come cheaply, but still agreed to roughly $1.5 million less than Joseph's 1998–99 salary with Toronto. In tonight's game, Cujo again was a clear winner. Philly outshot the Leafs 26-9 over the final two periods, but could not beat the man in the blue-and-white mask.

"Their shots went in and ours didn't," was Flyer coach Roger Neilson's succinct but lame evaluation of the match. In truth, Joseph made a half-dozen remarkable stops — game-savers, as it turned out — while Vanbiesbrouck looked feeble on both Maple Leaf markers.

But in the end, a rather innocent-looking, albeit childish exchange between pugilists Sandy McCarthy and Tie Domi left an indelible imprint on this game, virtually destroying what had been an otherwise enjoyable night of hockey. Rosie DiManno outlined the bizarre scene in her *Toronto Star* column:

> From a distance, as an act of pantomime, it looked quite funny — in a drop-your-pants, pie-in-the-face, vaudevillian kinda way.
>
> The teams were lining up for a face-off in the second period and both coaches had sent out their tough guys — the "special ed" lines, as one pressbox wag has tagged them.
>
> The Maple Leafs had Tie Domi and Kris King abreast of Todd Warriner; the Flyers had Sandy McCarthy, Craig Berube and Mikael Andersson. Before the puck was dropped, McCarthy switched wings and lined up, quite deliberately, alongside Domi. Words were exchanged, threats delivered. Domi waggled his knees, as if to say, "Oh yeah, I'm shakin'!"
>
> Moments later, as McCarthy tried to goad Domi into a rumble, the Leafs' enforcer rolled his eyes and skated away. McCarthy ended the little skit by bending his arms and waving his elbows, in the universal gesture for "Chicken!"

From a distance, the repartee seemed like nothing more than an innocuous attempt by two role players to upstage one another. The crowd got a kick out of it and the game resumed. In reality, the consequences were much more grim.

Unaware that anything additional had resulted from the incident, I went down to the Maple Leaf dressing room after the game, primarily to speak with Thomas and Joseph, the principal figures in Toronto's victory. I then stopped by the Philadelphia room to gauge any frustration that might be emanating from the likes of John LeClair, Steve Duchesne or Rod Brind'Amour — players who'd been thwarted spectacularly by Cujo. As I was walking out of the room, I noticed, but chose to ignore, a small gathering of media around McCarthy. I guessed that he was discussing the theatrical exchange with Domi, but there were other, more significant, story lines to consider on this night. Or so I thought. What made me stop in my tracks was overhearing McCarthy say something about race. I pivoted around, clicked on my tape machine, and cautiously asked the perturbed Flyer to explain what he was referring to. His reply almost knocked me off my feet.

"Tie Domi yelled a racial slur at me on the ice," he said.

Unaware, at the moment, that McCarthy was of minority descent, I said, "*Racial slur?*"

"Yeah, he dropped an N-bomb on me. I can take anything in this game — high-sticks, punches, elbows. But when you attack my race, I won't stand for it. That's why I went after him like I did."

Still a bit confused, I walked away and asked a member of the Flyers' staff about McCarthy's heritage. "He's part black, part Indian," I was told. "His father is black, his mother native-Canadian." Nothing more need be said. I hurried back to the Maple Leaf room to see if Domi had yet been approached about the allegation, and ran head-long into a media maelstrom. A half-dozen TV cameras and roughly 15 reporters were clogging the main entrance, frantically obtaining Domi's side of the story.

"I never said anything racial to him . . . he's crazy," Domi insisted. "All he's doing is trying to get himself out of trouble for spitting in my face."

"He spit in your face?" asked about six of us, simultaneously.

"Yeah . . . a pretty good one, too. I went straight to the referee; I just left it hanging there. He told me to wipe it off. By no means did I say the N-word. I'm not that type of person. If [McCarthy] is trying to squirm out of trouble, that's a pretty lame excuse to use."

It required limited journalistic skill to realize I had stumbled across a story that was going to dwarf anything hockey-related from tonight's game. Sprinting to a near-by payphone, I called the radio station and quickly broke the news to my night-time colleagues, Norm Rumack and Marty York, who, by coincidence, were on the air with long-time hockey host/broadcaster Dave Hodge. We talked about the incident for a few minutes, after which I went looking for series supervisor John D'Amico. Informed that he was going to meet with the referees and linesmen, I walked over to the officials' dressing room in a small corridor beside the entrance-ramp to the arena.

Standing there was hockey writer Lance Hornby of the *Toronto Sun,* who'd been designated as pool-reporter for the print-media throng now entrenched in the story. As I waited for D'Amico to arrive, a woman standing 25 or 30 feet to my right began shouting angrily at me. Obviously having noticed my microphone flag, she yelled, "Hey, Fan-590, that Domi's a real classy guy . . . why don't you go tell him how classy he is for using the N-word?" Figuring the woman was a Flyers supporter who'd gotten wind of McCarthy's allegation, I purposely chose not to respond in any way. I stood facing the dressing room, feeling slightly uncomfortable as the woman continued her verbal assault. "Domi's a pretty big asshole, and you can tell him that, too."

After another minute or so of invective, I stole a quick glance her way and could hardly believe my eyes. Standing right beside this venom-spewing female was none other than Sandy McCarthy himself. Obviously, she was either a friend or a relative, and he had chosen to let her prattle on. As if I'd had anything to do with the incident.

A few moments later, D'Amico arrived looking like he'd seen a ghost. He was on his way into the officials' room when I asked him for a brief comment on the incident.

"I talked to [referee] Paul Stewart and he told me directly that he didn't hear any kind of racial slur," said the supervisor. "He also told me that he did not see McCarthy spit on Domi, even though he did see some saliva around his chest and face area. We're going to look at a [video]tape to determine if we can see some kind of conversation between the two players. Right now, I don't have any answers as to what action the league may or may not take."

Somewhere in one of my reports tonight, I'm going to have to mention that the Leafs won Game 3 of this playoff series.

Tuesday, April 27, 1999
Philadelphia
One of the truly bizarre moments of my career covering the Maple Leafs took place today, replete with a conspiracy theory. All I could do was laugh.

With the 76ers in town for a basketball game tonight, we were informed yesterday that the Leafs would be practicing today at a local rink somewhere in the boonies. During the second period of last night's game, Anthony Alfred of the Leafs' publicity department handed out photocopies to Toronto media in the First Union Center pressbox. They were printed directions to a facility called "Twin Rinks" in Warminster, Pennsylvania, and we were told to expect a 45- to 50-minute drive. This was not unusual, as most practice rinks around the league are a fair distance from the main city core. The directions read:

> *Interstate 95 north to Street Rd., exit (about 25 miles) . . . Make a left*
> *on to Street Rd. Go about eight to ten miles until you pass a navy base*
> *on your right side. Go about a half-mile to Mears Rd. and make a right.*
> *Twin Rinks is about one to two miles on your right side.*

The Maple Leaf bus pushed off from the hotel around 12:15 this afternoon, and I was offered a ride to the practice rink by photographer Peter Power of the *Toronto*

Star, who had a rental vehicle. In fact, four of us piled into Peter's car — myself, reporter Bill Cole from Toronto radio station 680 News, and Peter's *Star* colleagues Rosie DiManno and Ken Campbell. Kenny and I had a road-map laid out in the back, while Bill tried to navigate from the front passenger seat.

Peter leisurely began following Anthony Alfred's directions, and none of us paid much attention to the drive for the first 25 minutes or so. At every green road-sign after that, we began looking for the "Street Rd." turn-off, and figured it would be the next exit ahead. Five or six exits later, some mild concern set in, as we realized there was either no "Street Rd." exit, or we had simply missed it and gone too far up Interstate 95. When we came upon a sign that read "New Jersey State Line, Straight Ahead," mild concern turned to moderate panic.

We turned around and began circling through towns named Morrisville, Yardley, Langhome, Newtown — everything *but* Warminster. By then, our 45- to 50-minute excursion had stretched to well over an hour, and we were lost and starving. We finally came upon the naval base outlined in Anthony's directions and Peter pulled into a convenience store. We loaded up on junk food and were told by the store manager that Warminster was, indeed, the next town up ahead.

A narrow, winding road took us roughly a mile, and we finally saw our coveted destination — the white-topped Twin Rinks. But when Peter pulled into the parking lot, it became obvious something was terribly amiss. The first clue was the absence of a team bus. While it took us 90 minutes to find the arena, there's no way the Leafs could have gotten there, practiced, and left — even while we were circumventing half of Pennsylvania. The second clue was the sight of long-time CFTO-TV broadcaster Joe Tilley stomping around like a wild man in the parking lot — steam coming out of his ears.

We pulled up alongside Joe who, incredibly, was talking on his cellphone to Alfred while the Leafs were skating at Twin Rinks . . . in Pennsauken, New Jersey! About a half-dozen of us Toronto media wags were standing outside a perfectly empty arena — 25 miles north of Philadelphia — while the hockey club we were supposed to be covering was practicing at a rink virtually across the Delaware River from the First Union Center. Tilley was close to a stroke when we calmed him down and realized, among ourselves, that all we could do was head back to Philadelphia and hope the Leafs had dressed at the sports complex. If so, we'd probably be able to meet them there when they returned.

Racing back down Interstate 95, Peter's mood had deteriorated. His assignment was to photograph the Leafs during their workout, and that was no longer a possibility. In the back-seat, me, Ken and Rosie were experiencing some unusual G-forces as Peter practically kept pace with jetliners — parallel to us — on final approach to Philadelphia airport. Once back at the First Union Center, we hurried inside and were immensely relieved when the Maple Leaf players began streaming in 15 minutes later, with wise-ass expressions.

"I hear you guys had a nice tour of the countryside," chided Kris King, as he headed for the dressing room. Pat Quinn walked past with that sly grin of his — fully aware of the adventure we'd just been through. Suddenly, good old Anthony Alfred appeared, looking like a little sheep-dog.

"Uh, sorry guys," he mumbled. "Here's what happened . . ."

Turns out that Alfred had asked one of the pressbox attendants at last night's game for directions to Twin Rinks — not realizing there were a half-dozen facilities of the same name in the Philadelphia region. The attendant must have been a real genius, as he presented Anthony with instructions on how to find the furthest such arena. The Leafs were actually on their way to Warminster as well, until their bus driver informed them of the error. Obviously, there was no way for Anthony to relay the blunder to us, and we were shit-out-of-luck. But there were no hard feelings. Besides, it's practically impossible to get mad at Anthony. Gibe the hell out of him, yes. But get mad, no.

A few moments later, Quinn came out to do his daily media scrum. By that time, the Warminster voyage was all but forgotten — until the smoke began rising again from Joe Tilley. The veteran TV man wormed his way to the front of the scrum, jabbed his microphone in Quinn's face, and asked, "Now, Pat, did this little mistake have anything to do with last night?"— clearly implying that Quinn had orchestrated the Warminster affair to diffuse the Domi-McCarthy scandal.

"No, of course not, it was just a mistake from what I understand," he replied.

To be honest, our little escapade served as comic relief from the dreadfully unpleasant chore of following up Domi-McCarthy. What an awful thing to have to talk about in the middle of a playoff series. But that's all anyone seemed to be concentrating on here today. As he did last night, Domi feverishly professed his innocence in another dressing room scrum. He did so in the face of McCarthy stepping up his own claim of hearing a racial slur, and a defaming vilification of Domi by a black columnist in the *Philadelphia Inquirer.*

Claire Smith, a former baseball columnist at the *New York Times,* took it upon herself to pass judgment on Domi, even though she was not at last night's hockey game, and certainly had no additional evidence to support McCarthy's claim. It's understandable why a black person might react emotionally to such a story, and no white person, including myself, could even pretend to understand the outrage and profanation attached to the N-word. Still, it's hardly an excuse to omit one's journalistic integrity, as Smith did in her column:

> The expressions were all too familiar, the wounds too real. No one this side of Laurence Olivier could have feigned the pain, anger and humiliation written all over McCarthy. This was not a play for publicity or even a quest for vengeance against a fellow tough guy. It was a deep-rooted anguish that belied McCarthy's usual swagger; the kind that can be understood only by those, whether black, white, red or brown, who have had to spend even one second of their lives fending off the effects of such debilitating attacks. In that one instance, McCarthy understood, whether he wanted to or not, what Jackie Robinson, Hank Greenberg and Henry Aaron had hoped to eradicate.

Smith based the tone of her entire column on the assumption that Domi uttered the racial epithet, despite his own fervent denials, the fact he had never been accused of a similar misdeed in hundreds of on-ice squabbles, and that the NHL, itself, concluded an investigation today by stating that no person on the ice last night — not even a Philadelphia teammate — could corroborate McCarthy's assertion.

It's one example of some incredibly biased reporting by members of the Philadelphia media, who have become house-men (and women) for the Flyers. A loss to the Maple Leafs in this series would be a personal catastrophe for many of those with the apparent responsibility to be journalists.

An exception is veteran hockey writer Les Bowen of the *Philadelphia Daily News*, who is able to analyze the game objectively, and have a bit of fun with it, too. In his notes section today, Bowen cracked me up when describing the physical appearances of the two head coaches. "Somehow, Pat Quinn and Roger Neilson both got really bad haircuts for this series," he wrote. "Neilson looks like a poorly trimmed poodle. The sides of Quinn's head look like he fell asleep in his yard and was run over by a lawn mower."

When Quinn bumped into the veteran reporter after practice at the First Union Center, a hilarious scene developed. "C'mere, Les," the coach summoned with a fiendish grin. TV cameramen gleefully turned on their equipment. "To be honest, I don't care how you describe me, but you'd be lucky to live if another Quinn [*his father*] ever got a hold of you." Everyone got a laugh out of the little exchange and it served as more comic relief from last night's shenanigans.

The *Daily News* also ran a clever double-entendre on its back page (the front page of its sports section): "CURT CHILLING" the headline said, referring to Joseph's 40-save performance in Game 3. Curt *Schilling,* of course, is the ace of the Philadelphia Phillies' pitching staff. Bowen's quip and the witty headline contrasted with the Domi-McCarthy affair, but only briefly.

"He called me a big, fucking nig . . .," McCarthy repeated today, choosing not to finish the word. "There's no doubt whatsoever. You can't mistake that word for anything else. Domi's like a rat trying to hide — a little weasel. If he's a real man, he has to tell the truth. I used to look up to Tie, but I have no respect for him anymore."

Domi held his composure again, amid the continued accusations from McCarthy, the incriminating Smith column, and another gaggle of TV cameras.

"First of all, I didn't even know [McCarthy] was black," he said. "I would never say a word like that, anyway. I work with young black kids all the time, and I don't want them thinking I said these things. Everyone on [the Flyers] knows what I'm like and have respect for me. But I'll tell you one thing: if McCarthy is trying to egg me on to a big fight, he'll get one down the road. He's been on three different teams in a year, and now everyone knows why."

Wednesday, April 28, 1999
Philadelphia
Mercifully, the focus returned to hockey today, and the Flyers were merci*less* in their thorough destruction of the Maple Leafs tonight in Game 4.

A 5-2 Philadelphia romp tied this series at two games apiece — the only redeeming fact for a Toronto club that's been completely dominated in 11 of the 12 periods played in this series so far. Tonight's effort was abominable, as my old Warminster pal, Ken Campbell, summed up so well in the *Toronto Star*:

> This was all part of the Toronto Maple Leafs' grand playoff plan. It had to have been, because there is no other way to explain how the Leafs performed here [tonight]. Instead of burying the Philadelphia Flyers, they dug a nice little bunker for themselves with a lame performance in a 5-2 loss . . .

It practically defies logic that the Maple Leafs are square with Philly in this series. One can only imagine what might be if the Flyers had received better goaltending in the first two games, and if Eric Lindros had been present. There is plenty of reason to think it could all have ended tonight in a four-game sweep. Game 4 was strictly a case of men against boys. The Philadelphia forwards set up shop in front of Curtis

Joseph and could not be moved. John LeClair was like a fixed monument in the slot area, scoring two goals. As Ken Campbell put it, the Leafs were simply "lame." Can they possibly turn it around back at home?

"Our worst game of the series, by far . . . we totally lost our composure," said Mats Sundin.

The Leafs did compete to a degree in the first period — twice answering Philadelphia goals with quick responses of their own. Sergei Berezin and Steve Sullivan offset markers by Craig Berube and LeClair. But Joseph's brilliance kept the Flyers from running away with it early, as the home side poured 18 shots at the Maple Leaf net in the opening frame. The only physical altercation between Domi and McCarthy did not turn out well for Toronto, as it sent Philadelphia on its way to the lop-sided victory.

After the Leafs' pre-game skate this morning at the First Union Center, Domi vowed that he would not drop the gloves with McCarthy. "I doubt that I'll ever fight him again," Domi said. "After what happened, I have zero respect for him." The two foes did come together early in the second period tonight, as they briefly jostled in the neutral zone. As Domi got up, he foolishly gave McCarthy a face-wash with his glove, and was sent off for roughing.

On the ensuing powerplay, Eric Desjardins beat Cujo with a screen-shot from the point, breaking a 2-2 tie. Philly led the rest of the way.

Domi uncharacteristically bolted for the team bus and refused to talk with reporters after the game. In his absence, Steve Thomas said, "I think it was a case of Tie just losing his cool for a moment. He was really bothered by the racial slur allegation and probably overreacted when he collided with McCarthy. This is an emotional game even without a controversy like that."

McCarthy had mixed feelings afterwards. "It felt pretty special when Eric scored that goal [with Domi in the box], but I still would like something to come of it," he said, referring to the NHL's fruitless investigation of the incident. "I know there weren't any witnesses who heard what Tie said, but at least the word is out there for everyone to hear."

Thursday, April 29, 1999
Toronto
Pat Quinn told his players to stay away from the rink today, as the Maple Leafs chartered home late last night after the drubbing in Philadelphia. Sadly for the coach, reporters covering the series were not given the day off, and the big Irishman had to "entertain" the hordes for a few minutes. Dressed in a checkered shirt, Quinn held court in the press lounge at the Air Canada Centre, and tried to deflect criticism from his players for their lethargic effort in Game 4.

"We wanted to keep them away from you guys," Quinn smirked. "All that other crap [*Domi-McCarthy*] has really become a side-show, so I told them to go shopping today. The Flyers seem to find ways to have distractions and you guys gobbled up that racial thing. Instead of one scrum, you had reporters in the corridors and hotel lobbies. I wanted to keep them away from that today."

Strangely, Quinn was blaming the media for the Domi-McCarthy affair — consistent with his modus operandi, but a bit below his level of intellect.

"There were some accusations and they became a whole side-show," he grumbled. "They provided something for . . . everyone interested to get their own private stories. It had nothing to do with the game, and the players shouldn't have to go through that."

Damien Cox took Quinn to task in his follow-up column in the *Star*:

> Presumably, Pat Quinn will be handing out congratulatory stogies to members of the local media [tomorrow night] if the Maple Leafs triumph in Game 5 against the Philadelphia Flyers.
>
> For if said media pundits contributed to the Leafs' defeat in Game 4 because of their "distracting" coverage of the Tie Domi-Sandy McCarthy slur/spit incident/non-incident, well then surely a Toronto victory [tomorrow] will mean the scribes and broadcasters tailored their work more suitably to Leaf interests and should be part of the victory celebration. All of that is, of course, nonsense. As was Quinn's diatribe yesterday. . . .
>
> He found the usual target. The media. It's us against the world, boys. Everybody's out to get us. Circle the wagons. And so on.

We'll see if Quinn's ploy has any effect tomorrow night.

Meanwhile, gleeful members of the Philadelphia media were writing off the Leafs today — perhaps with justification. Sports editor Jack McCaffery of the *Delaware County Daily Times* penned a column entitled, "Maple Leafs Cannot Survive Much Longer." He wrote,

> Once again last night . . . the Leafs were clobbered in a hockey game, losing 5-2 to the Flyers. While that made the first-round playoff series even at two victories apiece, it also made the Maple Leafs 4-for-4 in pitiful postseason performances. . . . For the good of hockey, the sooner the Leafs are eliminated, the better. And through 240 minutes of playoff hockey, there has been no sign that

Toronto is capable of seeing a second round. . . .

The Leafs cannot — they simply cannot — be long for these playoffs, not as they have played in the first four games.

I wonder how Quinn feels about *that*.

Friday, April 30, 1999
Toronto

Maybe we *were* to blame, after all.

Whatever it was that prompted the passion to return to the Maple Leafs worked. And the timing couldn't have been better. The most scintillating game of this less-than-scintillating series ended tonight at 11:51 of the first overtime period, when Toronto centerman Yanic Perreault scored yet another weak goal on John Vanbiesbrouck. Taking a pass from linemate Gary Valk, Perreault skated wide into the right-wing side of the Flyers' zone. From a difficult angle, he fired a routine backhand shot at the net and it somehow drifted past Vanbiesbrouck over his outstretched glove-hand. The rush appeared to present no danger at all, and the Air Canada Centre exploded in dumfounded ecstasy. Toronto had won the game, 2-1, to capture the pivotal fifth match of the series.

"That was a lucky one," said a beaming Perreault afterwards. "I was just hoping to get the puck on the net and maybe produce a rebound opportunity. I was very surprised when it went in. We knew this series would be very close — with not many scoring chances — so every goal is important."

Vanbiesbrouck, somewhat understandably, had no desire to re-live the play in his post-game media session. "It went in, that's about it," he lamented. "Does it matter how I describe it? Not really."

Flyers defenceman Eric Desjardins felt his club played Perreault in a textbook manner on the goal. "We kept him to the outside and in that situation, you're trying to *force* a backhand shot," he said. "Of course, you don't want to allow any type of shot, but if you have to give one up, that's the way to do it — prevent the player from switching to his forehand. The Leafs have had some lucky bounces in this series."

Whereas the Leafs had been passive and reticent in Philly on Wednesday, they skated with abundant resolve tonight and were able to rebound emotionally from a quick goal against. The actual start of the game was delayed for nearly 10 minutes when a large segment of the arena lights failed to illuminate after the national anthems. The switch for the TV lights had been accidentally turned off and they required time to warm up. Once the puck was dropped, it took only 1:52 for the Flyers to seemingly reclaim their momentum from two nights ago. Keith Jones converted a wrap-around on the game's first shot, and silence befell the Air Canada Centre.

But Dimitri Yushkevich calmed the nerves before the midway point of the period. The Flyers were sloppy in a clearing attempt and Yusky's drifting shot beat Vanbiesbrouck through a screen. It was a powerplay goal, with Steve Duchesne of Philadelphia serving a roughing penalty, and it clearly jump-started the Leafs. From that point on, the boys in white and blue outhustled the visiting team and played their best transition game of the series.

Like always, Toronto had to rely on some timely excellence from Curtis Joseph. In a nerve-wracking sequence near the midway mark of the third period, he made impressive saves off John LeClair and Mikael Renberg, and then brilliantly foiled Rod Brind'Amour from close in, as the Philadelphia center appeared to be lifting a backhander into the net. "Actually, the guys did a great job in front of me tonight," Cujo said afterwards. "I was able to see the puck all night long." The Leafs' ability to control LeClair — who'd been an overwhelming force in Game 4 — was another key to the victory.

Yushkevich missed the overtime session after his right arm was cut above the elbow by Keith Jones's skate in a third-period collision. "I'll play in the next game, no problem," he said afterwards. "I would have come out for the overtime but the doctors were still stitching me up when Yanic scored."

The Leafs can eliminate Philadelphia for the first time in four playoff meetings with another victory Sunday night at the First Union Center.

Saturday, May 1, 1999
Philadelphia

Today's routine was identical to last Sunday's: the Leafs practiced at the Air Canada Centre after a satisfying win, then flew here to Philadelphia later in the afternoon. The difference is, they could be going home tomorrow night to prepare for the second round of the Stanley Cup playoffs.

I came here this afternoon as well with a horde of my media buddies. Air Canada flies its smallish CRJ (Canadair Regional Jet) aircraft between Toronto and Philadelphia, and the 50-seater was jammed with print, broadcast and TV technical people heading back for Game 6. We were told by Maple Leafs travel coordinator Mary Speck that the Sheraton Society Hill was sold out and unable to accommodate the media on this shorter trip. So, most of the Toronto contingent has been booked into a Hilton hotel in Cherry Hill, New Jersey, a 45-minute drive from downtown Philadelphia. My desire was to stay much closer, and I checked into the Westin Suites at Philadelphia airport, where I stayed during the 1993 World Series between the Blue Jays and Phillies.

There's a major drawback at my hotel this weekend, however, as the device that codes the room-key cards is not working, and they can't get anyone to fix it till Monday. As a result, each time I return to my room, I have to be escorted up by a hotel security man. Glamour all the way.

I had a very enjoyable experience tonight. As the NHL and NBA seasons clearly overlap, I've not had the opportunity to become much of a basketball fan during the four-year existence of the Toronto Raptors. In fact, prior to tonight, the only Raptors game I'd been to was the club's very first exhibition contest at SkyDome, against Atlanta, back in October 1995. But The Fan-590 obtained the Raptors' radio broadcast rights this year and we hired a superb play-by-play man named Chuck Swirsky away from WJR Radio in Detroit. Coincidentally, the Raptors played their second-last road game of the regular season here in Philly tonight, and Chuck invited me to attend.

For the first time, I sat at the court-side press table, as the hometown 76ers qualified for the NBA playoffs with an exhilarating 103-96 victory — eliminating Toronto from post-season contention. In no other professional sport can you experience a perspective quite like the one accorded the basketball media, which is literally right on top of the action. Raptors coach Butch Carter paced back and forth all night directly in front of me. It was fascinating to witness the correlation between Carter and veteran power-forward Charles Oakley each time the play went up and down the court. And the whimsical by-play between the court-side spectators and the game officials was quite humorous.

More than anything else, however, this basketball neophyte thinks he saw a miniature Michael Jordan tonight. Rarely, in any sport, have I seen one player electrify a crowd the way 76ers point-guard Allen Iverson did. Chants of "MVP! MVP!" loudly echoed through the First Union Center as he came out of the game late in the fourth quarter. What a spectacular athlete.

Sunday, May 2, 1999
Philadelphia

There's a terrific irony in today's date, being the 32nd anniversary of the night the Maple Leafs last won a Stanley Cup. I was eight years old on May 2, 1967, when the Leafs upended Montreal 3-1 at Maple Leaf Gardens. Sitting at the foot of my parents' bed, watching on television as George Armstrong scored his now-legendary empty-net goal to cinch the victory, remains among my earliest — and fondest — hockey memories.

Similarly, young Maple Leaf fans of the current generation may one day reflect on where *they* were when Sergei Berezin tallied — as he did tonight — one of the truly dramatic goals in the club's playoff history. The Leafs and Flyers skated through more than 59 minutes of breathless hockey . . . neither side able to solve the other's netminder. Overtime seemed all but a certainty when Berezin alertly pounced on a loose puck to the right of the Philadelphia net and snapped it past John Vanbiesbrouck with only 59.2 seconds remaining on the third-period clock. The Maple Leaf bench exploded in euphoria and Toronto hung on to win, 1-0, for a six-game triumph in this Eastern Conference quarterfinal.

"I don't know how the puck came to me, I just shot," said Berezin in a delirious post-game dressing room. "I was looking for loose pucks all night long. This is a great feeling but it's just the first stage."

Berezin was in perfect position when Bryan Berard's shot bounced off the leg of Flyers defenceman Adam Burt. He moved in a stride and planted the loose puck between Vanbiesbrouck's pads before the goalie could react. Steve Thomas and Mats Sundin almost crushed Berezin in celebration. Up in the press box, the Maple Leaf contingent (Ken Dryden, Bill Watters, and the club's public relations staff) let out a whoop that might have been audible throughout the stunned arena. The Flyers were finished.

The goal was scored with Philadelphia winger John LeClair serving a contentious elbowing penalty, and it spawned one of the truly remarkable cases of post-game histrionics ever seen. It sent Toronto to the second round of Stanley Cup competition for the first time since 1994, and sets up a conference semifinal engagement with either Pittsburgh or Boston. The Penguins avoided elimination against New Jersey this afternoon when an ailing Jaromir Jagr scored in overtime — forcing a Game 7 showdown at the Meadowlands this Tuesday. If the Devils win, the Leafs play Boston. If Pittsburgh prevails, Toronto gets the Penguins.

Unfortunately, this Maple Leaf conquest could be remembered less for Berezin's goal than for the emotional meltdown afterwards of Flyers owner Ed Snider. An unrestrained harangue aimed at veteran referee Terry Gregson in the Philadelphia dressing room will surely cost Snider copious amounts of money. It was Gregson who nailed LeClair for elbowing at 17:06 of the third period. Under normal circumstances, there would be no debate over the call, as LeClair clearly and somewhat violently cuffed Mike Johnson in the head behind the Philly goal. It was a foolish act, with Gregson standing roughly three feet away, and the ref did not hesitate in raising his arm. But the call lacked consistency, as merely seconds before, Toronto's Derek King had gone unpunished after mugging Rod Brind'Amour: a misdeed that would have unquestionably been called earlier in the game. With the apparent onset of

"Hudson Bay" rules for the final moments, it came as a momentary shock when Gregson penalized LeClair. Berezin scored the series-winner with five seconds remaining in his infraction.

For such a critical game, it *was* strangely officiated by Gregson and Rob Shick — both of whom were remarkably whistle-happy. Penalties were assessed in bunches to both sides. The Flyers took three consecutive calls in the first half of the second period, then the Leafs were handed four of their own in less than an eight-minute span before the period ended. A fifth call in succession went to Mike Johnson (for tripping) at 10:17 of the third frame, presenting Philadelphia with a glorious and timely chance to break the scoreless tie. Incredibly, neither club could capitalize . . . until the final minute.

Frustration and anger spilled over in the Flyers' dressing room after the game, and I don't think I'll soon forget how it all unfolded.

After getting tape from a number of Maple Leaf players, I walked down the hall to the Philadelphia room — chiefly to ask LeClair for a reaction to his fateful penalty. But the only player attending to the media was the inactive Eric Lindros — standing in street-clothes in a far corner — discussing what might have been if he were healthy. The main part of the room was the sole domain of Ed Snider, who appeared to be smoldering with rage as he paced back and forth. A large semi-circle of Philadelphia media (TV reporters, cameramen and writers) gave him a wide berth, standing back 10 or 15 feet.

It was my belief that Snider had already addressed the local reporters, as none of them were making any attempt to seek his comments. Sensing I might have missed a one-time chance, I quickly debated the notion of re-approaching him. I had met Snider on a couple of previous occasions and remembered that he was friendly and obliging. Of course, it was under much different circumstances. But the worst he could do in this situation — I figured — was tell me to go screw, so I took the chance and carefully walked up to him.

"Uh, Mr. Snider, could I speak with you for a moment?" I asked, the words barely escaping from my throat. To my relief (and utter astonishment), he calmly looked up and said, "Sure, who are you with?" I apprised him of my affiliation and quickly sensed the entire mob of Philadelphia media closing in around the two of us. Obviously, the locals had *not* talked to him. Courageous bunch. Speaking as if he'd rehearsed his comments — and his delivery — the owner began slowly and quietly, but his trembling body quickly gave rise to a crescendo of absolute rage.

"First of all, let me congratulate the Toronto Maple Leafs . . . they are a fine hockey club and they played hard in this series. But I am absolutely sick to my stomach over the way tonight's game ended. Terry Gregson chose to decide the game on his own and not let the players [do it], and it's a disgrace to the league, the citizens of Philadelphia, and our fans. I'm sick of this crap with these officials and I'm not going to take it anymore. [Gregson] made a chicken-shit call on John LeClair, one of the cleanest players in the league. They can't control Gregson. The man has an attitude . . . thinks he's greater than God. And he stinks as an official."

Snider then took a deep breath, but he was just warming up.

"I know I'm going to get fined for this, but I don't care. Gregson decided to determine the game. Where was he born, Toronto? [*actually, Erin, Ontario — near Guelph*]. I don't know what I can do about it, but I'll tell you one thing: everyone in the arena knows what this guy did. There's not one fan who doesn't know what this official did tonight. John LeClair was mugged the whole night long and they didn't call a thing. Just a few minutes before, Jody Hull nearly had his head taken off and it wasn't called. Gregson — I hope he can sleep well tonight, because you all know what he did. He's incompetent and I don't mind saying it."

Snider's impetuous outburst was clearly the most acerbic of its kind in the recent annals of hockey. In fact, it was strongly libelous. Back in the old six-team days, it was commonplace for coaches and managers (like Punch Imlach and Toe Blake) to launch into seething tirades, and local newspapermen were more than obliging to highlight and corroborate their remarks. Nowadays, with the trend towards grievous fines and suspensions, hockey people usually choke back their sentiments. But Snider entertained at least a half-dozen waves of reporters after tonight's game, and his message did not fluctuate. More than 15 minutes after his initial diatribe, he could still be heard blathering away in the Flyers' room.

I've known Gregson for several years and was pretty sure he would not respond to Snider's outrage. Just in case, I waited for him by the exit-ramp of the arena and he materialized roughly 45 minutes after the game — encircled by a cluster of beefy security men. Our eyes met and his right arm emerged from the human enclosure. "Hello Howard," he said as we shook hands. We talked for a brief moment (not on tape) and he claimed the penalty call on LeClair was an obvious one, regardless of the circumstance. He did look beleaguered and seemed happy to be on his way out of town — heading to Phoenix to officiate Tuesday night's Game 7 showdown between the Coyotes and St. Louis Blues.

The Maple Leafs, meanwhile, scurried to the airport for their chartered flight home. They had pretty much escaped this series, thanks to a precipitous edge in goaltending. Toronto established a dubious club record for fewest goals scored in a six-game series (nine), but Curtis Joseph was brilliant in the opening round for the third consecutive spring. He blanked the Flyers for the final 129 minutes and 59 seconds of the series (more than six full periods), stopping the final 59 shots he faced.

Vanbiesbrouck, on the other hand, may have a sleepless summer when he considers the quality of shots that eluded him. Three fateful backhanders — all easily stoppable — proved to be his (and the Flyers') undoing: the Steve Thomas goal that tied Game 2 in dying moments; Mike Johnson's goal that quickly brought the Leafs even in Game 3; and Yanic Perreault's overtime winner in Game 5. It just wasn't meant to be for the veteran puckstopper.

"A lot of people doubted whether our club could get the job done," said Leaf coach Pat Quinn. "We didn't play the free-flow offensive style that worked so well during the season, mainly because Philadelphia took it away from us. But we did prove that we can win ugly if we have to. We played their [style] of game and still made it through. Sure, we got some bounces in the series, but you don't win a best-of-seven just on luck. We battled hard and got great goaltending."

Tuesday, May 4, 1999
Toronto
After a light, optional workout this afternoon at the Air Canada Centre, the Maple Leaf players and staff spent the evening watching Game 7 of the New Jersey–Pittsburgh series on TV. The Penguins scored three second-period goals at the Meadowlands to eliminate the Devils, 4-2, and will now face Toronto in the second round of the playoffs. Jaromir Jagr is supposed to be incapacitated by a groin injury that forced him to miss three games of the New Jersey series, but he was a major factor in the deciding match, setting up two goals.

"Pittsburgh will be tough for us," Pat Quinn said late tonight. "They are pretty much a lay-back hockey team, but where they excel is in their counter attack — much like Ottawa. The Senators were maybe the best team in the league this year at laying back, setting their trap, and then sticking it down your throat. That's where the Penguins' success comes from. They obviously have a few talented players, and probably the best player in the game [*Jagr*]. But they really prosper with their discipline and defensive coverage. They'll present us with a different type of challenge than Philadelphia did."

Speaking of the Flyers, it took the NHL disciplinary office less than 48 hours to respond to the voluminous criticism of Sunday night. A total of $76,000 in fines was levied against the club: $50,000 to Ed Snider, $25,000 to coach Roger Neilson (for able and willing support), and $1,000 to player Keith Jones.

When asked for a comment on the financial forfeiture, Snider would only lament, "I've said enough already."

Neilson was more glib. "I think we're going to have to raise the registration at our hockey camps to cover this," he quipped. "I mean, 25 grand . . . wow! That's 35 thousand for me alone this year [*Neilson was fined $10,000 by the league for hurling a stick at referee Bill McCreary during a game in St. Louis, March 16*]. For some people, that's an annual salary. We had our say, though, and probably shouldn't have. I guess you've got to pay the penalty."

Wednesday, May 5, 1999
Toronto
The Leafs started preparing today in earnest for the Penguins. Maple Leaf management was hoping to begin the series tomorrow so that Game 2 could be played during the traditional *Hockey Night In Canada* slot on Saturday. But the Christian rock group D.C. Talk has long been booked into the Air Canada Centre for tomorrow, and is unable to reschedule its concert. Therefore, the Leafs and Penguins will face off Friday night here in town, with Game 2 on Sunday.

Toronto and Pittsburgh have a history of playoff meetings that dates back to the same era as the initial Toronto-Philadelphia match-ups. The Maple Leafs and Penguins met in consecutive springs (1976 and '77) during a best-of-three preliminary round — part of a format that spanned five playoff years beginning in 1975. Back then, the regular-season first-place finishers in the four divisions (Norris, Adams, Patrick, Smythe) received automatic byes into the second round. The second- and third-place teams in each division were aligned, 1-through-8, based on points in the regular season, comprising the preliminary round (1 vs. 8 . . . 2 vs. 7, etc.). It was played on a 1-1-1 rotation — the higher-point team skating on home ice in Game 1 and (if necessary) Game 3.

In 1975–76, the Leafs finished only a point ahead of Pittsburgh (83-82) and gained home-ice advantage in the preliminary series. The Penguins scored a team-record 339 goals that season, tied with Buffalo for second-most in the NHL. Three Pittsburgh players — Pierre Larouche, Jean Pronovost, and Syl Apps, Jr. — placed among the top 10 regular-season scorers, with Larouche and Pronovost surpassing the 50-goal mark.

It was roughly midway through the '75–76 season that the Maple Leafs began to assert themselves. The Sittler-McDonald-Thompson line evolved into one of the top forward units in the league, and a journeyman goalie obtained prior to the season from Montreal — Wayne Thomas — suddenly came of age. Thomas was brilliant in the three-game preliminary round ouster of Pittsburgh. Toronto limited the high-flying Pens to just three goals (one an empty-netter), and Thomas spun a 4-0 shutout in the deciding match at Maple Leaf Gardens.

The Leafs and Penguins tied in points (81) the following year, spawning another first-round match-up. This time, Pittsburgh had home-ice advantage based on a 34-33 edge in regular-season victories. Toronto again prevailed, with the home team going winless. What I remember most about that series is being wildly busy on the day of Game 2 at the Gardens. It was held April 7, 1977 — several hours after the Toronto Blue Jays played their first-ever baseball game (against the Chicago White Sox) at Exhibition Stadium. I attended both, and felt much warmer in the Gardens.

The Leafs romped to a 5-2 victory in the deciding game at Civic Arena two nights later. Sittler and McDonald dominated the entire ice — the Toronto captain selflessly feeding McDonald for a clinching empty-net goal on a two-on-nothing break in the final minute. It allowed McDonald to register a hattrick, and Sittler received a telephone call afterwards from an impressed and touched Bobby Orr, who had seen the game on TV.

Sittler's role on the current Maple Leaf team belongs to Mats Sundin, who skated through a singularly unspectacular series against Philadelphia. He scored only one goal (the dramatic, last-minute winner in Game 2), and managed to avoid criticism mainly because his uninspired play was overshadowed by other elements (Domi-McCarthy; Vanbiesbrouck's struggle, etc.). Sundin's inability to step forward was particularly disconcerting in view of the fact the Flyers' best player, Eric Lindros, was not in the series. Facing Pittsburgh, the fans and media will spotlight Sundin against the ailing Jaromir Jagr, and it won't be a favorable comparison if he continues to perform with a general lack of spryness.

The NHL's regular-season award nominees were announced today, and Quinn is up for coach of the year. Not bad for a guy who had to be talked out of retirement.

Friday, May 7, 1999
Toronto
There were probably few eggs in the dinosaur era quite as large as the one the Maple Leafs laid tonight at the Air Canada Centre.

For the sell-out audience on hand, a disgraceful 2-0 loss to the Penguins was excruciatingly similar to the series-opening defeat against Philadelphia, only worse. Once again, the Leafs' potent regular-season attack went M.I.A. In seven games (and 21 periods) of regulation time thus far in the playoffs, the boys in blue have struck for a grand total of eight goals (the other being scored by Perreault in overtime).

Sundin's misery intensified. Not only was he invisible in the attacking zone, but he actually contributed to Pittsburgh's first goal when he crossed in front of Curtis Joseph, providing an unintentional screen. Dan Kesa scored on a howitzer from the high slot at 10:52 of the opening period (a powerplay goal), and it was all the Penguins needed.

The Sundin-Thomas-Modin line has combined for only four points in the play-offs so far, increasing wonderment at how the Maple Leafs are in the second round of the post-season.

"It makes you worried when you're not able to get the job done," Sundin admitted after the game. "Our line is expected to be producing goals and scoring opportunities and we haven't been able to do that. For sure, we're worried about it. No one has to tell *me* how I played. I feel it myself."

Toronto Sun columnist Steve Simmons encapsulated the feeling around town after Game 1, under a headline, "TINY EFFORT FROM BIG MATS":

> Dan Kesa and Mats Sundin are tied for goals scored in the playoffs. That isn't necessarily a good thing.
>
> That is, however, a most troubling sign for the offensive threat that used to be the Toronto Maple Leafs. A new playoff series began last night with the same old offence. No hits. No runs. Too many errors. And nobody left on base.
>
> It is not particularly funny because this is the time of year that players are not paid, and Mats Sundin isn't earning his playoff salary.

A microcosm of the entire evening occurred with 2½ minutes left. Rookie defenceman Tomas Kaberle passed ahead to Perreault, who noticed linemate Gary Valk streaking into open ice up the middle. A nifty pass found Valk's stick, but the defensive-minded forward fired the puck into the Penguins' zone without first gaining the red line. It was icing . . . and lights out.

Saturday, May 8, 1999
Toronto

Not surprisingly after last night, Sundin appeared to have a target-pattern attached to him today. And like always, he stuck out his chest and took the darts, straight on. The Maple Leaf captain is now officially and profusely under siege for his lack of authority and production in these playoffs. A humongous squash of media from Toronto and Pittsburgh descended, vulture-like, on the Swede after this morning's somber workout at the Air Canada Centre.

Like the warrior he is, Sundin stood for minutes on end in front of his dressing room locker — beads of sweat on his forehead — trying to make sense of it all. He's been down this road before, and likely will be again, as expectation and reality continue to clash. How such an immensely talented player with his size and presence can be made to look so ordinary is a genuine puzzlement.

"It's harder to figure out for me than anyone else," Sundin agreed. "I know my job is to score and set up goals and I put lots of pressure on myself to get the job done. When things aren't working out, like right now, you somehow have to live with it, and that's not easy.

"As far as the team is concerned, I don't think there's any problem with confidence or belief in each other. We've shown all year long that any time we have a bad game or a let-down, we come back stronger. And I'll tell you what: there hasn't been a single game in the playoffs so far when we've come into the dressing room afterwards feeling like we played our best. I fully expect us to come out hard and be much better in Game 2 of this series."

It appears that Quinn has finally grown weary of anticipating any sort of breakthrough from Fredrik Modin. The young Swede has looked frightfully out of place in the post-season, and he had many of us in the media scratching our heads after practice today.

When questioned about his performance, he said, "I feel good when I'm out there and I think I'm doing good stuff when I'm out there."

Huh?

"It's not like I'm skating around thinking, 'I haven't scored a goal, so I suck,'" he continued. "I'm working hard and creating some chances, I just need to score. You keep on trying and sooner or later, the puck will go in."

But not as soon as Modin will go into the press box.

Late today, the Leafs called up center/left-winger Lonny Bohonos, who led St. John's of the American League in scoring this season with 34 goals and 82 points. They did not summon him to play with Kris King and Tie Domi. Chances are Bohonos will skate on the top unit tomorrow night, looking to add a touch of spark to Sundin. It has to be considered a long shot, but with nine goals in seven playoff games, anything is worth trying.

Sunday, May 9, 1999
Toronto

The captain has spoken. Finally.

Responding to the most extreme vilification of his four-plus years in a Toronto uniform, Sundin was party to all of the Leafs' goals tonight in another bounce-back victory. He scored twice and had two assists in a 4-2 win over the Penguins, squaring this best-of-seven series at one game apiece, and prompting the *Toronto Sun* and *Star* to coincidentally print duplicate headlines on their front sports pages: "MATS MORE LIKE IT!"

Paul Hunter of the *Star* wrote:

> Mats Sundin hadn't been reading the newspapers. He'd avoided sports talk on the radio and television. He didn't need it. He already knew.
>
> He could sense a panicked hockey city was targeting him. But that was almost irrelevant. What mattered most, what caused the genuine anxiety, was what he understood in his own heart. He wasn't playing well.

All of that changed tonight — for the time being, anyway. Set against his most recent standards, Sundin was a man possessed. He formed an immediate connection with Lonny Bohonos in their first playoff game together. Bohonos had skated alongside Sundin and Steve Thomas for a brief spell just prior to the All-Star break in January, and he performed well. His commitment to the game has come under scrutiny since a lethargic performance at training camp last fall. And he's facing a potential legal dilemma after being charged with assault by Michel Therrien — coach of the AHL Fredricton Canadiens — who alleges he was roughed up by Bohonos in a St. John's night club on April 30.

All of Bohonos's problems seemed immaterial based on his unanticipated effort tonight. He got off to a great start by shoveling a Daniil Markov rebound under Tom Barrasso just 6:06 into the game. On a powerplay 8½ minutes later, he deflected a Dimitri Yushkevich point shot — slowing it down — and allowing Sundin to sweep the loose puck between Barrasso's legs for an all-important 2-0 lead after one. A fair bit of fortune then smiled on Bohonos in the dying minutes of the game. The Penguins were trailing, 3-2, and seriously threatening to tie the score, when Bohonos upended Alexei Kovalev at the Leaf blueline. A seemingly blatant tripping penalty went uncalled and Bohonos sped away on a 3-on-2 with Sundin and Thomas — the latter ripping a slapshot high into the net at 16:50.

The Pittsburgh bench — led by coach Kevin Constantine — went ballistic after the goal: Constantine applauding referees Paul Stewart and Don Koharski in sardonic fashion. As the Penguins filed off the ice after the game, I happened to look down just in time to see Matthew Barnaby give Stewart the "finger." The official responded by handing out a misconduct penalty.

"I think I was able to help out with my speed tonight," Bohonos said. "I got in behind their defence a couple of times and created some scoring chances. That helped ease the nerves I was feeling before the game. I'm not afraid to shoot the puck and go to the net; I don't go looking for fancy plays."

Sundin had difficulty hiding an immense grin afterwards. Relief was written all over his face in the Toronto dressing room. "You wonder a bit when you're not feeling on top of your game," he said. "I know when I'm not playing well, because I don't get the usual number of scoring chances. I don't have to read about it or hear about it to understand the situation, but I guess that comes with the territory. Tonight, I felt a lot better."

Not at all lost in Sundin's bounce-back performance was another stellar night's work by Curtis Joseph. He was splendid in the second period, stopping 13 of 14 Pittsburgh shots with an array of acrobatics. A goal by Kip Miller cut into Toronto's 3-1 lead midway through the middle frame. Seconds later, Joseph came up with the key save of the night — whipping out his goal-pad to thwart a slapshot by Tyler Wright. Another blast, by Brad Werenka, was turned aside.

"If you compare tonight to Game 1, we had two or three times as many opportunities," moaned Penguins forward Rob Brown. "Joseph stood on his head and made some great saves, and I thought he stole the game. He's a lot like Dominik Hasek at times — some nights he gets hot and is almost impossible to beat. We've got to throw some more pucks and bodies at him next game."

Jaromir Jagr saw an enormous amount of ice time again tonight, despite his alleged groin problem. And he was as dangerous as ever. Privately, some of the Leaf players are accusing Jagr of "playing possum." Either that, or he has an unparalleled pain threshold. "I think the Penguins are pouring it on a little too thick about Jagr," said one Leaf. "He doesn't look the least bit hampered to me out there, even though I know he was injured during the New Jersey series."

Tonight's festivities at the Air Canada Centre began on an ominous note. Or, should I say, a silent one. Anthem singer John McDermott's microphone cut out only a few lines into his rendition of the "Star Spangled Banner." He soldiered on and continued singing, even when a second mike was handed to him and *it* failed! And they kept the poor bastard up on the video scoreboard during the entire painful episode. The crowd took up the slack for McDermott and began singing "O Canada" before power was finally restored.

These new rinks!

Monday, May 10, 1999
Pittsburgh

Here we are, in the midst of what could be a dynamite playoff series, and the front pages of both Pittsburgh newspapers are chronicling the financial plight of the Penguins. The club has gone into insolvency, and a group spearheaded by Penguins legend Mario Lemieux is angling to buy it, but not at optimum market value. As such, a local bankruptcy court has given the club's creditors only until the end of this month to resolve the issue. If not, the franchise could conceivably be dissolved while still active in the Stanley Cup hunt.

I came here today with my wife, Susan, and 2½-year-old son, Shane. The Maple Leafs also arrived this afternoon and are staying at their usual Pittsburgh hotel, the Westin William Penn, a stately old fortress within a five-minute walk of the Civic Arena. I'm staying with my family at a Sheraton in Station Square, Pittsburgh's equivalent of the Queen's Quay Terminal in Toronto. An old, gutted factory has been remodeled into a shopping mall, and the hotel spectacularly overlooks downtown Pittsburgh from the south bank of the Monongahela River.

This city had a rather nondescript history in the NHL until the early '90s, when Lemieux, Jagr, and Ron Francis formed the heart of a championship team. The Penguins were born as part of the 1967 expansion that saw the NHL double in size from six to twelve teams. The club encountered dire circumstances in the early '80s — worse, even, than today — when crowds of less than 6,000 per game were commonplace at the Civic Arena. Lemieux's arrival in 1984 as the league's No. 1 overall draft choice served, initially, as a stabilizing force, and ultimately, as the dynamism that produced back-to-back Stanley Cups in '91 and '92. Pittsburgh flourished as one of the NHL's marquee franchises for nearly half a decade — an additional balcony of seats required at each end of the Arena to accommodate the masses. Then Lemieux retired. And the momentum began to wane.

The Leafs will want to forget their last trip here. They began the post-All-Star break portion of this season with a hideous 6-0 loss to the Penguins in what many of the players agree was their worst performance of the year. With Joseph and Glenn Healy both nursing injuries that night, Jeff Reese and Francis Larivee were the Toronto goaltenders, and the club appeared to quit on Reese after he allowed a soft goal early in the game.

"The Penguins will come out with a vengeance and probably try to crash the net tomorrow night," Joseph predicted after the Leafs' practice today. "It's not something I dwell on too much, but I've got to expect it."

Tuesday, May 11, 1999
Pittsburgh

"Good game, Kerry."

Those were the words of an unusually acerbic Curtis Joseph as the Maple Leafs stomped off the ice at Civic Arena tonight, bitter 4-3 losers to the Penguins in Game 3 of this Eastern Conference semifinal.

To a man, the Leafs feel they were hoodwinked by referee Kerry Fraser and the off-ice officials at 10:42 of the second period, when several moments of chaos and confusion resulted in a game-tying goal by Pittsburgh defenceman Kevin Hatcher. Maple Leaf president Ken Dryden had Charles Manson eyes as he frantically sought an explanation in the dressing room corridor afterwards.

"You can call it the 'phantom' goal," groused coach Pat Quinn.

Here's what happened . . . or *appeared* to happen:

On a Penguins powerplay, forward Rob Brown received a pass from Jagr behind and to the left of the Toronto net. With his stick parallel to the goalline, he fired the puck into the crease, where it hit the left skate of defenceman Alexander Karpovtsev. It caromed off the right goalpost, straddled the entire length of the goalline, and was swept away by the blocker-glove of Joseph. Leaf defenceman Bryan Berard cleared the puck out of harm's way as the red goal-light flashed on. Without making decisive signals of any kind, referees Fraser and Dave Jackson raised their arms to stop play, and skated over to the penalty timekeeper's bench.

What ensued was an incomprehensible delay of four minutes and thirty-two seconds, as every conceivable video angle crossed the TV screen of replay judge Dale Ruth and series supervisor Charlie Banfield. Fraser spoke first over a phone receiver, then hung it up and donned a head-set. On and on it went. The players were growing beards while awaiting a decision, and the fans began to wail in agony after about three minutes. Finally, Fraser disconnected himself and pointed to center ice, signaling a goal. Hatcher was given credit, as he had taken a swipe at the puck after it bounced off Karpovtsev's skate.

A close look at several replay angles did not show the puck completely crossing the line — the requisite for a permissible goal. Roughly two-thirds of the way across the line, the puck began angling towards the net, and had the far post been six or seven inches further away, it would have certainly curled in. But even the overhead television camera could not determine if the puck had gone fully across the red line, as it seemed to briefly vanish beneath the skirt of white-nylon canvas laced around the bottom of the goal-frame. Joseph instinctively swept the puck away with his glove before it re-appeared.

Considering how contentious the issue would be after the game, there was a comparatively mild reaction from the Maple Leafs. Fraser skated directly over to the Toronto bench and conferred with Quinn, who seemed more stunned at the call than outwardly disturbed. Not only was it a questionable decision, but the goal occurred just more than two minutes after Leaf winger Mike Johnson had banged in a Derek King pass to break the scoreless tie. King and rookie Adam Mair — playing his first NHL game in place of the injured Steve Sullivan — added second-period goals for Toronto, while Bobby Dollas scored another for the Pens.

A 3-1 lead after two would have been far more comfortable for the Maple Leafs than a one-goal edge, and offset the narrow loss produced by unanswered goals from Jagr and Jiri Slegr in the third. Instead, the visitors found themselves behind again in the series, and thoroughly aggravated over it.

Dryden has probably never presented himself in public quite like he did after tonight's game. The Maple Leaf president stomped through the myriad of hallways near the dressing room looking for a league representative. Pent-up rage was clearly evident in his skin-color (crimson), his expression (crazed) and his lips (tightly pursed). When he finally came upon some hapless member of the off-ice crew, Dryden spoke in a forceful, monotone inflection. "No! I want an answer NOW!" he tremored, when told the league would look at the tape and speak with him tomorrow. "You have a machine with the video, right?" he asked. "Then let's take a look at the goal." With that, he barged into a room full of A-V equipment.

Meanwhile, I waited outside the officials' room (yet again) for Banfield to make some sort of comment. The supervisor was huddling with Fraser and Jackson to get their stories straight. He materialized about 15 minutes later and calmly explained the officials' position. "In essence, we could not make a proper determination on the goal based on the replays," Banfield said, discussing his painstaking review with the video judge. "Believe it or not, even with all this technology, there are times when we can't tell for sure if a puck enters the net, and tonight was one. Overhead view; side view, we just could not tell."

With no other recourse, the play went back down to the ice, where the initial perception of goal judge Gary Steffenhagen prevailed. Steffenhagen — of the Chicago Blackhawks' off-ice crew — had immediately flicked on the red light, but Fraser hadn't seen the puck cross the goalline himself, and decided to go upstairs to invoke Rule 93(a) of the official NHL rulebook, which simply states:

The following situations are subject to review by the Video Goal Judge:
a) Puck crossing the goal line.

When no determination could be made by Banfield and Ruth, there were many who believed the spirit of the rule should have negated the goal. After all, there was no conclusive evidence that the puck had completely crossed the line. It was explained, however, that the next course of action is to send the play back down to the ice, though a thorough perusal of this season's NHL rulebook (all 160 pages' worth) presents no such directive. Rule 57 ("Goals and Assists") clearly denotes (under sub-heading "a"):

> *A goal shall be scored when the puck shall have been put between the goal posts . . . and entirely across a red line the width and diameter of the goal posts drawn on the ice from one goalpost to the other.*

Under Rule 37(c), pertaining to goal judges, it reads:

> *In the event of a goal being claimed, the Goal Judge of that goal shall decide whether or not the puck has passed between the goal posts and entirely over the goal line.*

But that's it. Nowhere in the book is there an outlined procedure for the circumstance that arose tonight — indecision by the video goal judge. It must be noted that the integrity of this particular judge (Dale Ruth) has come into question on several occasions. The usually mild-mannered Cliff Fletcher was ready to kill him one night a few seasons back when Ruth overruled a Maple Leaf goal at the Civic Arena. Fletcher stormed out of his glassed-in enclosure, tramped past a row of Toronto reporters, and angrily slammed on the window of Ruth's cubicle. When an invitation to discuss the call did not materialize, the Maple Leaf GM returned to his position mumbling a stream of obscenities.

Fairly or not, Ruth has garnered a reputation for bias. Whispers around the league claim that he'll rule against the Penguins only under the most obvious of circumstances. His non-decision on the "phantom" goal occurred after he had already wiped out a Toronto marker in the first period. At 14:42 of the opening frame, Leaf defenceman Sylvain Cote fired a wrist-shot past Tom Barrasso, but Gary Valk clearly had a foot in the crease. It could have easily been determined, however, that Kevin Hatcher used a fair amount of muscle to prevent Valk from moving, thus invoking Rule 93 (h):

> *The On Ice Officials or Video Goal Judge may be consulted to establish if*

> *an attacking player has entered the crease prior to the puck, and subsequent goal . . . Any information as to the position of the attacking player may be "overruled" if the Officials have determined that the attacking player was pushed or held in the crease at the time of the goal being scored.*

Ruth determined that Valk had *not* been pushed or held — news that most visiting GMs or coaches would figure to be less than a bulletin. "Hatcher held Valk in the crease, so we lose one there," grumbled Quinn. "And then there's the phantom goal that never crossed the line. We could have nine referees out there. I guess that'll be the next step." Asked what Fraser explained to him after allowing Hatcher's goal, Quinn said, "Kerry just told me it went in. He saw it go in. There's nothing as far as I know on any replay that shows it crossed the line."

The fact that Fraser was center-stage in tonight's controversy — more of a coincidence than anything else — only added to the ire and misgiving of Maple Leaf fans. It's unlikely the Sarnia, Ontario, native will ever be forgiven in Toronto for the torturous memory of May 27, 1993. The Leafs and Los Angeles Kings were early in overtime in Game 6 of the Campbell Conference final at the Forum that night — Toronto leading the best-of-seven series, 3-2, and needing just a goal to advance to the Stanley Cup final for the first time since 1967. Waiting for them was the same opponent of 26 years earlier, the Montreal Canadiens.

As he positioned himself opposite Doug Gilmour for an offensive-zone face-off, Wayne Gretzky accidentally brought his stick up under the chin of the Maple Leaf captain, opening an ugly gash. A chilled hush overcame the Forum as Gilmour's blood dripped to the ice — fans realizing that, based on the NHL rulebook, the Great One would be banished from the game. To this day, Maple Leaf fans abhor Fraser for somehow overlooking the infraction. More than six years later, it seems no less bizarre that Fraser and his linesmen — Ron Finn and Kevin Collins — could miss what everyone else in the arena (and those watching on TV) had clearly seen. With the Kings already on a powerplay, Gretzky added salt to Gilmour's wound by scoring the overtime winner himself — sending the series back to Toronto for a seventh and deciding match two nights later.

A grandiose performance by No. 99 at Maple Leaf Gardens lifted L.A. to an anticlimactic final against the Canadiens, and left permanent scars, it seems, on the hockey fans of Toronto.*

---

* In early September 1999, my Fan-590 colleague Gord Stellick (the former Maple Leaf executive and GM) posed a question to his afternoon radio audience: "What is the most gut-wrenching sports moment you can remember?" At least half of Gord's callers named the Gretzky-Gilmour incident as the one that stuck in their craw, and identified Fraser as the enduring villain.

More than 90 minutes after tonight's game, Dryden finally emerged to discuss the Hatcher goal with reporters. "I've looked at all the replays and they tell me the puck never crossed the line," insisted the Leaf president. "The images up there [in the video booth] were not difficult to read. We have the technology in place; the process; the people. Everything was there to make the right call, but the wrong call was made. If I were the NHL, I'd be embarrassed."

Lost in all the commotion was a terrific moment for young Adam Mair. His first-ever NHL goal, at 12:58 of the second period, gave Toronto the 3-2 lead it took into the third. Mair bulled his way to the net and seemed to bump goalie Tom Barrasso out of position with his rump before backhanding in a Tie Domi rebound.

"It was a great feeling to score, but the game ended in a disappointing way," said Mair, politically correct. "I know a whole ton of family and friends were watching the game on TV back home [in Hamilton] and I'm sure I'll hear from a lot of them tonight and tomorrow."

Mair was the Maple Leafs' second choice (84th overall!) in the 1997 entry draft. This season alone, he has played for Owen Sound of the Ontario Hockey League, in the World Junior Hockey Championships for Canada, and with the Maple Leafs' farm team in St. John's. Just 20 years of age, he was understandably nervous after this morning's skate, when he found out he would definitely be playing in place of Steve Sullivan, whose back problems have re-emerged.

"It's quite a jump for someone like me," he said. "One day, you're skating with the Black Aces, and the next, you're playing in the second round of the Stanley Cup playoffs. You've got to be ready for the unexpected."

Wednesday, May 12, 1999
Pittsburgh

Today was one of intense reflection on Game 3, and the *Toronto Sun* took up the Maple Leafs' cause. Following its own thorough investigation of Kevin Hatcher's disputed goal, the tabloid flashed a headline across the top of its front page: "PHANTOM GOAL: PUCK DIDN'T GO IN; NET-CAM REPLAY PROVES LEAFS WERE JOBBED." Hockey writer Tim Wharnsby detailed a review session he attended this afternoon:

> *Hockey Night In Canada* producer Paul Graham invited a number of reporters to an afternoon screening (only the *Toronto Sun* and the *National Post* attended) of what his staff had discovered.
>
> The net-cam view showed that Hatcher whacked a loose puck off the right post and the puck made its way along the goal line. The

spinning puck started to dip across the line as it approached the left post, where it hit the protective padding, spun out, and then was raked out by Toronto goalie Curtis Joseph's glove. At no point did it appear the puck crossed the line completely, which it must in order to be a goal.

In the *National Post,* columnist Cam Cole wrote:

On the morning after the night before, ESPN was claiming to have exclusive footage showing the puck crossing the goalline . . . But the mother of all replays is a digitally expanded shot taken by CBC's in-goal camera, which shows — as clearly as can be — that part of the puck remains at all times in touch with the goal line. Which means that whatever the goal judge, Gary Steffenhagen of Chicago, thinks he saw from a vantage point considerably worse than the net-cam's, it was not white ice between the puck and red line. And the game should not have been tied, 1-1.

So, he was guessing. Or extrapolating on where he thought the puck must have been heading. Just as Kerry Fraser was guessing, otherwise he never would have sent the play upstairs for a second opinion.

The Leafs practiced this afternoon at the Civic Arena, after which Quinn held court with reporters in the Zamboni corridor. As per usual, his comments were to the point . . . perhaps excessively. CFTO-TV reporter George Bryson took the brunt of Quinn's wrath when he quite sensibly implied that Hatcher's goal did not entirely influence the game's outcome. Quinn's response was hasty and insensitive.

"Are you *nuts*?!" the coach thundered, causing Bryson to turn a flaming shade of crimson (Quinn later apologized to Bryson).

Expanding on his feelings about the phantom goal, Quinn may have come perilously close to crossing the line of tolerance in the league's head office. "It's a disgrace for it to happen," he said. "This is a Stanley Cup final [almost], there's a lot at stake here. We know mistakes happen, but it's the cover-up afterwards that you hate. That's the type of crap you have to deal with and there's an immunity built in where no one ever has to own up for their mistakes, except the players, and that's not the way it should be.

"[The rulings by the officials on and off the ice] were all fabricated," Quinn continued. "[Hatcher's goal] didn't go in. There's no proof in all their angles that the puck ever went in the net. And that's exactly why we put cameras up there, to help these guys out. But if they take it on their own to conjure up a situation, then there's not much you can do about it. The league should do something, because we can't do anything about it now."

As per Bryson's observation, the Leafs indeed contributed to their own demise in the third period with some sloppy defensive work. The mathematics of the situation is open to debate; obviously, the Leafs would not have been beaten if Cote's goal stood and Hatcher's marker had been disallowed. But several missed assignments and a poor choice of line matching by Quinn contributed to Toronto blowing the 3-2 lead it held with 10:57 remaining in regulation time.

Jiri Slegr's winning goal had been scored with a peculiar tandem of Leafs on the ice. Three virtual freshmen — Lonny Bohonos, Tomas Kaberle, and Adam Mair — were out against Jagr's line. Had this arrangement resulted from a change on the fly, perhaps it could have been rationalized. But Quinn placed his skaters on the ice in a 3-3 tie, following a 90-second television time out.

"It was my fault, I had the wrong guys out there," the coach admitted.

The Leaf players were in a mind-set to forget the exasperation of Game 3 and look ahead to tying the series tomorrow night. "No matter what anyone thought of the call, it's over and there's no sense dwelling on it anymore," said Steve Thomas. "We haven't allowed anybody to beat us three games in a row this year. This team has always been able to bounce back from adversity. We have the ability in this dressing room to beat that team over there."

Thursday, May 13, 1999
Pittsburgh
There is an intermission feature that runs on *Hockey Night In Canada* during the Stanley Cup playoffs called "Overtime Magic." It is a compilation of overtime goals as called by the various CBC broadcasters like Bob Cole, Chris Cuthbert and Don Wittman. The Maple Leafs added a segment to the feature tonight, while extending *their* season-long trend towards overtime magic.

Sergei Berezin scored one of the easiest and most significant goals of his young career to prevent the Maple Leafs from heading home in this series facing elimination. The Russian-born winger pounced on a loose puck and slammed it into a wide-open Pittsburgh net at 2:18 of the first extra period, giving Toronto a 3-2 victory and a 2-2 deadlock in this Eastern Conference semifinal. Counting the regular season, the Leafs have now played in sixteen overtime games — winning an incredible eight of them. They were 6-1-7 during the season, and are 2-0 in the playoffs — a far cry from what Maple Leaf fans endured in a previous era.

Anyone my age (40-ish) will practically shudder when recalling the grief and despair of the 1970s, when the Leafs were repeatedly conquered in overtime. Toronto missed the playoffs only once during the decade (1973), but was able to win only four of fourteen games that went into extra time. That is why the goal scored by Lanny McDonald to eliminate the New York Islanders in the 1978 quarterfinals remains a legendary moment. Sure, it happened in Game 7, and on the road, and allowed the Leafs to reach the semis for the first (and only) time in the decade. But it also followed a string of five consecutive overtime losses — dating back three years. The images of Andre (Moose) Dupont, Reggie Leach, Rick MacLeish, Mike Bossy, and Bob Nystrom each firing a stake through the hearts of Maple Leaf fans were finally vanquished by McDonald's unforgettable tally.

Times have sure changed. While the Maple Leaf Stanley Cup drought is 31 years and counting, there have been abundant overtime thrills in the 1990s — beginning with the goals, in Detroit, by Mike Foligno and Nikolai Borschevsky during the Leafs' first-round conquest of the Red Wings in 1993. Foligno won Game 5 of the series at Joe Louis Arena, and the smallish Borschevsky, whose promising career was derailed by a ruptured spleen early the following season, scored the overtime winner in Game 7 — becoming the first Maple Leaf to accomplish the feat since McDonald.

The sight late this evening of Berezin standing triumphantly beside the Penguins' net — arms extended in victory, a wide smile on his face — must have mirrored the emotions of Maple Leaf fans watching the game on TV. It caused nothing more than a sickly groan from the previously rabid audience here at the Civic Arena — a place that quickly grew so silent, you could easily hear the Maple Leaf players bellowing in ecstasy as they poured off the bench.

Tomas Kaberle's shot from the point was tipped by Gary Valk, cruising in front of Tom Barrasso. The puck slithered beneath the Pittsburgh goalie and two Penguin players — Greg Andrusak and Jan Hrdina — pounced on Valk. Berezin had eluded defenceman Bobby Dollas in the corner, and he emerged to the right of the Pittsburgh net just as the loose puck dribbled into the crease. He gleefully slapped it home for his first goal of the series.

"It was like a dream come true," said Berezin. "I was so tired, but I went to the net and the puck was waiting for me. Even my son [*six-year-old Justin*] wouldn't have missed that shot. Our line hasn't had too many scoring chances lately, it's been so tight-checking. Hopefully, this will change things."

The Leafs won a game they clearly dominated — outshooting Pittsburgh 30-14 on the night, 15-4 during the third period and short overtime. For the first time in the series, Toronto proved capable of beating the Penguins' suffocating trap, but the

Maple Leafs trailed 1-0 until 16:57 of the second period, when Mats Sundin fired in a Lonny Bohonos rebound. Bohonos and Brad Werenka then traded goals in a 1:42 span early in the third, leading to the extra period.

As per usual, a sequence of heroics from Curtis Joseph went somewhat unnoticed after the dramatic conclusion. But a breakaway stop on none other than Jaromir Jagr in the first period — followed by a tremendous pad save on Matthew Barnaby a few minutes later — prevented the Maple Leafs from falling behind early by three goals.

"Winning this game was huge," sighed Gary Valk. "You can't go down 3-1 in a series and expect to win. We were the better team all night long, but it was getting a bit nerve-wracking until Mats finally broke the ice. Now, we have home-ice advantage back."

After playing decently in Game 3, Tie Domi had a difficult time accepting a demotion to the sidelines for tonight's game. Moments before the puck was dropped, Quinn told Domi he would be replaced by Fred Modin in the interest of more team speed. It marked the first time the popular pugilist has been chosen to sit out a game since he was acquired from the old Winnipeg Jets — for Mike Eastwood — back on April 7, 1995.

"It was very disappointing for me not to play," Domi frowned, amid the jubilation of his teammates afterwards. "I've been a part of this team all season long and I think everybody was shocked in the dressing room. The thing is, I have no idea why I was scratched; nobody gave me an explanation. And having it happen right before the game was a downer. If I'm going to sit out, I wish they would tell me in the morning. I think I deserve more respect than that."

Even while dressing for games in the playoffs, Domi has been used quite sparingly — usually seeing less than five minutes of total ice time. "I guess they wanted to create a shake-up by keeping me out, but after playing two and three minutes a game, is that really going to cause any type of shake-up? I think with my leadership on the bench and in the dressing room, I contribute more than playing four minutes a game. I'll deal with the situation tomorrow."

Quinn's reasoning for sitting Domi: "Tie has struggled in the sense that he has an injury that hasn't been announced [*likely a strained knee*]. We wanted to get some skating in there tonight, and that's why I put Freddy [Modin] back in. I also wanted to keep young Mair in because we're so thin at center at the moment with Sullivan, McCauley, and Korolev out."

Domi did not view the game from the press box, as most "extra" players do. Instead, he watched on a TV in the Leafs' dressing room while working on a crossword puzzle.

Friday, May 14, 1999
Toronto

One of the clear advantages of a playoff series between the Maple Leafs and Penguins — for everyone involved: players, media, fans — is the wonderful lack of travel time. A flight that manages to evade air traffic delays takes exactly 38 minutes to soar between Pittsburgh and Toronto. That's roughly the time involved in *driving* to the Pittsburgh International Airport from downtown.

The Leafs departed after last night's overtime victory, and had an optional skate this morning at the Air Canada Centre. After sleeping on his emotions, Tie Domi was in his normally jocular frame of mind, pulling a complete about-face with his words and actions. "That was totally blown out of proportion," he said, concerning reports of his discontentment last night. "We won the game, that's all that matters." Of course, Tie is media-savvy enough not to expect any of us to buy that pile of baloney. Still, he was sticking to his story.

"It's a situation where I'm not 100 percent, and Pat felt he should put in some-one who is 100 percent," Domi calmly rationalized. "I've been around for 10 years, and it's always been a rule not to talk about injuries at playoff time. But I will admit that after being a big part of this team, and a part of these playoffs, it was tough to swallow not being out there. You have to take it as it goes."

With another day between games, the *Toronto Star* took the opportunity to examine what has been a growing concern around the Leafs — the observable lack of relationship between Dryden and associate GM Mike Smith. Under a front-page headline in the sports section that read, "VIEW FROM THE TOP," Ken Campbell and Rosie DiManno profiled the two men and discussed their ostracized existence. Wrote DiManno: " The Prince and Princess of Wales, in those final horrible months of their marriage, had more warmth for each other in public than do these two proud, stub-born, and perhaps fatally foolish men."

This will be something to keep an eye on once the Leaf season is over.

Saturday, May 15, 1999
Toronto

Anyone who is even a casual fan of hockey knows that Jaromir Jagr is the most tal-ented player in the game today. What we all discovered tonight was his unrevealed sporting versatility. Jagr, it turns out, is one hell of a javelin thrower. Or at least he appeared to be late in the first period of Game 5, when he chucked his hockey stick into the penalty box — freeing a chest-load of confined fury.

Jagr is clearly indisposed with his groin injury and tonight, at the Air Canada

Centre, he encountered a resolute, inflexible pest by the name of Dimitri Yushkevich. The Maple Leafs' Russian defencemen harassed the Penguins' Czech winger to utter distraction — completely nullifying Jagr in a resounding 4-1 Toronto victory. Like they did in the last round against Philadelphia, the Leafs have made a crystalline statement in the pivotal fifth match on home ice. They can knock off the Penguins on Monday night in Pittsburgh, and advance to the Stanley Cup semifinals for the first time since 1994.

"They were the better team from the very first minute," acknowledged a downcast Jagr after the game.

A potential Jagr-Yushkevich embrace was the subject of a short, pre-game chat between Bob Cole and Harry Neale on *Hockey Night In Canada*:

COLE: Well, Harry, this is another wild, Saturday night in Toronto. The playoffs move along and the games get bigger and bigger, and this one is the biggest so far . . . they've got to stop Jagr, somehow.

NEALE: Well, I don't think you're ever going to stop him, but you can contain him, and the Leafs' defence pair of Yushkevich and Markov have done a pretty good job. But when you get the assignment to handle him one-on-one in the defensive zone coverage, your problems just start. Jagr can win this game by himself, and he just may.

Yushkevich has been paying increasingly close attention to the Penguins' megastar in recent games, and he became a virtual silhouette tonight. Realizing that Jagr was already frustrated by his own lack of mobility, Yushkevich launched a systematic verbal assault on the Pittsburgh captain — the result of which became dramatically evident in the final minute of the first period.

Skating through the neutral zone on a line change, Penguins forward Dan Kesa headmanned the puck to Jagr along the right-wing boards. Jagr had to briefly look behind him for the pass and was checked by Lonny Bohonos before he crossed the blueline. His momentum, however, carried him into Maple Leaf territory, where he was rocked against the boards by Yushkevich. He went to the ice, momentarily stunned, and recovered to his knees — a startled expression on his face. As Yushkevich left the zone, he purposely brushed Jagr and whispered another sweet-nothing in his ear. Jagr's face crinkled in rage and he took a fairly harmless whack at Yushkevich with his stick. But the mild slash to the leg was clearly noticeable — drawing a boisterous reaction from the fans — and referee Terry Gregson sent him off for two minutes.

Cole and Neale called the sequence on *Hockey Night*:

COLE: There are just 40 seconds left in the period. Moran stickhandling
         out of his own zone . . . to Kesa . . . yup, and Jagr was hit hard . . .
         he doesn't like it and took a swing at the Leaf player, Yushkevich, and
         the captain of Pittsburgh is drawing a slashing penalty.
NEALE: And a selfish one at that. At this time of the year, when your team is
         on the ropes, you can't be taking those types of penalties. We all
         admire Jagr's poise, but we didn't see much of it there.
COLE (*watching replay*): He was down — hit hard — and you'll see it now
         . . . it took him a while to get up . . . that's a pretty legal, tough hit
         on Jagr. Now he's down . . . now, he thinks about it, and says "I can't
         take it," and there's the slash.

It turned out to be the defining moment of tonight's game. The Leafs came out
strongly and built a 2-0 lead by the 10:48 mark of the opening period. Sylvain Cote's
floating slapshot found its way through a screen, and a nifty deflection of
Yushkevich's point shot by Mike Johnson increased the Toronto advantage less than
four minutes later. Johnson's goal would prove to be the winner.

The first-period Maple Leaf edge included a rare component, when Kris King and
Pittsburgh agitator Matthew Barnaby dropped their gloves at the 16:40 mark. Actually,
Barnaby came looking for the scrap — gently cross-checking King inside the Toronto blueline — and the Maple Leaf ruffian was more than willing to oblige. Both players landed a
flurry of punches in the lively skirmish, with King garnering a slight decision. As Barnaby
left the ice, he responded to the cat-calls by gradually extending his arms, like a symphony
conductor in the tumultuous climax of a musical score. The man is a character.

"You don't want to risk changing the momentum of a game by fighting, especially in the playoffs," King explained afterwards. "But I just couldn't resist the invitation. It was definitely there, on the table. There is no love lost between us and I
knew I could kick his ass. So I wasn't backing down."

King's loathing of Barnaby is not just played out on the ice. I had the Leaf scrap-
per in the radio studio a couple of years ago, and he checked his political correctness
at the door. "I have no respect for Barnaby, I think he's a fool," King said, matter-of-
factly. "He runs around mouthing off all game long — you can even hear him yap-
ping on the bench. He will fight, but he tends to become a lot more courageous once
he's in the grasp of a linesman."

Barnaby *is* a crackpot on the ice, but it's difficult not to like the guy away from it. Regardless of the circumstance, he always makes himself available to the media, and doesn't soften his stance over the air, or for publication. Last week in Pittsburgh, I asked Barnaby about giving referee Paul Stewart the "finger" after the Penguins' loss in Game 2. Most players would have tip-toed around such a question, or avoided answering it altogether. Not Barnaby. "I was upset at the way the game ended and wanted to show [Stewart] the way I felt," he explained. "Do I regret it? Not at all. The referees can be pretty confrontational themselves. It's an emotional game and, sometimes, stuff like that happens."

Late in tonight's game, another fight broke out that shocked many of us. Leaf rookie Ladislav Kohn dropped his gloves and tonged on Penguins center Tyler Wright in front of the Toronto bench. Kohn had played only 16 games during the regular season, compiling a measly four penalty minutes. "I had a lot of energy left and the fight was a way to burn it off," shrugged Kohn, who saw only 5:11 of ice time during the game. "It just happened."

The evening's emotions were clearly in contrast after the game. In the happy Maple Leaf dressing room, Yushkevich stood for many long minutes, entertaining waves of reporters. Repeatedly given the opportunity to gloat about his effective maltreatment of Jagr, the defenceman chose a different tack.

"Jagr may be injured, but to me, he's healthy as a horse," Yusky said. "He is so strong and so good on every shift. I try to play against him like he's any other guy, but also remember that he's the best player in the world. Even if he's injured, he plays great. To keep him off the scoreboard is very hard to do."

Yushkevich chose to downplay his verbal strategy. "I don't remember what I said to [Jagr]," he confessed, appearing uncomfortable with the question.

Down the hallway in the Penguins' room, I waited more than 20 minutes with a swarm of media for Jagr to emerge. The Czech star is a bit of an enigma. There are times when he simply will not speak with reporters, even after happy occasions. But when he's willing to talk, his cheerful, effusive personality is an absolute delight. And he has a smile that can illuminate a pitch-dark room. That smile had to be forced during his brief tête-à-tête with reporters tonight.

"We kept saying how much we love each other," Jagr joked, when asked about his running dialogue with Yushkevich. "He does everything he can to stop me and I do everything I can to beat him. That's the way it should be."

Jagr admitted that he's growing increasingly weary as this playoff round progresses. His usual mobility is hampered by the groin injury and he realizes how much the Penguins miss their other sidelined players, particularly forward Alexei Kovalev, who suffered a deeply bruised foot by blocking a shot in the final seconds of Game 3.

Kovalev skated in the warm-up prior to tonight's game, then decided his foot was still too tender for him to play.

"We really miss Kovie," Jagr said. "We have guys playing who are from out of the NHL and are out of shape. That's frustrating. Nobody knows where to play . . . we have centers playing the wing, wingers playing center. The [forward] lines just aren't right."

But Jagr isn't conceding anything to the Maple Leafs. "I love Toronto too much, and want to come back for Game 7," he grinned. "It's the best city."

Sunday, May 16, 1999
Pittsburgh

The blissfulness of the short flight between Toronto and Pittsburgh was effectively negated by traffic congestion on the ground at Pearson International Airport late this afternoon. First, they had a problem closing the door on the Air Canada CRJ, then we taxied out to runway 6-Right and waited 45 minutes in line before taking off. It's not often that a flight is shorter in length than a delay, but the quick hop down to western Pennsylvania took 40 minutes.

One of the truly majestic sights on the hockey trail is here in Pittsburgh, on the drive into downtown from the airport. An incredible contrast unfolds when you emerge from the dreary Fort Pitt Tunnel and get smacked in the face by the triangular panorama of America's steel city. Glassy skyscrapers line the north shore of the Monongahela River, while giant Three Rivers Stadium basks in virtual solitude on a point just west of the city center.

Shrouded by a conclave of office towers, and perched on an incline at the northeast end of downtown, is the venerable Civic Arena: now the oldest rink in the NHL. Nicknamed the "Igloo" for its unique spherical design and its primary tenant (Penguins), it opened in 1961, and became the patriarch of hockey arenas when Maple Leaf Gardens closed for business in February 1999. As a result of Mario Lemieux's predominance in the '80s and '90s, spectator seats are jammed into every visible cranny of the building — primarily rust-orange in color. The low-angle positions between the bluelines have been converted into rectangular sections of dark-blue "club" seats. Large balconies were added to both ends of the arena in the early '70s; smaller ones (the "Lemieux Balconies") were built in the late '80s, just prior to the Penguins' championship years.

Conspicuous by their absence are the private luxury boxes that fuel the pro sports economy, and the Penguins have long claimed they are saddled with a burdensome lease that is currently threatening to disable the franchise.

That subject was broached by hockey writer Joe Starkey in the *Pittsburgh*

Tribune-Review. He wrote: "With a victory [tomorrow night], or in Game 7, the Maple Leafs might become the answer to a trivia question: Who was the last visiting team to play in the Civic Arena? Given the dire circumstances surrounding the Penguins' bankruptcy, this could be the final match at the 39-year-old Igloo."

The Leafs practiced at the Air Canada Centre this morning before flying here to Pittsburgh. The Penguins skated at their practice facility in Southpointe, Pennsylvania, and had to cut short the workout when their Zamboni malfunctioned right in the middle of an ice-surfacing trek. "As for the Zamboni, it pooped out on its second lap [today], leaving the smoke and the smell of a car repair shop," wrote witness Tim Wharnsby in the *Toronto Sun.* "'The ice wasn't that bad, it was the carbon-monoxide out there,' defenceman Ian Moran deadpanned."

There wasn't a lot to do here late today. I watched in my hotel room at the Westin William Penn as the Utah Jazz held off an NBA playoff challenge from the upstart Sacramento Kings, winning the deciding game of a series in overtime. Tonight, I went down to the lobby and ran into several of my colleagues — David Amber and (cameraman) Tim Moses of TSN, and Paul Hunter of the *Star.* We went for dinner at Mallorca, a Spanish restaurant southeast of downtown. I had garlic soup and garlic chicken. Should be a riot doing interviews tomorrow.

Monday, May 17, 1999
Pittsburgh

Move over Lanny McDonald and Nikolai Borschevsky — you've got company. For the third time in the past generation, the Maple Leafs have won a playoff series with an overtime goal. Unheralded (but extremely hairy) winger Gary Valk — a pro hockey outcast only nine months ago — forever etched his name in Maple Leaf legend here tonight. He swept a rebound past Tom Barrasso at 1:57 of extra time, stunning an overflow crowd at the Civic Arena, and lifting Toronto to a berth in the Stanley Cup semifinals for the first time in five years. The 4-3 victory clinched the series over the Penguins in six games.

"This is awesome!" enthused Valk, whose square jaw, steely expression, and playoff beard give him the look of a serial killer. "Coming from where I've been — sitting at home last summer with no job — to get this far in the playoffs is unbelievable. I've never been a part of anything like this before."

McDonald and Borschevsky had scored their overtime winners in Game 7 situations, but Valk's goal here seemed no less dramatic. Center Yanic Perreault, who has done nothing but win face-offs for the Maple Leafs in these playoffs, did it again — cleanly beating Jan Hrdina to the right of Barrasso. He drew the puck behind him on his backhand and Sergei Berezin instinctively moved in a couple of strides to gain control. From the high slot, Berezin briefly lost, then re-gained possession, and fired a quick, low shot at Barrasso.

The Penguin goalie flung out his right pad, but rather than kicking the puck out of harm's way, he inadvertently stepped on it and carried it back across his body under his right skate. Seeing the loose puck, defenceman Jiri Slegr awkwardly sprawled to try and smother it, but crashed feet-first into Barrasso. Valk's eyes must have been the size of frying pans as he shoveled the inviting disc into the open right side of the net while tumbling over Slegr's right arm.

The Leafs' newest hero got up and raised his arms in triumph, facing the Toronto bench across the ice. Berezin quickly jumped on him, and the linemates wildly embraced in the right-wing corner. In descending order, Berezin and Valk were pounced on by Perreault, Alexander Karpovtsev, Bryan Berard, Daniil Markov, and Mats Sundin. Then the rest of the ecstatic team, including Tie Domi in street-clothes (he was scratched again for tonight's game). Wearing a stud in his left ear and a white Penguins uniform, a local fan seated in the front row of corner seats stood up, pressed his nose against the glass, and yelled obscenities at the blue-clad villains celebrating mere inches in front of him. He supplemented his verbal barrage with an impassioned display of his middle finger — all of it caught on national television in Canada.

Lonny Bohonos and Kevyn Adams were the first Leaf players off the bench. Derek King, Adam Mair, and Kris King briefly stood behind, jumping for joy. Mair embraced Kris King, while Derek hugged Mike Johnson, who'd already leapt on the ice. A member of the Penguins' training staff walked in front of the Toronto bench and shook hands with Pat Quinn, and the Leaf coach was then doused with a cup of beer from the seats behind him, the suds splashing onto the left shoulder of his suit-jacket.

The only noise in the building — and it was considerable — came from the several-thousand Maple Leaf fans who had made the trek south. They were dancing in the aisles — cheering, high-fiving, waving their banners — as the locals filed out dejectedly. The traditional handshakes took place down the center of the ice and the triumphant visitors scampered off to their dressing room.

I quickly made my way down to the cramped corridor outside the room, and was standing in back of CBC reporter Scott Oake when Valk came out to be interviewed live on *Hockey Night In Canada*.

RON MACLEAN: Here's the hero of the hour with Scott Oake.

OAKE: And what a story he is, Ron. Gary Valk was temporarily — with emphasis on *temporarily* — retired in September. He's the hero tonight with two goals including the winner in O.T. Go ahead and make your statement.

VALK: Oh my God [*laughs and shakes his head*] . . . I'll tell you what, tonight was the first time I've scored in the playoffs. Kris King gave me a pat on the butt going out before O.T. and said, "Y'know, I scored an O.T. winner in this building one time; I think you can do it yourself, kid." It's a dream come true for me, I don't know what to say. I'm just so proud of the way our guys battled tonight. We were down 2-0; we came back and were fighting the whole way.

We stayed with each other [*Valk then looks at replay of his winning goal on monitor in front of him*]. Y'know, Sergei lets a shot go there and I just tried to battle to the front of the net and go for the loose rebound. It's just hard for words to describe that feeling right there.

OAKE: You got a shot with this team, and as I said earlier, you were temporarily retired in September. How far away does this seem now from where you were at that time?

VALK: Y'know what, this is a real tough series for me to play . . . I have some friends on that team. But . . . when a team kind of gives up on you, you want to really win it; it's kind of a personal thing, too. Just to be able to perform and to get a good chance to play in this series was so much fun for me, and then to win it [with an overtime goal] was just a bonus.

Quinn came out of the dressing room just as Valk finished, and Oake began to interview the coach. Valk re-entered the room and his teammates all exploded in cheer. I caught a glimpse of the celebration before the door closed, as the jubilant players embraced Valk in the middle of the floor — most of them still wearing their shoulder and elbow pads.

While tonight was a coming out for Valk, he certainly is no stranger to the NHL. In fact, it's been almost 12 years since the Edmonton native was drafted by the Vancouver Canucks (108th overall in '87). He played parts of three seasons in Vancouver and was claimed by expansion Anaheim in the October 1993 waiver draft. The Mighty Ducks' inaugural season of 1993–94 remains Valk's best so far in the NHL. He had 18 goals and 27 assists for 45 points — all career highs. He remained with the Ducks until February 21, 1997, when Pittsburgh acquired him for defence-man J.J. Daigneault. But he never fit in with the Penguins — playing only 39 games last season — and was cast adrift at its conclusion. Thus the palatable vindication he's experiencing here tonight.

Any feeling of euphoria in the Toronto dressing room is punctuated by the fact the Maple Leafs seemed so far *out* of tonight's game in the first period. It was, unquestionably, their most inept 20-minute segment of the playoffs so far — and the fact they trailed only 2-0 at the buzzer was, once again, a tribute to Curtis Joseph. Completely overwhelmed by a dizzying Penguin onslaught, the Maple Leafs should have been wearing neon-orange, as Quinn kept sending out five pylons to accompany Cujo.

"We *told* them the building was going to be wired," the coach stressed. "Said we had to be alert so we don't give them any gifts early and hopefully quiet down the crowd. Obviously, it didn't work out that way."

But it could have been, and *should* have been a lot worse. Outshot 15-8, the Leafs yielded only a pair of goals — to Rob Brown (on the powerplay) at 5:04, and Alexei Kovalev at 14:08 (Kovalev returned to the Penguins' lineup following a two-game absence). Otherwise, Joseph barred the door in spectacular fashion, his acrobatics preventing an irreversible humiliation. "If Curtis Joseph isn't there, we go up 3-0 or 4-0 and they don't have a chance," accurately surmised Penguin coach Kevin Constantine. Added Rob Brown: "Cujo was unbelievable."

Mats Sundin could only shake his head afterwards. "I'll tell you, that first 10 minutes, it was old-time Pittsburgh hockey," he marveled, reflecting on the halcyon days of Lemieux, Jagr, Francis and Co. "That might be the best stretch of hockey I've seen in my life. It's amazing we were still in the game after that, and we can thank Cujo once again."

The partisan fans in the Civic Arena obviously believed the Penguins had fashioned some invincibility in the opening period. As I walked around in the mid-level corridor during the first intermission, the locals mercilessly taunted Maple Leaf supporters sulking in their blue and white garb.

"See ya in Toronto on Thursday."

"You may as well leave now to get back for Game 7."

"Toronto sucks!"

Had the Leaf players chosen to, they could have adopted a similar stance and taken their chances at home in the deciding match. But they aren't on their way to the Stanley Cup semifinals by pondering surrender. This is a club that has proven to be remarkably resilient all season long. When a tailspin appeared imminent, the '98–99 Maple Leafs unceasingly righted themselves — never losing more than three games in succession during the regular season. Neither did they reel off lengthy unbeaten streaks, but they preyed on Western Conference teams (20-4-2 in 26 games), poured in many more goals than expected, and were bailed out by Joseph on numerous occasions. It all added up to a 45-30-7 record for 97 points and a team record for victories in a regular season.

And it was the club's penchant for reparation that brought it back from the dead again tonight. The events of the second period came without warning. The Leafs somehow reversed the tide and scored three goals in the first 3:52 of the middle frame, one of which was nullified by video replay judge Dale Ruth (a shocker). The call was correct, however, as rookie Kevyn Adams fell into the crease a nano-second before Mike Johnson flipped in his own rebound. That reversal — coming after the pitiful opening period — might have flattened a lesser team. But the Leafs rebounded almost immediately.

Lonny Bohonos fired a laser over Barrasso's glove-hand just 1:08 after the disallowed goal, and the Leafs were officially on the board. Only 26 seconds after that, Valk muscled towards the Pittsburgh net and stuffed the puck in from a bad angle. The unassisted endeavor silenced a thoroughly confounded audience of Penguin supporters — none of whom had expected the swift reversal of fortune. Sergei Berezin's hard shot deflected in off Barrasso's glove at 11:43 of the period, giving Toronto its first lead of the game.

"When we were down 2-0 we could have packed it in," mentioned Valk. "Could've gone into the dressing room and said, 'Let's wait for the home crowd in Game 7.' But we fought adversity again and came out on top."

The Penguins didn't roll over either, and Jagr's fifth goal of the playoffs (off a Sylvain Cote turnover) re-upped the score three minutes after Berezin's tally. A scoreless and cautious third period by both sides spawned the overtime, and Valk's early heroics.

As Jagr passed his nemesis, Yushkevich, during the post-game handshake custom, he broke into a wide grin. "I told him that he's a great player and that I hoped I didn't hurt him while doing my job in the series," Yushkevich recalled afterwards. "Against us, he showed why he's the best player in the world. Even though he was bothered by the groin injury, he was still dangerous on almost every shift and he had another great game tonight. I couldn't lose my focus on him for a moment."

About the only Maple Leaf who had difficulty enjoying the post-game euphoria was Steve Thomas. He glided off the ice doubled over in pain after an innocent-looking collision with Jagr in the first period. Though he later returned, he had his shoulder wrapped like a mummy afterwards, but would not confirm the extent of the damage.

As Curtis Joseph filed out of the dressing room late tonight, he analogized this entire Maple Leaf experience. "It feels like a Cinderella season, but the clock never seems to strike midnight," smiled the club's fairy godmother.

POSTSCRIPT
May 1999
Toronto/Buffalo

One night after the Maple Leafs' ouster of Pittsburgh, the Buffalo Sabres eliminated ex-Toronto coach Pat Burns and the Boston Bruins in Game 6 of their Eastern Conference semifinal at Marine Midland Arena. It set up an Eastern final match-up, and a first-ever playoff meeting, between geographical rivals Toronto and Buffalo — further inciting hockey emotions in southern Ontario, the Niagara peninsula, and western New York state.

From the outset of Buffalo's NHL existence, the Maple Leafs and Sabres have been natural foes — though they faced one another so infrequently while Toronto resided in the Campbell and Western Conferences between 1981 and '98. Not long after gaining entrance to the NHL as an expansion club on May 22, 1970, the Sabres hired George (Punch) Imlach as general manager and coach. Imlach had been GM and coach of the Leafs throughout the 1960s, fashioning a glorious epoch in Toronto's hockey history. Under his dictatorial and autocratic administration, the Maple Leafs won four Stanley Cups in six years, including a dynastic three in succession between 1962 and '64.

But as the team began to regress after an unanticipated Cup triumph in '67, so did Imlach's stock. His bombast and tyranny grew ineffectual, and when the Leafs were demolished by Boston in the playoff quarterfinals of 1969, he was promptly fired by owner Stafford Smythe. The Maple Leafs hired Jim Gregory as GM and John McLellan as coach for the 1969–70 season and missed the playoffs altogether. Imlach re-surfaced with the new Buffalo franchise in 1970–71 and laid a relentless thrashing on his former team in the first Toronto-Buffalo encounter.

Hockey fans in both cities still talk about the night of November 18, 1970, when Imlach's Sabres pounded the Maple Leafs, 7-2, at the Gardens. The former Leaf boss received a boisterous standing ovation when he first appeared behind the Buffalo bench, and that was only the beginning. The Sabres fell behind early, but quickly recovered to trounce the Leafs and present Imlach with one of the most satisfying victories of his NHL career. One-time Toronto prospect (and former Marlboro junior star) Gerry Meehan scored twice for Buffalo, as did North Bay, Ontario, native Larry Keenan. Don Marshall, Steve Atkinson, and Paul Andrea had the others. Garry

Monahan and Mike Walton replied for the Maple Leafs on that stunning night, and a rivalry was instantly hatched.

In the mid to late '70s, the Sabres developed into one of the elite teams in the NHL, sparked by front-line players Gilbert Perreault, Richard Martin, Rene Robert, Danny Gare, Don Luce, Craig Ramsay, and Jerry Korab. Stricken by two heart attacks, Imlach had turned over the coaching reins to Floyd Smith (the Sabres' first captain) by the time Buffalo advanced to the 1975 Stanley Cup final against Philadelphia. The Sabres and Flyers matched up well everywhere but in goal, and Bernie Parent steered Philly to its second consecutive championship.

At the same time, the Maple Leafs were beginning to flourish for the first and only time in Harold Ballard's ownership reign. On a shoestring budget, Jim Gregory proved to be a shrewd hockey man — assembling the Toronto teams of Sittler, McDonald, Salming, Turnbull, Williams, and Palmateer. One can only imagine how potent those clubs may have been had Ballard not misjudged the resolve of the World Hockey Association. Parent had been a Leaf, as had young defencemen Jim Dorey, Rick Ley (the current assistant coach), and Brad Selwood. All were allowed to escape to the WHA, along with feisty center Jim Harrison. A disgraceful 1972–73 Maple Leaf season resulted, but Gregory somehow managed to right the ship the following year. By the middle of the decade, the Leafs were strong enough to compete against Imlach's splendid Buffalo squad.

Members of the electronic media in both cities enhanced the burgeoning rivalry with good-natured partiality. What Maple Leaf fan of that era can forget the exaltations of Buffalo TV anchors Chuck Healy, Rick Azar and Mike Nolan? As the Sabres progressed through the 1975 playoffs, a would-be songwriter sent a ditty to the TV stations and "We're Gonna Win That Stanley Cup!" was played to oblivion. Like a wounded racehorse, it was humanely destroyed after the Sabres lost to Philadelphia in the finals.

Both the Sabres and Leafs fell on difficult times at the tail-end of the '70s, but they continued to face one another five and six times per season. Regardless of their position in the standings, there was something special in the air when the teams hooked up in Maple Leaf Gardens or the Memorial Auditorium.

All of that changed, however, with a heartless decision made by Harold Ballard in the summer of 1981. The NHL chose to carry out a divisional re-alignment in order to group its 21 teams in a more sensible territorial arrangement. The Norris Division, for instance, was all over the map — housing Montreal, Pittsburgh, Detroit, Los Angeles, and Hartford (which had replaced Washington in 1979–80). During the process, the Maple Leafs had the opportunity to be placed in the new Adams Division with Boston, Montreal, and Buffalo. The move would have spawned half-a-dozen match-ups per season with their most intense rivals (old and new), and hockey fans in Toronto were excited about the prospect.

But Ballard — whose alienation of Leaf fans was limitless — chose to enter the Norris Division as a courtesy to his long-time friend, Detroit Red Wings owner Bruce Norris. Naturally, a large sum of cash accompanied this "favor." It grouped the Leafs with Detroit, Chicago, St. Louis, Winnipeg, and Minnesota, and effectively mothballed any competition with the Habs, Bruins and Sabres.

For much of the decade prior to 1998, Toronto and Buffalo would face each other in a cursory two games during the regular season — once in each city. The games were practically meaningless in the standings, and the geographical juices — which had fueled the rivalry — slowed to a trickle. Only Ken Dryden's resolve was able to re-establish a more intrinsic arrangement. It ranked among his primary deeds on becoming president and GM of the Leafs, and he pulled it off with masterful persuasion.

In the 1998–99 season, a re-alignment saw Toronto join the Northeast Division with Buffalo, Boston, Ottawa, and Montreal. Only the Leafs and Sabres were standing when the Eastern Conference playoff-dust settled. Ninety minutes of highway travel stood between summertime and a shot at the 1999 Stanley Cup championship.

* * *

To the misery of hockey fans north of the border, the build-up for the Toronto-Buffalo series wound up flattering the actual event. The Maple Leafs had nothing left to offer the Sabres, who romped to an easy five-game victory and a berth in the Cup final against the Dallas Stars. Buffalo proved to be more polished and resolute than Toronto, the Sabres' invaluable experience derived from the 1998 playoffs an obvious determining factor.

When the series is reviewed by history buffs, it will be firmly noted that the Leafs pretty much blew any chance for victory when they lost Game 1 at the Air Canada Centre. For the sake of the Toronto players and their descendants, the particulars of Game 4 in Buffalo will mercifully vaporize with time, as it ranks among the most calamitous efforts in Maple Leaf playoff annals.

The flags of both teams were raised at the Peace Bridge border crossing, and that may have been the highlight of the entire experience for the Leafs and their fans. When the Sabres bussed over the Niagara River into Fort Erie on May 22, they carried with them a concealment of epic proportions. It became evident only when the teams skated out to warm up for Game 1 the following afternoon. A buzz radiated through the Air Canada Centre when fans and media gradually noticed that Dominik Hasek was not on the ice. Dwayne Roloson and Martin Biron were the two

Buffalo goalies in the pre-game skate, causing a great deal of momentary bafflement. Where was the world's very best netminder?

As the Stanley Cup playoffs develop, those still in contention evolve into emotional manipulators . . . some better than others. Coaches, especially, go to all lengths to shroud and modify information they consider potentially damaging. Silly mind games become habitual, the media willingly playing the jester's role. Could Hasek's non-appearance in the Game 1 warm-up be the preeminent tease of all time? That was the first consideration racing through my flustered mind — that the Czech luminary was lounging, fully dressed, in the Buffalo room with an evil snicker on his face. Common sense then prevailed and I consulted with Sabres media relations director Gil Chorbajian in the press box. The official word was that Hasek would not dress that afternoon — he was suffering from a groin injury — and his status for the remainder of the series would be determined on a daily basis.

It was difficult, at that moment, not to envision a Stanley Cup parade up Bay Street to Toronto city hall. Clearly, there was an unseen force guiding the Maple Leafs through this improbable playoff chase. First, it was Eric Lindros skipping the Philadelphia series with his lung ailment. Then, Jaromir Jagr hobbling on an injured groin and Alexei Kovalev suffering a bruised ankle during the Pittsburgh series. And now *Hasek*?!! Surely it could only be a matter of time before Mike Modano and Brett Hull crashed into each other in a Dallas practice — paving the way for an easy Maple Leaf conquest of the Stars.

Oh, to dream.

Reality proved to be a cruel slap in the kisser for all fans of the blue and white. When the Leafs failed to win the series opener with Roloson in the Buffalo cage, Toronto's '99 playoff karma took an irreparable turn. Potentially, six games remained in the Conference final, but the Sabres had garnered an emotional lift that would see them through a sloppy defeat in Game 2. The Leafs would follow up by melting down in mortifying fashion when the series shifted to Buffalo, and allowing the Sabres to overcome a second-period deficit back in Toronto to clinch a berth in the Stanley Cup final.

A brief recap of all five games:

Game 1, at Toronto
Sunday, May 23, 1999
As mentioned, this was the ultimate killer for the Maple Leafs — a 5-4 loss to the Hasek-less Sabres in a rare matinee encounter. Compounding the dreary afternoon for Leaf fans was the frightful recognition that Roloson had outplayed Curtis Joseph. The

game's defining moment occurred with the Sabres holding a one-goal edge just past the midway mark of the third period. Buffalo forward Geoff Sanderson, who appeared to have little retro-rockets affixed to his skates all afternoon, sped down the ice and motored around Leaf defenceman Sylvain Cote. His left hand effectively hooked by Cote, Sanderson maintained control of the puck with his right hand and deftly flicked it past Cujo, who attempted a futile poke-check. The outrageous goal gave Buffalo a 5-3 lead and astonished even the most die-hard of Maple Leaf supporters.

"He just flicked his wrist and the puck went around his curve," Joseph shrugged after the game. "Everything they shot seemed to go in today."

While the Sabres played quite well in Hasek's absence, the Leafs were left to wonder why they could not capitalize on a golden opportunity. "Maybe our guys saw [Hasek] wasn't in there and felt it was going to be easier," Pat Quinn mused. "I don't know that to be a fact, but it's clearly a possibility."

Added Dimitri Yushkevich: "All of a sudden we look, and one of the best goalies in the world isn't playing. We probably thought we were going to win easily. It's hard to fight that kind of feeling."

Was it a reasonable justification for the loss? Perhaps. Considering, however, this marked the third consecutive series in which the Leafs dropped an opener on home ice, maybe there was more to it. Joseph seemed out of sync all day, and he uncommonly admitted so afterwards.

"I have to battle more to see the puck," he said. "I needed to make the big saves and they didn't happen. I know I can be sharper."

While the Maple Leaf powerplay awakened with three goals, it was still not enough to justify an edge they received in penalty calls. Wrote columnist Dave Perkins in the *Toronto Star*:

> When people were calling this the QEW series, was anyone wondering if that stood for Quick Enough Whistle? . . .
>
> The Leafs basically admitted they couldn't find the highest setting on their dials because the greatest goalie in the world didn't show up. (And neither, it should be mentioned, did the second-best, as some are calling Curtis Joseph). But here is what the Maple Leafs also missed out on when they lost 5-4 to the Sabres: Winning a game [referee] Don Koharski and, to a lesser extent, Rob Shick kept them in. Without the zebras' calls, the Leafs might have been embarrassed. . . .
>
> The Leafs spent more than 15 minutes on nine separate powerplays and three times, the sentence was shortened by someone beat-

ing Roloson. On one of those occasions, two Buffalo men were nabbed simultaneously, providing the Leafs with the maximum advantage permitted: Two men for two minutes.

The Sabres, by comparison, had four personnel advantages, lasting 6:15. It is easy to say that this stuff evens out over the long run, but if it does, that's another disadvantage for Toronto because it suggests the Sabres are owed a couple of calls.

The Maple Leafs held the lead in the game for only a 4:07 span of the second period, after a Bryan Berard slapshot put them in front, 3-2. Stu Barnes tied it for Buffalo before the period ended and Curtis Brown fired a shot over Cujo's shoulder at 5:21 of the third to provide the Sabres with a lead they would not relinquish. Mats Sundin had the Leafs' other two goals.

Game 2, at Toronto
Tuesday, May 25, 1999

When reflecting on this series, it's intriguing to wonder if a 6-3 victory in Game 2 had the same effect on the Maple Leafs as Hasek's unexpected absence prior to the opener. Suddenly, it appeared as if nothing could go wrong. Though it was still Roloson in goal for Buffalo, the Leafs were able to flash their offensive brilliance and knot things up on home ice for the third straight playoff round.

This game turned wild in the third period. Yanic Perreault scored early to give the Leafs an apparently safe 4-1 lead. But Stu Barnes of Buffalo popped in consecutive powerplay goals less than three minutes apart, and it was suddenly a one-goal game at the midway point of the period.

Steve Thomas rescued the Maple Leafs and brought the crowd back into the picture when he blasted a shot over Roloson's shoulder on a 3-on-1 break at the 12:17 mark. Gary Valk then cemented the win with an empty-net tally.

Joseph returned to form by making several important saves early in the game — two of particular note off Sanderson and Barnes. "I think, because we lost the other night and there were questions whether Cujo had an off-night, it was important for him to make those early stops," Pat Quinn said. The Leafs capitalized on Joseph's sharpness by striking for a pair of goals 18 seconds apart midway through the opening period — Steve Sullivan and Sylvain Cote doing the damage, and throwing a crimp in Roloson's confidence. The Sabre stand-in was beaten five times on the first 22 shots he faced, magnifying the issue of Hasek's unavailability. Wrote *Toronto Sun* sports editor Scott Morrison:

Perhaps the groin is a vital organ after all.

While the Buffalo Sabres insist there is more to their being than just a superstar goaltender with a pulled muscle in a very sensitive area . . . there's no denying that a tender groin last night brought them to their knees.

True, they were able to survive the absence of all-world goalie Dominik Hasek in the opening game of this Eastern Conference final . . . But all of that changed last night, pretty much as everyone knew it would. It's no different than a goaltending match-up between Bill Ranford and Patrick Roy. Give it time and you know who will win. It's the same with Roloson and Joseph.

The victory guaranteed a fifth game at the Air Canada Centre five nights hence, May 31. The Leafs had never previously played later than May 29 in any one season (they lost Game 7 of the Campbell Conference championship to Los Angeles on May 29, 1993). "I don't care if we play right through to next training camp, as long as we win the Stanley Cup," said Steve Thomas.

Little did anyone realize the Maple Leafs had tasted their final bit of success in the 1998–99 season.

Game 3, at Buffalo
Thursday, May 27, 1999

All season long, dire predictions about the Maple Leafs' inability to play competent defensive hockey failed to materialize. Some observers felt they'd be fodder in the playoffs if there was even the slightest deterioration in the magic of Curtis Joseph. Yet, here they are in the Stanley Cup semifinals. Well, all of the Maple Leaf fears came to roost at the Marine Midland Arena tonight.

A 4-2 Sabres victory in Game 3 occurred almost solely as a result of panic and disarray in the Toronto end of the ice. Yes, Dominik Hasek was back in goal for Buffalo, and his mere presence gave the home side an immeasurable boost. But Hasek could have been facing Jagr, Kariya, Selanne, Lindros, and LeClair tonight and probably have won the match. That's because the Maple Leafs took the opportunity to self destruct in front of a strangely ordinary Joseph.

The visitors went to pieces early in the second period, throwing away a 1-0 lead forged by Yanic Perreault's third goal of the post-season at 16:08 of the first. Veteran Sylvain Cote suffered brain-lock when pressured in his own zone by Michal Grosek of the Sabres. Inexplicably, Cote threw the puck directly in front of the Toronto net

— a poor enough decision made worse by the fact young Tomas Kaberle was looking in the opposite direction when the pass arrived. It allowed Miroslav Satan to move in for an easy goal, tying the game.

Not 40 seconds later, fellow defenceman Alexander Karpovtsev suffered either an hallucination or momentary anoxia. The Maple Leafs were working on a powerplay when the big Russian apparently saw something blue and white standing at the left point. He threw the puck across to this person, who turned out to be an apparition. Sabres captain Mike Peca swooped into the picture, gathered up the gift, and sailed uncontested down the right wing. He faked Bryan Berard to the inside and fired a slapshot that Cujo kicked out. Karpovtsev and Berard both gravitated to Peca, allowing Joe Juneau to convert the rebound for a 2-1 Buffalo lead. Two goals off two gargantuan mistakes in 35 seconds.

"We lost the game in less than a minute," confirmed Mats Sundin in the funereal Maple Leaf dressing room. "I thought the Sabres were the better team. They made less mistakes than we did."

While the Toronto defensive gaffes were mind-boggling, this game will probably be remembered for what happened in the waning seconds. All night long, the Leafs were trying to get under the skin of Hasek. Knowing how emotionally volatile the Sabres' goalie can be, players like Tie Domi, Kris King, and Kevyn Adams were brushing against him and jabbing him with their sticks at every opportunity. These tactics combined with the escalating Maple Leaf frustration to cause a tempestuous outbreak with 12.6 seconds to play.

Obviously making no attempt to avert an emotional scene, Quinn sent Domi and King out for a face-off in the Buffalo end. Hasek made a routine save and Domi purposely bumped into him. King followed suit, and all hell broke loose. A wild melee erupted with Domi, King, Adams, Dimitri Yushkevich, and Daniil Markov piling into the corner-boards with Buffalo adversaries Eric Rasmussen, Rhett Warrener, Jay McKee, Michal Grosek, and Brian Holzinger. No actual fights broke out (this is the playoffs, after all), but some fairly violent pushing and shoving ensued, with players falling on top of one another. All 10 combatants were banished, with Domi receiving a minor penalty for goaltender interference, a double-minor for roughing and a 10-minute misconduct.

When play resumed, Sabres defenceman Alexi Zhitnik appeared to fire the puck directly at Leaf winger Mike Johnson in the neutral zone, prompting the normally placid Perreault to doff his gloves and pounce on the Russian rearguard. Zhitnik got the better of him in the ensuing scuffle, but Perreault showed some grit by defending his teammate.

As soon as the final buzzer sounded, Buffalo coach Lindy Ruff ran down to the glass separating the two players' benches and began screaming at Quinn. A Leaf player later told me Ruff said, "You better be ready 'cause Cujo's a dead man next game." To prevent the same from occurring to Hasek, Ruff removed his meal-ticket and inserted Roloson for the final dozen seconds.

Emotions continued to run high in the post-game media sessions. When asked about the Leaf-spawned brouhaha, Ruff countered with a single word.

"Classless," he said, in a direct reference to Quinn. "I don't think we did anything for them to react like that. I guess they don't think they can beat us by scoring goals." Then, for effect, Ruff repeated, "Yeah, it was classless."

Quinn later shrugged off Ruff's denunciation. "He said *that*?" the coach asked. "Well, then, no comment." But Quinn did have a few choice words about Hasek. "I don't understand why he thinks he can wander out of his net with complete immunity," mused the big Irishman. "He goes into the corner to get the puck and jumps in the way of attacking forwards. Then if he's even touched, he launches into theatrics. It's a bunch of crap to think we were trying to do any of that stuff at the end of the game on purpose."

In the *Toronto Sun,* columnist Steve Simmons felt that Ruff's sentiments towards Quinn were uncalled for:

> Lindy Ruff sat calmly behind a microphone and called Pat Quinn classless. Then he said it again, just in case his opinion had not been clearly conveyed the first time. Ruff was talking about the final seconds of what was otherwise a playoff game of substance. Ruff objected to Quinn's choice of a line-up in the final seconds of a playoff game that was already decided in Buffalo's favor, 4-2.
>
> "I didn't think we did anything for them to react that way," Ruff said. Ruff is right about one thing. He didn't think.
>
> What Quinn did in the final seconds [of the game] might be classless in the real world, but it is just another night of real hockey. Live with it. It happens all the time, every playoff spring, by almost every playoff coach, including Ruff — just check the films from Game 2. . . .
>
> There is no reason to do what Quinn did and there is no reason not to do it. For all my life and yours, this has been going on in hockey . . .
>
> Ruff never did mention Alexi Zhitnik's inaccurate slapshot [aimed at Johnson] after the game. I wonder what he would have called it? Classy, it wasn't. Hockey, it was.

There were some people who wondered if the Maple Leafs were a bit tired in Game 3. The club stayed at the Adam's Mark Hotel in downtown Buffalo — a facility undergoing a massive renovation and reconstruction. From 8 a.m. to suppertime, the place sounded like a war zone, with jackhammers, drills, and earth-moving machines pounding away. One reporter dubbed it the "Hotel Beirut" — hardly a location conducive to the Maple Leaf players relaxing on the afternoon of a game. Compounding the noise was a major construction on the northbound 190 freeway, roughly 150 yards from the hotel.

The Leafs' usual home in Buffalo is the Hyatt Regency Hotel, located a mile or so east of the Adam's Mark, in the heart of downtown. But rooms were unavailable during the Buffalo leg of the Eastern Conference final.

Game 4, at Buffalo
Saturday, May 29, 1999

Oy vay!

It was difficult to conceive of the Maple Leafs playing any more sloppily than they did in Game 3, but it actually happened. In fact, the third match was a veritable showpiece compared to the catastrophe of Game 4. A 5-2 Buffalo win revealed an element of the Leafs rarely witnessed during any part of the '98–99 season — surrender. Or, as Harry Sinden would say, capitulation.

"Our bodies were out there tonight, but our brains weren't," succinctly analyzed Bryan Berard after the embarrassing Leaf performance. Added Sundin: "There was only one team on the ice."

For reasons that were becoming increasingly apparent, the Maple Leafs simply failed to show up. The Sabres had systematically stolen any emotional edge the Leafs could attain, and they did so from the outset of the series. First, it was Hasek's unannounced absence from Game 1, and Toronto's inability to beat his rusty stand-in, Roloson. Then there was the star goalie's much-ballyhooed and triumphant return for Game 3, which served to further energize an already boisterous gathering at the Marine Midland Arena. These two factors augmented the clear dominance Buffalo exhibited with its overall belligerence and ability to rattle the Toronto players when racing in on the forecheck. The latter ingredient caused several moments of absolute panic for Toronto in Game 4.

No example of this was more striking than the gaffe by expectant father Steve Sullivan in the second period. For one of the few times all season, Curtis Joseph had let his teammates down by allowing a soft, albeit well-placed shot by Dixon Ward to beat him while the Sabres were shorthanded late in the opening frame. The goal offset some earlier brilliance by the netminder, whose personal standards throughout the season made any soft effort appear ghastly. Despite being outshot, 13-6, however, the Leafs were still very much in the game before Sullivan's ugly error.

At 2:51 of the middle period, the Leaf centerman simply threw the puck in front of his own net, obviously without looking. Brian Holzinger of the Sabres could hardly believe his eyes when the wayward pass wound up directly on his stick, and he fired a sharp, low shot past a startled Joseph. It took just more than two minutes for the Maple Leafs to completely unravel once again. Blatant defensive miscalculations led directly to goals by Rob Ray and Geoff Sanderson, 22 seconds apart, and it was lights out for Toronto.

Wrote the *Star*'s Paul Hunter about the Leaf meltdown and chances to rebound in the series: "Hemlock would be quicker. And far less painful."

And the Toronto players knew it. "We just aren't playing smart," Berard said. "For the first time since I've been here, we look like a nervous hockey team. Our passes are off and, mentally, we just aren't sharp at all."

Lindy Ruff concurred. "Toronto's giveaways have been the key to the series so far," said the Buffalo coach. "We've been very opportunistic and have taken advantage of them."

Magnifying the defensive indifference was the abject inability of any Maple Leaf front-liner to step forward against the Sabres. Sundin scored a pair of third-period goals in Game 4 — one on a penalty shot — to make the final count appear infinitely more flattering to the Leafs. But he had not been a factor when the game still mattered. It prompted the following observation by Cam Cole in the *National Post*:

> One day, when he's on a team that has all the necessary ingredients to win a Stanley Cup, no doubt Mats Sundin will.
>
> Until then, people will be asking him to produce qualities he does not possess, expecting him to overcome gaps in his team's make-up by exerting his will, by doing more, being meaner or at least more assertive, more tenacious on the puck, more demonstrative — in other words, they will keep expecting him to be more like the classic NHL captain, and he will keep falling short.
>
> No matter what he may utter in public, Pat Quinn must sense the truth of that now.

One other truth is without dispute: The Maple Leafs faced elimination for the first time in the playoffs heading home for Game 5.

Game 5, at Toronto
Monday, May 31, 1999

The Maple Leafs' unanticipated pursuit of the Stanley Cup ended with a third-period breakdown in Game 5 that would have been heart-wrenching had it not seemed so inevitable.

Eric Rasmussen of Buffalo fired a rebound past Curtis Joseph at 11:35 of the final frame to break a 2-2 tie and send the Sabres to their second Cup final in franchise history with a 4-2 triumph. Cujo stopped Brian Holzinger's shot from the left-wing circle, but the puck boomeranged to the right-wing side where Rasmussen converted a backhander. Defencemen Tomas Kaberle and Sylvain Cote and backchecking forward Fredrik Modin were helpless on the play.

Dixon Ward — a one-time Leaf — punctuated the entire series by sliding the puck the length of the ice and into the vacated Toronto goal with 1:02 left on the clock. The Sabres were shorthanded at the time.

Thus ended a relatively courageous Maple Leaf effort — one far superior to the collapses of the two games in Buffalo — and, ultimately, the longest season on the calendar in franchise history. Second-period goals by Steve Sullivan and Kris King had the Leafs in front, 2-1, but Vaclav Verada connected for a deflating powerplay marker with 3:16 to play in the middle frame. It handed the Sabres the momentum they'd enjoyed for much of the series, and Rasmussen's winning tally in the third period seemed ordained.

"THE PARTY'S OVER," screamed a huge headline on the front sports page of the *Toronto Star*. It had lasted, arguably, a month longer than many people figured it would, and (temporarily) washed away the sour taste of failures past. And of frugal ownership. But will it be the first step towards ending the NHL's second-longest Stanley Cup drought? (Only Chicago has gone longer — 38 years — without sipping champagne.)

"One great thing about winning," said Ken Dryden — he of the six Stanley Cups as a goaltender with Montreal — "is that losing feels worse."

Horrible enough for a true and determined endeavor by the Leafs to finally *end* the losing? Only time will tell.

Chapter 4

Stanley Cup Travesty at the Marina

*The final full National Hockey League season of the century — and millennium —
may be remembered for the most shameful of incidents: a tarnished goal that ended the
championship series and dissolved the Stanley Cup aspirations of one of its participants.*

Sunday, June 20, 1999
Buffalo

The longest season in the 81-year history of the National Hockey League ended at
exactly 1:31 a.m. EDT this morning — the decisive play unfolding directly below
my auxiliary press box location at Marine Midland Arena.

The Stanley Cup then made its final appearance of the 20th century.

As I stood watching the Dallas Stars parade the old mug around the ice, neither
I nor anyone else had the faintest idea of the emotional upheaval taking place in the
catacombs of this arena. The lamenting of foul play from the Buffalo Sabres' dressing room would reverberate for hours.

It's been an 11-day grind through northern Texas and western New York, on the
heels of Toronto's advancement to the Eastern Conference final. For the first time in
my career on the hockey beat, I've covered all four rounds of Stanley Cup competition, and it's been a hoot. But I'm glad it's over!

A member of one of hockey's pre-eminent bloodlines was responsible for putting
an end to tonight's action, 5½-hours after it began. Thirty-eight years after the legendary Bobby Hull won his only Cup with the Chicago Blackhawks, Brett Hull followed his famous dad by going one step further. He swiped his own rebound past
Dominik Hasek at 14:51 of the third overtime period of Game 6, ending the second-
longest match in the history of the Cup finals. It eliminated the Sabres and earned
the Dallas franchise its first championship since joining the NHL as an expansion
entry from Bloomington, Minnesota, in 1967.

Hull scored the goal, it was later revealed, while enduring a partially torn knee
ligament and two severely injured groin muscles. Ostensibly, he was in no condition
to be standing upright, let alone finessing his way to the front of the net for the season's climactic tally. Unfortunately, his courage quickly became a footnote in the face
of a nightmarish episode for the National Hockey League.

Hull's Cup-winner was perfectly legitimate and artistically sound — the type natural goalscorers have been garnering since hockey was first played on frozen ponds almost a century-and-a-half ago. An instinctive maneuver that might well have been executed by Archie Hodgson or Haviland Routh — mythical figures on the first-ever Stanley Cup champion, Montreal's Amateur Athletic Association of 1893.

Somewhat cynically, it can be argued that hockey has not been played under rules of common sense since that time. And as a result, the final Stanley Cup of the millennium will be remembered for a series-clinching goal that should not have counted. You see, Brett Hull clearly had planted his left skate in the goalcrease before scoring on Hasek. Slow-motion replays from directly above the scene confirmed Hull's stance, rendering the goal illegal.

Game 6 of the Cup finals should have resumed with Dallas and Buffalo seeking to break an interminable 1-1 deadlock. Instead, the apparently victorious Stars poured off their bench to mob the moment's hero — their jubilation not to be interrupted by the game's dastardly penchant for video review.

And what a commotion it caused.

On hundreds of occasions over the past seven years, goals of a perfectly honest and legitimate nature have been nullified by Rule 78(b) of the NHL's official governance. Commonly referred to as the "in-the-crease" rule, it states:

> *Unless the puck is in the goal crease area, a player of the attacking side may not enter nor stand in the goal crease. If a player has entered the crease prior to the puck, and subsequently the puck should enter the net while such conditions prevail, the apparent goal shall not be allowed.*

Rule 78(b) was the NHL board of governor's ingenious antidote to the worrisome trend of goalkeeper interference. Acting on a recommendation from the league's general managers in the summer of 1991, the board — in its heartfelt wisdom — approved a transition from black to white. Goalies would no longer have to be physically jostled for a scoring play to be abolished. The mere presence in the crease of any portion of an attacker's anatomy — regardless of his complete univolvement in the play — would be sufficient to wipe out a goal. It was akin to having your car's transmission problem repaired by first removing all other cars from the road. A blatant and poorly conceived overreaction that spawned the most asinine rule in the history of hockey.

"It's been a source of aggravation for everyone," is how Ken Dryden so accurately described the rule after a numbing Maple Leaf loss in Montreal earlier in the season.

No other guideline in the rulebook had ever served to alter the very nature of the game. Hockey coaches since the beginning of time have instructed their pupils to aggressively pursue the front area of the attacking goal, where scoring opportunities abound. While this universally accepted strategy evolved to the point where netminders were indeed being physically harassed — and required appropriate amendment — hindsight clearly shows that a more moderate and carefully deliberated stance by rulemakers would have been preferable.

Instead, attacking skaters were now forced to accomplish several feats — all of them unnatural, and some even impossible. A form of visionary discipline was suddenly required to ensure that the mere tip of a player's skate did not come in contact with the plane of the goalcrease, even if such action occurred on the opposite side of a scoring thrust. Players whose momentum carried them toward the crease in a perfectly acceptable manner would now have to stop and change direction — sometimes in mid-air (try that, one day). And teammates, cleverly positioning themselves for rebounds, were required to somehow pause before converting loose pucks. Altering, once again, the nature of the game.

Compounding the problem within the past year was the inclusion of Rule 93(h) — the proverbial gasoline on the fire:

> *The On-Ice Officials or Video Goal Judge may be consulted to establish if an attacking player has entered the crease prior to the puck, and subsequent goal. The Video Goal Judge may initiate this information to the Officials by calling to ice level. The Video Goal Judge is to advise the Referee of the position of the attacking player when the puck enters the crease or is in contact with the crease line.*

Why not just take a poll of fans sitting in the seats around the goal areas? Or stage a best-of-three arm wrestling competition among the opposing general managers? Live, on the video scoreboard. Neither option would have cast any greater scorn on the league in the moments of confusion and gibberish after Hull's goal.

Almost immediately, it became the most notorious winning tally since the 1966 Stanley Cup final between Detroit and Montreal. Game 6 of that series — a matinee at the old Detroit Olympia — went into overtime with the Canadiens in an identical situation to this year's Dallas team: needing a sudden-death goal to win the championship on the road. Before three minutes had elapsed, Montreal veteran Henri Richard took a pass from linemate Dave Balon and was cut down inside the blueline by Red Wings defenceman Gary Bergman. As it was early in overtime, the ice surface was still quite slick, and Richard appeared to slide into the Detroit goal with the puck secured either under his glove or forearm.

As the red goal-light flashed on behind him, Red Wings netminder Roger Crozier sped towards referee Frank Udvari for an explanation. Sensing a possible reversal, Habs coach Toe Blake instantly instructed his players to pour over the boards in mass celebration, figuring that human nature might prompt Udvari not to suspend the season's climax. Nor did he.

Could the same emotions and sentiments have prevailed this morning, in spite of the obvious infringement of Rule 78(b)?

The scene in the immediate and subsequent moments after Hull's goal was chaos in its purest form. I remember it this way:

A feeling of considerable relief overcame me when Dallas scored to end the series. Having commiserated with several travel-weary colleagues during the copious intermissions of tonight's marathon, it became clear that only those with a strong allegiance towards the Sabres wanted any part of another trip to Dallas. Sure, a Game 7 showdown for the Stanley Cup would have been intriguing, but the overwhelming sentiment among those in press row was that hockey had run its course for the year.

When Hull finally won the game — and as is custom in the current age of mass media — a semi-ruly throng of television cameramen, reporters, and photographers barged through the Zamboni entrance and onto the ice. The Dallas players leapt unabashedly upon one another in the immediate euphoria of their triumph. The hugging and back-slapping continued for several minutes before the clubs aligned themselves for the traditional end-of-series handshakes. At no time during this familiar scene was there even a hint that something might have been amiss on the winning goal. NHL commissioner Gary Bettman presented the Conn Smythe Trophy to Dallas forward Joe Nieuwendyk and the Stanley Cup, several moments later, to Stars captain Derian Hatcher.

As the new champions paraded the Cup around the Marine Midland ice — passing it among themselves — reporters gathered their belongings and rushed towards the large freight elevator at the east end of the press box. While awaiting its arrival, I watched a live television interview with Hull at ice level; the latest Cup hero revealing his mixture of excitement over the goal, and pain over his physical plight. Again, no questions about a possible foot in the crease.

The packed elevator descended to ground level and reporters scurried to the corridor that housed the Stars' and Sabres' dressing rooms, as well as the media interview chamber with which we'd all become so familiar. It was in this brightly lit room that I first became aware of the unfolding saga. Clustered around three individually spaced televisions, reporters viewed replays of Hull's goal and were made aware — by the ESPN post-game telecast — that a major controversy had erupted. Word soon came that the Sabres had locked themselves in their dressing room and would not entertain the media until they received an official edict from the league as to why Hull's goal counted.

Without having to explain himself, NHL vice-president of communications Frank Brown informed those of us in the room that Bryan Lewis, the league's director of officiating, would — in due course — be coming in to make a statement and take media queries.

Quite surprisingly, Buffalo coach Lindy Ruff then entered the room and took his position at the interview podium. This is common practice after a playoff game, but Ruff was said to be holed up with his players in a state of flux over the series-winning tally. Obviously, no further explanations from the league were forthcoming.

"We want to protest this game," said Ruff in a pained but hollow reference to that which would never occur. "I mean, that's the worst nightmare right there — a man in the crease; the puck is definitely out of the crease. You can't explain that one to me. They've tried but it hasn't worked."

It was difficult not to feel for this man. Normally composed and relaxed in these situations, Ruff was simply beside himself. He did not rant or rave, but his feelings of helplessness, despair, and shock were so painfully obvious. "They're not taking back the Stanley Cup," he said, when asked again about a protest. "If they wanted to slow down the procedure, they would have reviewed it. Someone would've called [down] from upstairs and said, 'Listen, this is not a goal.' We've gone through that procedure so many times during the regular season and the playoffs."

Ruff then appeared to be hurt on a personal level. He was clearly seen storming out of his dressing room moments after viewing the replay of Hull's goal first-hand. Commissioner Bettman was waiting at the gate of the Sabres' bench to be introduced on to the ice for presentation of the trophies. "I wanted Bettman to answer the question as to why the goal was not reviewed," Ruff explained. "And really, he just turned his back on me. It almost looked to me like he knew that this might be a tainted goal and there was no answer for it."

Meanwhile, the Sabres' dressing room had finally opened and Dominik Hasek looked as forlorn as could be. "I congratulate the Dallas Stars, they played well, but I'm very bitter to have to lose like that," he confided to a gaggle of silent reporters. "You play for two months [in the playoffs] and the video judge didn't do his job. I don't know what he was doing; he must have been sleeping.

"This is very hard to imagine right now. I didn't know [Hull] was in the crease right away, but then I saw the replay in the trainer's room and I was about to go back on the ice because I couldn't believe it."

As Lindy Ruff left the interview podium, Frank Brown announced that Bryan Lewis would be next in the room, but Nieuwendyk then entered, carrying the Conn Smythe Trophy. He was followed by Dallas coach Ken Hitchcock and star player Mike Modano — neither of whom had even the slightest inclination to address the burgeoning conflict. Who could blame them? Finally, at 2:25 a.m., Lewis strode purposefully into the room with the look of a man about to be executed. Before his rump even settled into the podium chair, the league's officiating director launched a preemptive strike.

He talked quickly and disjointedly — uncharacteristic of this well-spoken, respected, and genuinely likable man. In fact, he almost slurred his words in an attempt not to be interrupted while saying his piece.

"I think it's important first of all to point out that every goal scored in the National Hockey League this year has been reviewed," Lewis began. This prompted a sudden but collective snicker, for it could have been taken as a literal claim. What Lewis meant, of course, was that video replay officials across the league consult their TV screens as a matter of course practically every time the puck enters the net.

"A couple of things I'd like to point out in terms of rules: the debate [tonight] would be, are there reasons that a guy can have his foot in the crease and score a goal? Absolutely. One example is coming down with possession and control, taking a deke, your left foot would go in, you would shoot and score even though the puck would be out; that goal counts.

"The debate here seems to be did [Hull] have possession and control. Our words from upstairs and our view was that yes he did; he played the puck from his foot to his stick, shot and scored."

None of these provisions, however, are spelled out in Section 78 of the NHL rulebook. But Lewis claimed a memorandum was distributed to all of the league's general managers "dated roughly March 25" outlining a dozen or so examples of goals that would or would not be permitted within the spirit of the rule. (Detroit GM Ken Holland later confirmed the memo.) Still, it was difficult for practically anyone to believe that a goal exactly like Hull's would've been allowed to stand during the regular season, or in any less chaotic situation. There were simply too many examples to the contrary.

During his brief media confab this morning, Lewis was either unwilling or unable to place an accurate timeline on just how long Hull's goal was officially reviewed by himself and the video goal judge. All he would confirm is that the play was looked at from varying angles "seven or eight times over." The consensus about the goal's legitimacy, he claimed, was unanimous.

Prompting the greatest amount of suspicion and doubt was the obvious departure from routine on the ice. Whenever a goal becomes the subject of a formal review, an identical scenario unfolds: the referee(s) and linesmen convene at the penalty bench area and expressly inform the team captains of the review taking place. At the same time, an announcement is made over the arena P.A. system, informing the fans and media in attendance. A tangible and often tedious delay occurs before the referee is notified of the video goal judge's determination. The ref then either waves off the goal with the long-standing "wash-out" motion, or points directly at center ice, indicating it will stand.

No part of that ceremony occurred after Hull's goal, prompting charges that the league simply choked under the obvious weight of the circumstance (Dallas players wildly celebrating their sudden-death championship live on national TV networks in Canada and the U.S.; a hundred or so photographers and television personnel on the ice recording the scene). Bettman, Lewis and Co. were said to have concocted a barely plausible alibi based on peripheral aspects of the in-the-crease rule (as outlined in the March 25 memo) — one that would have never prevailed in a more conventional situation. That may be a stretch, but Lewis tried unconvincingly to sound bold when queried on the matter of what most observers believed should have happened.

"This would obviously be the worse-case scenario you could think of," he conceded. "But, we've talked about it and our immediate reaction [to overruling the goal] would be to blow the horn [*stop the Cup celebration*], get the players back out there, drop the puck outside the blueline and play hockey."

Hollow words, indeed, for the Buffalo Sabres.

In reality, the ridiculous in-the-crease rule simply upped and bit the NHL in the ass at the most inopportune moment. And for all the world to see. I felt sorry for Lewis, because he was simply performing a verbal end-around for his bosses — the general managers and league governors — none of whom had either the balls or brains to properly amend the rule when presented with the opportunity. On at least three previous occasions, GMs' and governors' meetings could have resulted in a modification, but tee-off times and polo matches took precedence.

Despite bitching and moaning about the rule on a regular basis (after it stupidly cost their team a game), the GMs became apologists when confronted by the media. Brian Burke, now the Vancouver Canucks' GM, will remain in infamy for his rationalization of the rule (in late 1995) while working as the NHL's senior vice-president and director of hockey operations.

Asked about the zero-tolerance aspect of goalcrease infringement — when a skater's DNA is detected on the opposite side of a scoring play — Burke said, "Hey, you're either in the crease or not. It's like pregnancy. You can't be partially pregnant."

But you can be universally dumb. And that's what the NHL has been since 1991, by taking the legitimate concern of goaltender interference to an absurd extreme. Eliminating the discretion of its mostly competent on-ice officials, the league exposed itself to the ultimate humiliation: having a Stanley Cup influenced by the imprecise judgment of a wishy-washy rule. Eight years later, it finally happened.

A needless shame, indeed.

Monday, June 21, 1999
Toronto

While it will serve as no consolation to the Sabres or their legion of fans, the NHL board of governors finally deep-sixed the video review of goalcrease violations during their semi-annual meeting today in New York. Rule 93(h) died quickly and fairly unanimously. The governors and the commissioner claimed it had nothing to do with the fallout of criticism from Hull's Stanley Cup winner on Sunday. Yeah right! And seatbelt laws had nothing to do with drivers flying through their windshields.

It's amazing, the spin-doctoring that emanates from the NHL office. Gary Bettman has possibly been good for hockey — depending on whom you ask — but he must think the rest of us are morons. "The rule [on Hull's goal] was absolutely, correctly applied," he told reporters after today's meeting. "Everyone understands it was the right call."

What?

The governors' claim that it was merely a coincidence Rule 93(h) died on the table less than 48 hours after the Hull controversy is pure hogwash. Can you imagine Bettman emerging from today's meeting to tell the media, "We've kept the rule the way it is because it works just fine. The Stanley Cup–winning goal is a perfect example." Warheads would have been targeted for NHL headquarters in Manhattan.

During his state-of-the-game address to reporters covering the Cup final last week in Dallas, Bettman voluntarily questioned the impact video review was having on the sport. He expressed concern over the fans' spontaneity of cheering for a goal when so many were being reviewed. But even the commissioner — who is so sensitive to opinion that every article written about the league ultimately crosses his desk (someone once called him the "Xerox" commissioner) — could not have anticipated the hostile backlash from the Hull ruling.

Several examples:

Pasted across the top of the *Toronto Star* sports front page today was the headline "NHL COWARDICE TAINTS STARS' CROWN." In the accompanying column, Damien Cox squarely targeted Bettman:

> Bettman has allowed this league to suffer terribly through reckless expansion, which has produced the lowest goal-scoring totals in decades, and now the spinelessness of the organization he oversees has tainted a champion. . . .
>
> After looking as though he was heralding an era of progressive change in the early 1990s, he has become a leader like Bill Clinton who would rather spin than speak the truth. So the rest of the league follows his example. It has become the National Doublespeak Hockey League. No one believes a word these people say. The sport — not Bettman's little empire, but the sport — is in worse shape today than when he came to power.

Rosie DiManno of the *Star* wrote, "The players got game. They got guts. Too bad their league is gamey and gutless."

In the *Edmonton Sun,* veteran columnist Terry Jones pointed out what he believed was the obvious. "We didn't need a foot-in-the-crease controversy with printing presses rolling and editors screaming at 2 a.m. [after Hull's goal]. Didn't we all predict this would happen in triple-overtime of Game 7 in the Stanley Cup final? So it was Game 6. The NHL is going to wear this for a long, long time."

Only Al Strachan of the *Toronto Sun* — normally the most outspoken of critics when it comes to NHL decision-makers — supported the Hull goal as being purely representative of the rule. But he failed to mention whether a scoring play just like it would have been permitted to stand during the regular season, or in practically any other instance than the one in which it occurred. In that regard, Strachan's silence was deafening.

But if 93(h) was on life support before the Stanley Cup winner, there was no doubt in anyone's mind the plug would be pulled soon afterwards.

Sadly, it happened a couple of days too late.

Chapter 5

Fog in January, Snow in April:
Travel in the National Hockey League

The most appealing aspect of working as a full-time hockey reporter can also be the most appalling.

NHL teams currently play an 82-game schedule in the regular season — half of which (41) are away from home. Additionally, there are often four or five road contests in the pre-season, and anywhere from two to sixteen games on foreign ice during the play-offs. While most hockey reporters relish the opportunity to visit other cities in the league, the process of getting to these places can often be laborious and troublesome.

Flight delays, weather anomalies, and any variety of misadventures with personal luggage are not frequent affairs, but they do occur, and are inevitable. Late evenings quickly become early mornings, and even the most diligent attempts to eat balanced and timely meals are futile.

It's the wacky, wonderful, and addicting world of life on the road.

And most of us would have it no other way.

Pristine beaches on Florida's Gulf coast . . . immaculate golfing greens in picturesque, mountainous Arizona . . . and golden, face-warming sunsets on the Pacific in southern California. Can there possibly exist images of a more glorious nature for the snow-bound denizens of mid-winter Ontario?

As a full-time hockey beat reporter, these are not just the enticing photo composites on travel agency brochures, but an authentic dose of reality. During my six-year tenure on the road with the Maple Leafs, I've been lucky enough to experience the alluring and disparate elements of roaming our great continent. Be it sand and surf on the west coast, an alpine blizzard in the Canadian Rockies, or the wind-swept avenues of Chicago's Magnificent Mile, there is invariably something to anticipate while trekking to hockey games out of town. If, as they say, variety is the spice of life, then hockey travel is rosemary and thyme.

It can also be the most exasperating and monotonous exercise imaginable, replete with abrupt and unwelcomed distress. There is no joy to be had when a baggage agent informs you that your clothes, toiletries, and work equipment are in parts unknown. Or when an airline captain laments over the intercom that an ill passenger has prompted an emergency landing. Or that a blanket of fog in an area normally blasted by winter cold has canceled all of your flights.

These are several of the annoyances your trusty author had to endure in the 1998–99 season — and were grudgingly accepted as part of the job.

By and large, however, hockey travel is mostly routine and uneventful. Ken Dryden's triumphant bid in 1998 to re-locate the Maple Leafs in the NHL's Eastern Conference eased the travel burden on players and media. It precluded trips to the sunny climes of Arizona and California — a painful drawback — but enabled those who regularly follow the team to spend more quality time at home with their families. The tradeoff has been a welcome one.

The Leafs' 1999–2000 regular-season schedule is quite comparable to that of the previous year's. Once again, the club does not visit any of the five western U.S. teams (Colorado, Phoenix, San Jose, Los Angeles, Anaheim), nor does it pay its initial visit to Nashville (in the Predators' second NHL season). For the first time, the Leafs do not play in Dallas. This is a dramatic departure from the club's final season in the Western Conference (1997–98) when it made seven separate trips to at least the Mountain time zone — by far its most comprehensive and arduous travel agenda ever. Consider this logbook from the '97–98 season:

> Calgary-Vancouver-Edmonton, October 6–12
> San Jose-Calgary, November 4–5
> Colorado-Phoenix, November 21–22
> Colorado-Anaheim-Los Angeles-Phoenix, December 14–21
> San Jose-Anaheim-Los Angeles, March 8–13
> Phoenix-Dallas, March 23–27
> Edmonton-Vancouver, April 16–20

All of that for a team in the northeastern domain of the continent.

Whereas four- and five-hour flights were commonplace back then, most of the current-day trips take roughly an hour by air, with Pittsburgh and Ottawa reachable in 35 to 45 minutes, depending on the winds. As part of the agreement that saw Toronto move back to the east, the club agreed to continue visiting the western-Canada cities (Vancouver, Edmonton, Calgary) twice, while maintaining its old Norris Division rivalries (Chicago, Detroit, St. Louis) with three games apiece. Two visits to Florida and Tampa Bay prompt few howls of protest among players, management, or media.

As previously lamented, the Eastern schedule's liability is the absence of trips to the western-U.S. cities — all of which were highly anticipated. While it made for nightmarish newspaper deadlines, even the beat writers missed going to Colorado, California, and Arizona in the middle of winter.

Here's what I remember:

Denver

While the temperature was obviously cooler than in Los Angeles, Anaheim, or Phoenix, the Mile High city provided a bevy of activities during idle time. The Leafs stayed at the Westin Tabor Center, a hotel linked to a multi-level, 70-store shopping complex. A high-floor room — facing west — offered a breathtaking view of the Colorado Rocky Mountains, 40 miles in the distance, with the Denver sports complex in the foreground. The McNichols Arena played host to the Colorado Avalanche while the new Pepsi Center underwent construction. Across a parking lot, on the north side of the complex, was the giant Mile High Stadium — home of the Denver Broncos. A trip there in March 1997 was particularly memorable.

The Maple Leafs played in Phoenix on a Thursday night and chartered to Denver after the game. I flew there the next morning and had a chance to briefly tour Mile High Stadium on a brilliantly sunny and warm afternoon. I rode the Maple Leaf bus from the Westin to the arena and the players went in to suit up for their practice. I wandered next door to the stadium and introduced myself to a guard at the south security gate. Quite obligingly, he let me in and I stood in the south end zone bleachers, underneath the scoreboard. The empty, 75,000-seat colossus was mightily impressive in the late-afternoon glow — all of its chairs either blue or orange. I could almost envision John Elway leading one of his celebrated, late-game drives towards the closed end of the massive stadium, opposite to where I was standing.

I remember glancing at the south goalline, directly in front of me, and somehow recalling the day Earnest Byner of the Cleveland Browns fumbled away a sure trip to the Super Bowl in that very spot. It was January 1988, in the dying seconds of the American Football Conference championship game. Any fan of the Browns will tell you of the heartbreak all these years later. Byner was a mere step away from the end zone when the ball was torn from his grip. The Broncos escaped to meet Washington in Super Bowl XXII and got hammered.

My short stadium tour over, I walked back across to McNichols Arena and watched the Leafs practice. McNichols is the only arena in NHL history to be the home of two different franchises. It opened in the autumn of 1976, for the Colorado Rockies' initial season. The Rockies had moved to Denver that year after two ignominious seasons as the Kansas City Scouts, and would not garner any higher distinction in their new home. A six-year inhabitancy is remembered, most vividly, for the fact that Don Cherry held the coaching reins one season.

A dark, gloomy building devoid of frills, its seats retained the Rockies' color scheme of blue, red and yellow. The press box was an abomination — located at the very top section of the end zone, behind the north goal. I used to sit in back of the Leafs' radio broadcast crew of Joe Bowen and Mark Hebscher. They occupied the first two rows of the upper balcony on the east side of the building, just inside the blue-line. You could actually see the game from there.

On this particular trip, the Leafs and Avalanche were to face off at 5:30 p.m. local time — corresponding to *Hockey Night In Canada*'s 7:30 p.m. Saturday telecast back east. That weekend marked the conclusion of the 1997 major league baseball exhibition schedule and the Colorado Rockies (original, huh?) were playing the Kansas City Royals at Coors Field. Mark Hebscher and I decided to check out the brand new ballpark, about to open for its second season. With a one o'clock start, Hebsy and I figured we'd be able to watch roughly half the game before heading back to the hotel. We bought a couple of tickets off a guy outside and sat two rows in back of the Rockies' first-base dug-out; beyond us, a radiant and stunning panorama. Like its current-age brethren in Baltimore, Cleveland, and Arlington, Texas, Coors Field is a resplendent mixture of old-style charm and modern amenities. We watched four innings of the game, then left. But the baseball theme would re-define itself in stunning fashion later that night.

The Maple Leafs scored twice in the final five minutes of their game with the Avalanche to win, 3-2 — rookie Mike Johnson netting the decisive goal on a short-handed breakaway. The game ended around 8:15 p.m. local time and I had finished my post-game radio work at the Westin by 10. Wandering down to the hotel's lounge, I came upon Hebscher and a large group of technical personnel from CBC television. We sat around the oval bar area and had a late dinner.

As we were finishing up, an instantly recognizable figure walked in and began to survey the lounge. It was George Brett, the remarkable former Kansas City batsman, now a front-office employee of the Royals. He looked our way — as if we were long-time friends — and asked if we had seen a person that neither Hebscher nor I had heard of. He'd obviously been drinking elsewhere and was feeling little in the way of pain. We invited him over to sit with us till his party arrived and he accepted.

The CBC people soon left, and for the next two hours, Hebscher and I simply tried not to pinch one another. The greatest ballplayer in either of our lifetimes — a first-ballot Hall of Famer — regaled us with yarns and anecdotes from his extraordinary playing career. We talked about the infamous "pine-tar" episode, Brett's flirtation with a .400 batting average in 1980, and his single-handed annihilation of the Toronto Blue Jays in the 1985 American League playoffs. The alcohol had rendered him a trifle loose-lipped, and he seemed to enjoy telling his stories almost as much as we cherished listening to them.

It was an experience I'll never forget.

Phoenix

The Maple Leafs traveled to this stunning desert oasis five times in the Coyotes' first two post-Winnipeg seasons: 1996–97 and 1997–98. I remember watching Bank One Ballpark — beautiful home of the Arizona Diamondbacks — rise from the ground in stages: from a giant hole, to a steel frame, to an outer shell, to the finished product early in '98. The Leafs stayed at the Hyatt Regency in downtown Phoenix during the '96–97 season, four blocks north of the America West Arena and adjacent ballpark-to-be. A high room, facing east, afforded a great view of the stadium construction, with Sky Harbor International Airport three miles in the distance.

Apart from its aesthetic charm, downtown Phoenix was a colossal bore — a sleepy, sun-drenched grid, lined with countless palm trees. It was quietly pleasant and unusually clean for an American city, but civilization was hard to come by, especially after dark. The Leafs had a great idea in 1997–98 when they moved several miles north to a Ritz Carlton in the lively Camelback section of the city. The hotel stood across the street from a quaint outdoor mall, with a giant Border's bookstore and coffee house. Numerous restaurants and fast-food joints were just a five-minute walk west along Camelback Road. The only palpable drawback was its lack of proximity to the arena; the Hyatt Regency had been a three-minute stroll from the Coyotes' home rink.

Speaking of the America West Arena, it was probably the liveliest and most entertaining place to watch a game in the NHL. Sharp-image video screens at both ends of the ice were used smartly, and the music played during breaks encompassed many eras and varieties, from Elvis to Shania. When the home team did something of note, a recorded coyote-howl — "*AAAAAOOOOOOO!!*" — would echo through the building, and the fans would respond in kind.

America West opened in June 1992, and was built as a basketball facility for the NBA's Phoenix Suns. Jerry Colangelo, who owns the Suns and Coyotes, snookered himself to a degree in the construction blueprint. Hoping, at the time, to dissuade potential NHL investors, he sought and approved an arena design that would present logistic difficulties for hockey (obstructed seats). Therefore, when he purchased the

Winnipeg Jets franchise in 1996, these were problems he had to contend with. A perfectly symmetrical basketball facility is cockeyed for hockey. Seats at the north end of the building extend several feet over top the net, making it impossible to see the actual goal, or anything that happens behind it. Compounding matters, the upper-deck sections in the north end are partially obstructed by the protruding lower deck, creating what the team must sell as "limited view" seats, at a paltry $9.50 a ticket (next-lowest price is $18.75).

Like many other teams in the league, the Coyotes have built their own practice facility — the CellularOne Ice Den, in nearby Scottsdale. The facility was still being completed when the Maple Leafs skated there the day before a game against the Coyotes in March 1998. It was absolutely bone-cold in the arena, and the contrast outside was remarkable. I remember sitting on a giant boulder in the rear of the parking lot and shooting the breeze with Bill Watters. As the Maple Leafs were heading on to the ice for practice, it must have been 90 degrees in the sun, and a huge field behind the arena was filled with cacti and brush-plants of every variety. Nothing most people would associate with hockey.

Several hours prior to that March '98 game in Phoenix, the newly finished Bank One Ballpark was open to the public for a look-see. I took the opportunity to check out the stadium, with its retracting roof, its whirlpool in the centre-field bleachers, and natural grass field. It was something to behold.

Los Angeles/Anaheim

Speaking personally, no longer being able to visit southern California hurts the most — simply because I was often able to combine family and business on the same trip. My wife, Susan, is from the L.A. area and my in-laws, Peter and Maxine Straus, live in the San Fernando Valley community of Woodland Hills/Calabasas. A Maple Leaf trip to the western U.S.A. became a special treat for me, with an enjoyable routine.

One of the most memorable such journeys began in Denver just prior to Christmas, 1997. The Leafs played the Colorado Avalanche on a Monday night, and a majority of the fans in attendance spent the evening in the corridors of the McNichols Arena watching the Broncos play the San Francisco 49ers on TV. The next morning, I flew from Denver to Los Angeles and rented a car. I attended the Leafs' practice then drove to my in-laws' house, joining my wife and son. I spent the night there, then got up early the next day and drove 60 miles south to the John Wayne-Orange County Airport, where I dropped off the car. I took a cab to the Westin Southcoast Plaza in nearby Costa Mesa, where the Leafs stayed when they played the Anaheim Mighty Ducks. The Southcoast Plaza mall, a modern, up-scale shopping facility, was across the road from the hotel, and many Leaf players would head over there in T-shirt and shorts after the morning skate.

The Mighty Ducks play at the Arrowhead Pond of Anaheim — a gorgeous arena kitty-corner to and across the Garden Grove Freeway from Anaheim Stadium (now known as Edison Field). The arena's red-brick façade is accented by forest-green paneling, and the encircling parking lots are lined with palm trees. The interior of the Pond has been distinguished for its opulent marbled walls and ceramic tiling. The arena bowl itself comprises two levels of dark-red seats, angled steeply to the ice. The visiting dressing room presents a bit of a quandary, as media members must walk through the generally off-limits medical area to reach the players' lockers.

I remember a rather irksome, yet humorous scene from that dressing room in November 1996. After practice one day, Leaf rookie Sergei Berezin was just emerging from a leisurely shower, while the remainder of his teammates were already dressed and on the team bus. Assistant coach Mike Kitchen ran in and tried to hurry him along, but the language barrier got in the way. As Kitchen painstakingly motioned with his arms and attempted to talk Berezin into moving faster, the Russian native stood, butt-naked, in the middle of the floor with his head cocked, trying to interpret the gyrating coach. After 30 seconds or so, Kitch threw up his hands and stomped away in frustration.

In the days prior to Pat Quinn, when media members were allowed to travel on the team bus, I would accompany the club on the post-game jaunt from Anaheim to Los Angeles for the following night's game against the Kings. We'd bus to Santa Monica (in West L.A) and stay at a beachfront hotel that everyone on the trip detested having to leave. The trek north from Anaheim usually took 50 minutes to an hour and the environment on the bus was entirely predicated by that night's result against the Mighty Ducks. If the Leafs won, players would frolic to loud music and munch on the ubiquitous submarine sandwiches and pizzas that were delivered prior to leaving.

After a loss, it was so quiet you could hear someone burp 15 rows back.

I have vivid recollections of a couple of post-victory bus trips. Late in the lockout-shortened season of 1994–95, the Leafs won in Anaheim and I spent the entire journey to Santa Monica talking with Mike Gartner and Mark Hebscher about the early-1970s rock music we remembered from our youth. After another win over the Ducks in December 1997, Mats Sundin was given a pair of videos as a Christmas gift and he shared them with the rest of us (don't get excited). On the trip north to L.A., the triumphant Maple Leafs howled with laughter as they watched two episodes of *The Simpsons* on the bus TV.

As mentioned, there was no destination quite like the hotel we stayed at in L.A.

— the Loews Santa Monica. Located directly across a narrow street from busy Santa Monica Beach, and 15 minutes by foot north of trendy Venice Beach, it was a complete departure from the bustling mid-town hotels we normally stay at. In midwinter, the southern-California sun would turn a deep golden-yellow as it slowly set over the Pacific. As a result, I would always try to finagle at least a partial ocean-view room when we arrived late at night from Anaheim.

Naturally, the hotel preferred to set aside these chambers for guests who were paying more than a group rate, so it often required some negotiation and gentle cajoling. On one occasion, the front desk swore the hotel was completely full, even though there wasn't a soul to be seen in the lobby or adjacent bar. I was herded off to a street-level room that hung directly over busy Ocean Avenue, on the opposite side of the beach. I sent my post-game stuff from Anaheim to the radio station then went back to the lobby, and was told, again, that every room in the hotel was occupied. But the person relaying this information was not the least bit convincing. In fact, I'd seen more honest faces on bottles of iodine.

So, I decided to fight back. I went to a nearby payphone and called the hotel reservations desk. Pretending I was a tourist looking for a place to stay, I was informed — quite incredibly — that rooms of all sizes, locations, and prices were available, and to merely request my preference when I arrived. Confidently strolling back to the front desk, I asked the honorable clerk to fetch the night manager. Relaying my payphone information to them in no uncertain terms, I was met with a volley of guffaws and gagging noises. Because it was so late, the manager politely asked me to sleep in my assigned room, with the assurance of an upgrade in the morning. No problem, I said.

Susan was going to drive down from the San Fernando Valley and spend the following night with me, and I wanted a nicer room for her. After breakfast the next day, I received a profusely apologetic call from the hotel manager, who advised me to head up to an eighth-floor, ocean-front room. In it was a conciliatory bottle of champagne and fruit basket. The large suite was thoroughly magnificent, with an unparalleled view of the Pacific, and the Malibu coastline to the north.

But, alas, the hotel fates got even. Just as I comfortably settled into the lovely room, the skies above Santa Monica darkened and it wound up raining like a bastard the rest of the day. I stood forlornly at the window as the white-sand beach beyond me quickly became an expanse of light-brown sludge. Sheets of water poured down, turning the deep-blue ocean a sickly grey-green. I made a mental note not to scuffle for any such room on my next trip to town.

Luckily, the skies cleared later that afternoon, and the wispy clouds that remained actually intensified the gorgeous hue. There are few sights on earth quite as exhilarating as a wintertime sunset off the coast of L.A.

I may be the only person on earth who will miss the Great Western Forum — home of the Los Angeles Kings for 33 years; replaced by the Staples Center in downtown L.A. for the 1999–2000 season. An absolute palace of an arena when it opened in December 1967 (built by the Kings' first owner, Jack Kent Cooke), the Forum — in suburban Inglewood — maintained its '60s decor until the bitter end. On one side of the arena, seats were orange, with the opposite side gold. Curtains that corresponded to the color scheme were drawn shut during the game at ice level in the four corners of the building. The arena itself sat at the fringes of a south-central ghetto, one of the most forbidding sectors in the L.A. basin. Once the game was over and traffic cleared, Inglewood became a virtual ghost town.

Yet, I'll always have warm and wonderful memories of attending hockey games at the Forum during my long-distance courtship of Susan in 1990 and '91. In December 1990, I'd been working at the radio station for a year-and-a-half and happened to be visiting Susan when the Maple Leafs were on a west-coast swing. We had the Leaf broadcast rights back then, and our color-commentator at the time, Bill Watters, could not make that particular trip. As a result, I had the opportunity to fill in and do the Leafs-Kings analysis with the long-time voice of the Maple Leafs, Joe Bowen. It was the Wayne Gretzky era in Los Angeles, and the Forum was jammed to capacity each and every night.

More memories endure from covering the '93 Campbell Conference final between the Maple Leafs and Kings. Game 6 of that series (in the Forum) has been referred to earlier in this book, for the contentious manner in which it ended (Gretzky staying in the game after cutting Toronto captain Doug Gilmour with a high-stick in overtime, then scoring the winning goal himself). But that entire game was a rousing affair and remains the most electrifying playoff match I've covered in my years on the Leaf beat. The Buds were trailing by two in the third period, only to rally with the combined majesty of Gilmour passes and Wendel Clark goals. A third consecutive marker would have sent Toronto to the Stanley Cup finals for the first time in 26 years. But, it was not to be.

I was in the Forum for the final time on Thursday, December 17, 1998. Susan and I went to see the New York Islanders beat the Kings, 5-4, in overtime — on a goal by some defenceman named Bryan Berard.

San Jose

This sleepy little annex south of San Francisco became home to the Sharks in 1993, after the expansion club played its first two seasons at the archaic Cow Palace in Daly City, California. There's very little to say about San Jose, because nothing ever happens there. Just 41 hockey games a year. If you're walking in the downtown area and you look closely, another person will occasionally cross into view. The odd car passes by. And jetliners frequently whir over the main core on final approach to San Jose International Airport. But that's about it.

There's nothing particularly wrong with the place. It just happens to be a launching pad for the tourism capitals of northern California, as low-fare carriers like Southwest Airlines pour into the Silicon Valley. Just 15 miles up the road is quaint Palo Alto, home to historic Stanford University. Twenty-five miles further north is splendrous San Francisco. An hour's drive south takes you to the trendy outposts of Monterey and Carmel. When the Maple Leafs played the Sharks in the 1994 Campbell Conference semifinals, players, coaches, and media members from Toronto couldn't wait to get out of town during leisure time. The entire Maple Leaf contingent bussed into San Francisco one night for dinner at famed Fisherman's Wharf, while I along with several reporting colleagues drove down to Carmel on an off-day between Games 4 and 5.

What San Jose did have was one of the best hotels and nicest arenas on the NHL beat. The elegant, sand-stone Fairmont Hotel is the centerpiece of town and it housed the vast majority of traveling hockey parties. A high room, facing east, offered a lovely view of the Diablo mountain range, whose surfaces would green up spectacularly after the mid-winter rainfall.

The San Jose Arena, located on the western outskirts of downtown, was among the pioneers of the NHL's modern arena boom in the '90s. Clean and spacious, with great viewing angles, the Arena was consistently filled to capacity in the Sharks' early years — the club boasting of its 100th consecutive sellout for a game against the Maple Leafs, December 17, 1996. It was a far cry from the NHL's first venture into northern California, where the Oakland Seals played before sparse gatherings from 1967 to 1976. The franchise transferred to Richfield, Ohio, for two seasons (remember the Cleveland Barons?), then merged with the old Minnesota North Stars in 1978.

San Jose also had the best damned restaurant on the NHL trail. Original Joe's was a three-block stroll south of the Fairmont, and hockey players could be found within its walls at any time of day or night. I used to enjoy sitting on the revolving stools at the counter and gabbing with the short-order cooks. One day, I had lunch there with veteran defenceman Marty McSorley of the Sharks, and we prattled on endlessly about the Toronto-L.A. playoff series of '93. McSorley played in Los Angeles during the Gretzky era and will long be remembered for steamrollering Doug

Gilmour, and engaging in a dandy follow-up skirmish with Wendel Clark in Game 1 of that series at Maple Leaf Gardens.

California. Arizona. Colorado. They were grand places to visit during the Maple Leafs' old Western Conference days.

* * *

The NHL usually releases its annual schedule in mid-July. I often spend the better part of a day perusing the Maple Leaf agenda, and it's never difficult to isolate what might potentially be a trip from hell. For instance, near the end of the 1997–98 season, the Buds were well out of playoff contention when they had to make a four-day excursion to Dallas, Florida, and Carolina. All three flights — Toronto to Dallas, Dallas to Miami, and Miami to Raleigh-Durham — were more than two hours in length, the Dallas and Miami games occurring on consecutive nights. The only night off on that trip was spent in glorious Greensboro, North Carolina, where an exhaustive search turned up a decent Italian restaurant on the fringes of town. There was an ominous weather watch earlier that day, and it was the first and only time I've ever seen a funnel cloud — hovering menacingly over-top the city. If it had touched down, you'd have read about that, and not the Maple Leafs-Hurricanes game, the next day.

In January 1999, the Leafs had what appeared to be a pleasant six-game road trip, spaced over nine days, to Tampa Bay, Florida, Philadelphia, Carolina, Dallas, and St. Louis. At the end of the trip, I was to fly from St. Louis back to Tampa for the '99 NHL All-Star game. However, one of the most intense weather disturbances of the winter in the northeast and midwest sectors of the continent made it absolutely repugnant for travel. An experience I'll likely not soon forget.

The trip began unsuspectingly on Monday (January 11) with a two-hour-and-20-minute flight down to Tampa that was no problem, as we left Toronto and arrived on the Gulf coast of Florida amid clear skies. The Maple Leafs stay at the Wyndham Harbor Island Hotel in downtown Tampa — a short walk from the nearby Ice Palace, but a long trek from anything else of note. Like in San Jose, there's little more to do in the immediate area than rotate between the hotel and arena. A sandwich shop/convenience store, located in a remote office complex near the arena, offers the only culinary alternative to the hotel.

The Ice Palace — opened in 1996 — is a striking facility from the outside, with its 70,000 individual panes of glass. But, once inside, you wouldn't know if you were in Tampa, Washington, or Buffalo. All three new arenas (the Ice Palace, MCI Center, and Marine Midland Arena) are practically identical in appearance, with two levels of blue seats surrounding the ice. There are often more empty than occupied seats at Lightning and Capitals games, while Buffalo — a superior team in a better hockey market — attracts larger and more boisterous crowds.

The Maple Leafs began this early-1999 trip by rebounding from a 3-1 first-period deficit to edge Tampa Bay, 4-3. Up in Toronto, there was a grievous weather outlook, with the second major snowstorm of the month predicted to wreak havoc within 24 hours. The following day, I flew cross-state on Southwest Airlines from Tampa to Hollywood-Fort Lauderdale International Airport — a quick puddle-jump of 35 minutes.

The Florida Panthers played their first five NHL seasons in the Miami Arena, a rudimentary structure located in a less-than-ideal spot — the Overtown section of downtown Miami. There was a chain-link fence surrounding the employees' parking lot at the arena, and one's life was in peril upon venturing outside the smallish enclosure at night.

As such, taxi drivers generally avoided the area, even though fares were usually a slam-dunk after games (chances are, however, you'd get mugged long before a cab materialized). After a Maple Leafs-Panthers match in April 1998, NHL referee Dave Jackson, who I've known for several years, mercifully offered to drive me and my media colleagues back to the nearby Biscayne Bay Marriott. Otherwise, we may have been forced to bunk down for the night in the arena.

On earlier Maple Leaf trips to south Florida, Cliff Fletcher made sure the club ventured nowhere near downtown Miami, except for the actual games. In December 1995, the entire Leaf traveling party (media included) stayed at the Doral Ocean Beach Resort in north Miami Beach. And in March 1997, Fletcher had us at a gorgeous spot up the coast in Fort Lauderdale: the Marriott Harbor Beach Resort. Both were light years removed from the squalor of Overtown.

For the 1998–99 NHL season, the Panthers moved out of Miami and into their impressive new digs in Sunrise, Florida — a smallish community northwest of Lauderdale. The National Car Rental Center is the most exquisite arena — inside and out — in the entire league. Located in virtual solitude across from the giant Sawgrass Mills shopping complex, the Center is easily reachable by car and is surrounded by acres of parking. It's somewhat creepy to peer beyond the west boundary of the arena, into virtual nothingness, and realize that not more than seven miles downrange lurks the Florida Everglades — the forbidding, alligator-infested swampland that encompasses all but the border-fringes of the state. The immense N-C-R

Center can be seen for virtually miles in any direction, as it stands in the only conceivable spot for such an architectural monument.

The Maple Leafs stayed at a Sheraton Suites hotel in nearby Plantation during their two trips to south Florida in 1998–99. Situated off a large, multi-lane thoroughfare (University Drive), the hotel is conveniently linked to an unassuming shopping mall with a decent food court.

In the January 1999 trip, the Leafs blew a 3-0 third-period lead to the Panthers and had to settle for a 3-3 tie. The game took place on a Wednesday evening, and there was a three-day gap before the resumption of the road trip, Saturday night, in Philadelphia. As such, the Leafs chose to stay in Florida and practice on Thursday, before flying up to Philly on Friday. Somewhat surprisingly, after the third-period crash against the Panthers the night before, coach Pat Quinn decided not to conduct a team skate, allowing his players a complete day of leisure.

I took the opportunity to drive to Miami Beach and have lunch at an old haunt on 30th St. and Collins Ave., the Seville Hotel, where I'd spent Christmas breaks in 1974 and 1975 vacationing with family and friends. After a long, brisk walk along the beach, I went back to Plantation and spent the rest of the day and night wondering if I'd make it home the following afternoon. The forecast had been accurate and a ferocious snowstorm was blasting the Great Lakes region and eastern seaboard of the United States. Air traffic was at a virtual stand-still, and airports in the storm's path became unwelcome havens for thousands of stranded passengers. I wasn't anxious to join them.

My itinerary had me flying home from Miami the next morning (Friday), then out to Philadelphia later that night. I'm fortunate to have a good friend, Michael Ennis, who's a senior Air Canada captain living west of Toronto. Mike flies Boeing-767 aircraft primarily on long trips to Europe, the Caribbean, and the Middle East, and I met him on a flight home from San Francisco after a Maple Leaf trip in early 1995 (he was captaining the smaller Airbus-320 at the time). He has an air travel computer at home and was nice enough to repeatedly call me with updates on flight interruptions during that long, anxious Thursday evening in Plantation. Though I'd booked a restricted-fare ticket, Air Canada agreed to change my Toronto-to-Philadelphia flight from the following night to Saturday morning, removing some of the immediate pressure to get home.

I was booked on Air Canada #915, departing Miami International Airport at 11:05 Friday morning. The key to that flight operating was the plane's ability to leave snow-ravaged Toronto Thursday night and head south. Just before I hit the sack (around 11:30 p.m.), Mike called to say the aircraft was still stranded on the ground at Pearson International. But the actual flight to Miami had not been canceled, so there was a chance it could head south as I slept.

Thankfully, that's exactly what happened. Sometime after midnight, the snowstorm briefly subsided, allowing planes to depart Toronto. The Air Canada jet arrived in Miami in the wee hours of the morning, ensuring my trip home. In fact, Mike phoned around 7:30 a.m. Friday to give me the good news. He then had to scoot over to Pearson and fly a plane-load of passengers to Montego Bay.

I left Miami on schedule at 11:05, and roughly an hour into the flight, I was asked to identify myself over the plane's intercom. I rang my "call" button and a male purser — somewhat confused — brought me a Telex from the flight deck. Michael had FAXed the plane from his own jetliner, which had whizzed past us moments earlier on its way down to Jamaica:

> MESSAGE FROM AIRCRAFT 608 TO
> PASSENGER BERGER:
> Looks like we got lucky today . . . it's good to be prepared.
> —Mike E.

It's also good to have friends in high places (pun intended).

The Miami flight landed in Toronto in brilliant sunshine three hours after departing. A glance out the window on the descent turned up only two distinct colors — a crisp, blue sky and an entirely white tundra, as the thick blanket of snow from the previous day stretched to the horizon and beyond. The clouds had returned Saturday morning, but I got to Philadelphia with no problem for the Leafs-Flyers match that night (Toronto came up with a 4-3 victory to end Philadelphia's season-high 15-game unbeaten streak). And the weather held for the return flight to Toronto Sunday morning.

The second half of the road trip, however, was a nightmare — emotionally and logistically, one of the most exasperating adventures in my years covering the Leafs. It began on Monday morning (January 18) with a long and turbulent flight from Toronto to Raleigh for the Leafs' game that night against the Carolina Hurricanes. The storm system that dumped all the snow on the Great Lakes and eastern seaboard had drifted south, picking up warm air masses from the Gulf of Mexico. No one who flies even occasionally likes to hear that warm and cold air are clashing en route to a particular destination. It can mean only one thing — thunderstorms. And a seatbelt sign that never quits.

A flight from Toronto to Raleigh normally takes around an hour and 40 minutes, but this particular journey lasted almost 45 minutes longer, as the Air Canada captain zigged and zagged his trembling DC–9 in and around countless storm cells. Thick cloud formations of more than 40,000 feet surged into the sky, and there was simply no way to avoid all of them. The aircraft dipped and rose sporadically in the turbulent air, causing a young lady across the aisle from me to double over at the waist in terror. The flight attendants had been instructed by the captain to remain seated, but one of them staggered over to the woman and sat in an vacant seat next to her. I'm normally white-knuckled in rough air, until it reaches a point where I know things are not going to smooth over for a while. I somehow then become capable of surrendering myself to the feeling — realizing, logically, that the plane will not fall out of the sky. But rarely does any flight present more than a full hour of constant tumult, like that trip to Raleigh.

As mentioned, the Hurricanes played in Greensboro during the first two years after their transfer from Hartford. A whistle-stop hamlet 66 miles west of Raleigh-Durham International Airport, Greensboro was easily accessible by car along Interstate 40 — the ride taking little more than an hour. Anyone with even the slightest inclination towards U.S. college basketball could have a field day listening to radio on the quick drive, as it crossed directly through the heart of the Atlantic Coast Conference. There is an immense rivalry among N.C. State University (Raleigh), Duke University (Durham), and the University of North Carolina (Chapel Hill) — all located within 50 miles of one another.

The Hurricanes played their home games at the Greensboro Coliseum, part of a massive, internal sports complex that dominated an otherwise Spartan landscape. It quickly became evident to Hurricanes owner Peter Carmanos that hockey fans in North Carolina either did not exist, or were entirely unwilling to drive to Greensboro from larger surrounding cities like Raleigh, Charlotte, and Winston-Salem. Had Keith Primeau, Sami Kapanen, Sean Burke and Co. been NASCAR drivers, there wouldn't have been a problem. But hockey players were hardly coveted attractions in the early days of the Carolina franchise.

Lamentably, the Coliseum had an outrageous seating capacity of close to 21,000, and there appeared to be more ushers in the building than spectators on most nights. Rarely were 6,000 seats occupied for any hockey game, precluding an atmosphere conducive to a sporting event. Giant batches of light-green seats on both levels of the arena were empty; fans clustered, primarily, between the bluelines in the lower concourse.

When the Maple Leafs made their lone visit to Greensboro in the 1997–98 season (April 9), an announced gathering of 8,368 was on hand. Several rows of the upper deck on the north side were converted into a press box, and I can clearly envision glancing to my left at the masses of unused seats behind the east goal. Eight entire sections were completely empty. The P.A. announcer could have warbled through a spent toilet-paper roll and been heard. It just was not big league in any conceivable way.

The Hurricanes smartly curtained off most of the Coliseum upper deck for the 1998–99 season, dramatically improving the ambiance in the building. The club is banking on its permanent home — the Raleigh Sports and Entertainment Complex — to attract the large masses that refused to embrace Greensboro; it was scheduled to make its NHL debut for a game between the Hurricanes and New Jersey Devils, October 29, 1999.

Navigating through tiny Greensboro was never a problem for anyone with even a moderate sense of direction. But my pal Roy MacGregor — the famed Canadian sportswriter and littérateur — temporarily lost his bearings after the Maple Leafs-Hurricanes game in April 1998. Offering me a ride back to the Greensboro Hilton, Roy had to stay longer than expected in the Coliseum press room, as his computer malfunctioned. Still writing, at the time, for the *Ottawa Citizen,* Roy dictated his lengthy column over the phone then led me to his car.

The Hilton was no more than a two-mile drive from the rink — located in the midst of Greensboro's well-illuminated downtown core. When Roy failed to turn off at either of the first two exits, I was mildly surprised, but figured he had taken some other route. Five minutes later, as the lights of Greensboro were a faint glow in his rear-view mirror, I worried that I was being abducted. For some reason, I chose not to say anything, still trying to convince myself he wasn't lost. When we began seeing signs for Atlanta (I'm exaggerating), Roy finally snapped out of it and said, "Hey, where the hell are we?"

That's when I spoke up, and we thankfully had enough gas in the tank to double back to the Hilton. To this day, Roy has never explained to me just where the hell he was going that night.

Another media comrade, Alan Adams (now of the *National Post*), covered the Maple Leafs for the *Toronto Star* in 1997–98. To make the arduous, hour-long trek between Raleigh and Greensboro, Al rented a lavish town car for something like $220 a day. He was nice enough to offer rides in both directions, but the little wretch tortured me by playing the most revolting, abominable music cassette you will ever hear. Ostensibly, it was some newfangled country strain, but it sounded more like fingernails on a blackboard. Adams tapped along all the way to Greensboro and I was ready for a white coat by the time we arrived.

During the exasperating road swing of January 1999, the Leafs lost, 4-2, to the

Hurricanes. The routing on that particular leg of the trip (Toronto to Raleigh to Dallas to St. Louis, then to Tampa for the All-Star Game), could not be flown on any one carrier without making a connection somewhere along the way. To save money, I booked the remainder of the voyage — after Carolina — on United Airlines, choosing (unwisely, as it turned out) Chicago as a connecting point on every flight. The preposterous but economical itinerary came out like this:

> Greensboro - Chicago - Dallas - Chicago - St. Louis - Chicago - Tampa - Chicago - Toronto.

All in a span of six days.

No hint of annoyance occurred on the initial leg of the journey, and it was a delight not having to drive back to Raleigh first thing Tuesday morning (January 19). Instead, United had a flight to Chicago from the Piedmont-Triad Airport on the outskirts of Greensboro. The trip took one hour and 40 minutes in pre-dawn light, and I remember looking down and seeing empty Soldier Field on the final approach to O'Hare International Airport. I had breakfast in the O'Hare terminal and the fun began soon after re-boarding the Boeing-737 for the flight to Dallas.

Unlike the trip from Greensboro, the plane was now jammed to capacity, and no one was quite sure why maintenance people were running on and off the aircraft 20 minutes after our scheduled departure time. Finally, a stewardess came over the intercom and sheepishly explained that one of the rear lavatories had malfunctioned, and with such a full load of passengers, the airline wanted to ensure as much "convenience" as possible for the continuation to Dallas.

But workers were still hammering away on the damned toilet a half-hour later, by which time most passengers were inclined to endure some cramps for the opportunity to get up in the air. We finally took off 75 minutes late, and the first half of the excursion southward proceeded ordinarily. Many passengers were dozing when another attendant came over the mike and politely asked if there was a doctor on board. A moderately frantic scramble ensued at the rear of the plane, as someone had obviously fallen ill. "How ill?" many of us wondered. The answer arrived 20 minutes later, when the captain announced he had chosen to make an emergency landing in Tulsa, Oklahoma. "Once the passenger is safely off the plane, we'll head back to the runway and continue on to Dallas," he said.

Tulsa . . . site of the Maple Leafs' Central Hockey League farm team in the late 1960s. I had no more desire at that moment to visit the place than I'd ever had before, but my thoughts were confined to the predicament of the individual on-board, and once airborne again, Dallas would only be 40 minutes down the road. I watched out a portside window as a middle-aged woman was lowered from the rear of the plane onto the tarmac, and wheeled to a waiting ambulance. The captain explained she had suffered a severe asthma attack, but was expected to be just fine. Within five minutes, he was back rolling down the runway.

Arriving somewhat haggardly in Dallas just after the noon-hour, it was a pleasure not having a game to scramble to. The Leafs upset the eventual Stanley Cup champions, 6-4, the following night, and I later packed up for what I naively figured would be a routine trip to St. Louis the next morning.

After a good night's rest, I took a cab in steady rain to Dallas-Fort Worth International Airport. Upon checking in at United, I was given no indication of any delay or weather anomaly for my connection through Chicago to St. Louis. I had breakfast at a McDonald's in the terminal, then sat unsuspectingly at the gate area and read the morning paper. At some point moments later, I looked up and happened to notice that hardly anyone else was waiting with me. Glancing out a rain-splashed window, I saw there was no aircraft sitting at the end of the bridge-way, and I made a bee-line for the counter.

Without announcing it to the passengers already checked in, United had canceled the flight into Chicago because of a thick blanket of fog. In *January*??! I was told that even if I somehow got to O'Hare, my connection to St. Louis was delayed until very late in the afternoon, making it almost impossible to arrive at the Kiel Center on time for that night's game between the Leafs and Blues. As a courtesy, the United agent checked with TWA over her walkie-talkie and found me space on a non-stop flight up to St. Louis. But I had less than 15 minutes to make the switch, and had to first ask for my checked-in luggage to be returned. Somehow, it all worked out, and the fact we circled over St. Louis for 20 minutes prior to landing was immaterial after almost not getting there at all.

However, the accumulation of events on this trip was starting to wear on me. By the time I arrived at the Hyatt Union Station in downtown St. Louis, a fair bit of paranoia had set in. I was scheduled to fly back to Chicago, then down to Tampa the following day for the NHL All-Star festivities. I called a local weather service and was told that the fog in Chicago would likely dissipate overnight and not cause any further annoyances the next day. I enjoyed a delicious dinner at Lombardo's — an Italian restaurant near the hotel — with media colleagues Paul Hunter, David Shoalts, and Mike Ulmer. We then walked over to the Kiel Center and covered the Maple Leafs' 4-2 victory over the Blues.

When I was blasted awake the next morning by a thunderstorm over St. Louis, my instincts told me to call United, forthwith. I could only shake my head at the news. Chicago was still engulfed by mist, as a bizarre warm front refused to budge. My 11:20 a.m. flight there and my 1:10 p.m. connection to Tampa had both been canceled. I'd been re-booked on a consolidation that would have me in Florida sometime after midnight, luck permitting. In a kind gesture, the Hyatt offered me a room extension to 4 p.m. and I figured there was nothing to do but relax. I dozed off for a while, then re-packed my duffelbag and had lunch in the former train station, now a multi-level shopping mall attached to the hotel.

Arriving back in the room, my heart sank when I noticed the red light flashing on my bedside phone. In normal times, it could have been anyone — my wife, the office — leaving a message, but I somehow knew not to expect pleasant news from this particular communication. Typically, it was United, once again — this time informing me that my two late flights had been scrapped, and that no space was available on any of the non-stop TWA departures from St. Louis to Tampa until late the following afternoon. Considering that player availability at the All-Star weekend was the next morning, I had finally met my match. I called Air Canada and transferred on to a one-way flight home that evening.

What a trip.

Imagine having to miss the NHL All-Star game in Florida because of fog in Chicago in the middle of winter. Almost a year later, I'm still trying to figure that one out. Sure pays to try and save money, huh?

Perhaps I'd have been less confounded had I recalled a moment almost three years earlier when the same situation happened in reverse. On April 4, 1996, I awoke at home to a freak snowstorm — the tenacity of which we'd hardly seen in Toronto through the dead of winter. Crawling along Highway 401 to Pearson Airport for a late-morning flight to (where else?) St. Louis, I couldn't imagine the absurd weather persisting much longer. Just the previous day, it had been wonderfully springlike in southern Ontario, and this was obviously just a squall.

Right.

The white stuff continued to come down in sheets as I sat desolately in the Pearson terminal for more than three hours. No planes were landing, and while a number were departing in the storm, Air Canada would not fly its smallish Canadair Regional Jet (CRJ) in such conditions. My flight was officially canceled sometime after 1 p.m., and the next available connections (through Chicago) on either United or American were both oversold. Therefore, I did not make it to St. Louis for that night's game between the Maple Leafs and Blues.

Even more disconcerting was arriving in Dallas for the 1999 Stanley Cup finals without my clothing or radio equipment. Once again, weather played a fundamental role. I had booked an Air Canada flight from Toronto to Houston, with a connection to Dallas Love Field on Continental Airlines. As I was driving to Pearson Airport for the outbound trip, a violent thunderstorm passed over the area, choking off all air traffic in and out of Toronto.

By the time I parked, checked in, and got through customs, the weather had cleared, but there was no aircraft at our boarding gate. The departure time came and went, still with no evidence of a plane to take us to Houston. After an interminable delay, we were told that the Airbus-320 scheduled for our flight — in-bound from Bermuda — had proceeded to its alternate landing site (Niagara Falls, New York) during the thunderstorm. It was once again airborne and on its way to Toronto, and we'd be off to Houston within 45 minutes.

This obstacle thoroughly buggered up my connection plans to Dallas. As mentioned, I had booked a flight to Love Field, which is much closer to the main core of the city (known as the Dallas Metroplex) than the International airport in Fort Worth (D-FW). Anyone past the age of 40 will instantly associate Love Field with former U.S. president John F. Kennedy, who landed there with First Lady Jacqueline Kennedy the day he was assassinated in November 1963. At 5:45 p.m. — one full hour past our scheduled departure time for Houston — I realized there was no way I'd make my 8:30 connection to Love Field. I called Continental and was told of a 9:45 departure to D-FW: the airline's final one of the day. Had my luggage not already been checked to Love Field I would have re-booked on the later flight, but I decided to hang in for a bit.

Air Canada finally loaded us onto the A-320 and we took off into clear skies at 6:15 p.m. — 90 minutes late. The flight to Texas took longer than usual (3 hrs. 15 min.), as the captain had to navigate around numerous storm cells, and we landed at Houston Intercontinental Airport at 8:30 p.m. Central Time — exactly the moment my connection for Dallas was leaving. Knowing my chances to make it were bleak, I'd asked Air Canada to radio ahead, just in case the Dallas flight was delayed. As soon as I stepped off the plane and onto the passenger bridge in Houston, a man standing there asked if I was Howard Berger. He said I'd been re-booked on the 9:45 Continental flight to D-FW and pointed to a co-worker who (he claimed) was going to transfer my luggage between the two airlines.

My anxieties alleviated, I casually took the inter-terminal train over to Continental and checked in for the re-booked flight. That's when I knew I was in trouble. The agent said there was no record of anyone re-scheduling my ticket, but the flight had numerous empty seats and she'd make the switch. About my luggage?

She had no guarantees. I went down to the Continental baggage desk and asked the agent there to physically locate my duffelbag, which (according to Air Canada) had been transferred to the 9:45 p.m. Dallas flight. He couldn't find it, but said it might already be aboard the Continental jet.

Needless to say, I sat forsakenly at D-FW later that night, watching the luggage carousel make more laps than cars at the Indianapolis 500. Suitcases, golf clubs, birdcages . . . everything imaginable poured off that damned plane except my bag. If this ever happens to you, you'll immediately notice the comparative indifference of the airline baggage agent. This particular gentleman at D-FW was nearing the end of his shift, and likely had a fully comfortable dwelling to return to for the night. Me? I had a shirt, a pair of jeans, and some underwear. And my deodorant had worn off. Coolly, without a hint of concern or remorse, the man told me my bag would probably arrive sometime the next day. Then he added, "But, it could be lost. I've seen bags for Dallas wind up in all parts of the world. A buddy of mine once had his suitcase returned from Dubai [in the United Arab Emirates]. He'd been flying from Miami to Dallas."

Wonderful. The Stanley Cup final was starting in less than 24 hours and some sheik could be rummaging through my tape equipment. The baggage agent handed me an emergency toiletry kit — a frightful-looking thing that contained a comb, small tube of toothpaste, and a toothbrush with about six bristles on it. I nearly lacerated my gums a couple of hours later at the Hyatt Regency Reunion, before sulking off to bed.

Thankfully, the story had a happy ending. It took about six, high-strung telephone calls the next morning before Continental finally located my bag — on the tarmac at Houston airport! "Why not just leave it on the runway?" I thought. Fortunately, it had not been trampled by a taxiing aircraft and was sent to me on the next flight to Dallas. The only drawback came from having to use that toothbrush-from-hell one more time.

* * *

The primary exasperation of frequent travel — and it probably works both ways — is having to contend with the daft lot known as taxi drivers. While some are truly competent and courteous, most in my experience have been illiterate, unmannerly, and directionally challenged. Not to mention malodorous. Is it too much to ask a person to either shower or introduce some form of air-freshening quality to his vehicle? Evidently so.

Yet, riding taxis on a daily basis is essential on the hockey trail. In places like New

York and Chicago, where cabs seem to out-number private cars, all that's usually required by a customer is steely nerves. Or a stiff drink. These maniacs often know where they're going, and will get you there quickly, while disregarding minor obstacles like traffic, stop-lights, and pedestrians.

Then there's a place like the Meadowlands. When the Maple Leafs travel to play the Devils, they stay at an Embassy Suites in Secaucus, about three miles inland on the New Jersey side of the Lincoln Tunnel. For most taxi drivers, it may as well be Neptune. I'd like a nickel for every time I've hopped into a cab at Newark International Airport and proceeded to tour the entire west bank of the Hudson River. Bayonne, Jersey City, Hoboken, Moonachie . . . I've seen them all — without asking.

While this routine is always infuriating, it's easier to stomach in daylight hours. Much more so than at night, when your confused cabbie pulls into a darkened New Jersey alleyway to consult with a similarly disjointed comrade. And you're left sitting in the back seat, with ghastly visions of every late-night movie you've ever seen dancing through your head.

So as not to paint all these people with the same brush, I'll recount an incident that occurred recently in Calgary. I stopped there to cover a Canadian Football League game between the Toronto Argonauts and Calgary Stampeders after the Maple Leafs' exhibition tour of western Canada in September 1999. I had left McMahon Stadium after the game and was looking to hail a cab on busy Crowchild Trail. Adjacent to the stadium was a five-story motel, and I found a taxi driver letting off a customer in the parking lot. He agreed to take me back to the Delta Hotel at Calgary International Airport, but his dispatcher soon ordered him to pick up a call he'd been given moments earlier.

Apologizing profusely, he drove me to a nearby Holiday Inn and saw me into another cab. The two drivers — both of East-Indian descent — nodded to one another and off we went. Seconds later, panic ensued. I reached into my bag for my cellphone and couldn't find it. I looked in all the nooks and crannies, scoured the back seat and felt around on the floor. Nothing. Since I'd been using it while walking out of McMahon Stadium, I immediately figured I had dropped it in the first taxi. A sensible deduction. How to get the damned thing back was another story. That's when my friend in the turban took over.

He drove me back to the Holiday Inn, thinking the other cabbie may have noticed the phone and returned it there. Not so. But he somehow did remember seeing the taxi number on the car that delivered me to him. I called Checker Cab and issued the number. The dispatcher — typically harried — put me on hold, and came back three minutes later to say the phone had been found, and was being returned to my location. Whew!! My first cabbie was nice enough to immediately detour out of his way and return the phone. All he asked was that I make a call to his company, "for appreciation to me." I was only happy to do so.

The second driver took me to Calgary Airport, boasting the entire way that he'd worked with numbers in his native India. Good thing for that!

* * *

Traveling to hockey games out of town occasionally affords me the opportunity to attend other sporting events. And a rare and welcome chance to sit among spectators, away from the impassivity of a press box. There is often occasion, for instance, to attend an afternoon baseball game prior to an evening NHL playoff match. When the Leafs returned to Philadelphia for Game 6 of the 1999 Eastern Conference quarterfinals, the Phillies were hosting the Los Angeles Dodgers. I drove over to Veterans Stadium and bought a ticket in the upper deck down the third-base line. On a wind-swept, sunny afternoon, I was anticipating a monster pitching match-up between Curt Schilling and Kevin Brown, only to watch the home team slaughter the visiting multi-millionaire.

In April 1996, I saw the St. Louis Cardinals take on the Atlanta Braves at Busch Stadium prior to a Maple Leafs-Blues playoff game. It was before the Mark McGwire era in St. Louis and the stadium was mostly empty. I mentioned earlier the 1998 side-trip to Coors Field in Denver, and the subsequent encounter with Hall of Famer George Brett. While covering the 1988 NHL entry draft in Detroit, I got my first look at Tiger Stadium. And I still marvel at the fact I'm alive after nonchalantly walking back to the hotel in the dead of night along crime-ridden Michigan Avenue. Sure, there were four other people with me, but bullets don't discriminate. Nor are they frightened off by numbers.

A real treat is the rare opportunity to catch a National Football League game. The Leafs were in Philadelphia for a Sunday night match-up in November 1996, and the Eagles hosted the Buffalo Bills that afternoon at sold-out Veterans Stadium. I spent an exhaustive 45 minutes attempting not to be ripped off by the flagitious ticket-scalpers, and finally met up with a nice man who was going to the game, himself, and simply wanted to sell his second ticket at cost. We sat together at the 30-yard line on the east side of the stadium.

On the afternoon of the Maple Leafs' 1999 pre-season opener in Chicago, the Bears were hosting the Kansas City Chiefs. It was opening day of the '99 NFL regular season and Soldier Field was completely sold out. As one of the ancient facilities in all of sport, at least half the 60,000 seats at Soldier Field are located in the end zones. In a one-shot deal, my objective was to find a ticket-seller with a chair between the goallines, and it didn't look promising for the first 30 minutes. But with immense fortune, I once again succeeded. This time, a rather attractive female offered me a $47 ticket — the full value of which I'd been willing to spend. When she asked me for $20, I quickly obliged and sat at the 20-yard line on the west side of the stadium, behind the Bears' bench.

U.C.L.A. quarterback Cade McNown made his NFL debut for Chicago in the Bears' 20-17 victory — something I'll point out more frequently one day if he develops as many anticipate he will.

* * *

As you've seen, inclement weather can often ravage the enjoyment of travel and cause tangible displeasure. But a snowstorm, of all things, came as a particularly nice surprise during a unique side-trip with the Maple Leafs in October 1998.

After opening the regular season at home with a win over defending Stanley Cup–champion Detroit, the Leafs embarked on a three-city voyage to western Canada. The trip was scheduled rather oddly, with games Tuesday night in Edmonton, Friday in Calgary, and Saturday in Vancouver. Taking advantage of the three-day gap, coach Pat Quinn chose to set up camp at a mountain resort in Banff, Alberta, Wednesday and Thursday. Since the media must follow the team, reporters were compelled to rough it in similar fashion.

The Maple Leafs opened the roadtrip with a 3-2 victory over the Oilers, in goalie Curtis Joseph's return to the city he'd recently bolted as a free agent. The next morning, I flew down to Calgary and hitched a ride to Banff with *Toronto Star* colleagues Paul Hunter and Rosie DiManno. Banff National Park is located in the Canadian Rockies, about 90 minutes west of Calgary on the Trans-Canada Highway. Somewhere in its midst is the delightful Rocky Mountain Resort — an alpine lodge with suites featuring bedroom lofts, fireplaces, full kitchens, and wrap-around balconies. It was our home on October 14 and 15, 1998, and quite an awesome location, resting at the foot of giant Cascade Mountain.

Several times during that 48-hour span, I witnessed a truly wondrous sight: DiManno shopping. Single-handedly, and with astounding impulsiveness, Rosie strengthened the entire Alberta tourism industry. Hunter was driving us through town Wednesday afternoon on our way to Banff Memorial Arena, when Rosie — from the back seat — exclaimed, "Ooooo, look at that!" and asked Paul to pull over to the curb. With cat-like quickness, she dashed out of the car and into a clothing shop. Seconds later, Hunter and I watched in amazement as a scarlet overcoat disappeared from a mannequin in the front window. DiManno hopped back into the rear seat wearing the garish-looking outfit and we were on our way once again . . . a quick 200 bucks left behind in the till.

The Maple Leafs skated in the bone-chilling Banff arena both afternoons. We spent much of the first day dealing with a swap of defencemen between the Leafs and New York Rangers — Mathieu Schneider for Alexander Karpovtsev. Around 1 p.m. on the second day (Thursday), snow began gently falling on the park and it quickly developed into a full-blown blizzard. Not the type of weather Ontarians are accustomed to in mid-autumn, and a predicament for which we were wholly unprepared (all except Rosie in her blazing-red gabardine). Slip-sliding back to the lodge, we spent the late afternoon and evening hunkered down amid the elements. There was such a complete absence of wind and extraneous noise at our location, you could almost hear the heavy snowflakes landing on tree limbs and bushes. With the white stuff expected to continue through the night, there was some momentary concern that the Maple Leafs might be stranded in Banff, and unable to leave for Calgary Friday morning.

Travel of any sort was ill-advised, so we stuck around and made ourselves comfortable. I ordered a stack of wood from the front desk and spent Thursday evening in front of a raging fireplace in the living room watching the Green Bay at Detroit NFL game on TV. The breeze picked up overnight, and I briefly lay awake in the darkened loft watching and listening to the sheets of snow lash the upstairs window. It was all quite cushy.

By morning, the storm had passed through and left behind a spectacular panorama. A golden sunrise began shining on the summit of Cascade Mountain around 8 a.m. No part of the giant alp had been visible during the previous day's tempest, but it was now fully in scope, and magnificent. The contrast during the 90-minute trek back to Calgary was remarkable, as the snow-covering gradually disappeared. There wasn't a trace of the stuff anywhere near the city.

One other moment from that Banff pilgrimage remains etched in my mind, and I still laugh when I think about it. Naturally, Rosie was involved. Following the Maple Leafs' practice on Thursday, the media huddled in a cramped, narrow passageway outside the dressing rooms. At one point, Rosie happened to be leaning against the wall across from the room in which the Leaf coaching staff was changing. To her utter horror, the door somehow swung open and she caught a rear-scrotal view of Alpo Suhonen hovering over his equipment bag. An involuntary gasp escaped from her throat, prompting Suhonen to pivot in disgust — flash a dirty look — and slam the door shut. My revolted colleague did not appreciate the discourteous reaction from the Maple Leaf assistant, and was pissed off the rest of the day.

"Like I *wanted* to see that!" she griped.

* * *

Something I never want to see again almost ruined the longest roadtrip I've ever been on. The Fan-590 sent me to Nagano, Japan, to cover hockey at the 1998 Winter Olympic Games. There was some last-minute confusion over my accommodations, and I wound up renting a room at a Japanese ski resort from a Canadian travel agency just one week before departing. In spite of the 11th-hour aggravation, it actually turned out to be a superb set-up, with a couple of twin beds, plenty of desk space, and a large Jacuzzi in the bathroom. Located in the alpine village of Hakuba, it was also an hour's bus ride in and out of Nagano each day — an inconvenience I quickly grew to tolerate.

After a full day's work (which averaged 12 to 14 hours), I could always tell when we were nearing Hakuba at night, as you could see the giant ski-runs all lit up in the distance (Hakuba was the site of the downhill-skiing events at the Olympics). One night midway through the Games, the bus had to slow down because of a slight traffic snarl. As we inched forward, a gaggle of flashing red cherries came into view up ahead, indicating some sort of mishap. A sequence of flares re-routed traffic in an elliptical fashion around the accident site, which had been illuminated by floodlights. Seconds before we passed by, something instinctively told me, "Howard, don't look!" I wish I had followed my inkling.

In Japan, as in the British Isles and Australia, cars travel on the left-hand side of the road. A small Japanese-made automobile had obviously attempted to cross over the on-rushing lane and make a right turn into traffic. It was a hideous miscalculation. The car had smashed into an enormous dump truck and was in the shape of an accordion — roughly four feet from fender to fender. You'll hardly ever see a car demolished so compactly.

A closer look almost made me nauseous. Part of this conflagration was an obviously-former human being, whose crushed torso had squeezed his arms and head in a grotesque manner beyond the front edge of the vehicle. Those of us on board the bus could only gasp in horror and turn away. For reasons that were dolefully evident, rescue workers were in no hurry to free this person, who had instantly met his maker. But the mere sight of that individual cast a pall over me that I could not shake for almost a full 24 hours.

It just so happened that the following day was one in which I had not planned on going into Nagano (there were no hockey games or practices). And it couldn't have presented more unfortunate timing for me. I was, quite simply, an emotional wreck over what I'd seen the night before. I didn't want to be alone, and I didn't want to be in the company of anyone else. A cold sweat enveloped my entire body and would not evaporate. My ardor for anything related to the Games was sapped (temporarily, thank goodness). I tried walking around the picturesque resort, calling home, lying down, taking a bath . . . nothing could snap me out of the catatonic state.

"C'mon Howard, you never even *knew* that person," I kept on telling myself. It didn't work.

Finally, and without justification, the feeling was gone when I snapped awake from a mid-afternoon snooze. Not the sense of sorrow for the dead man and his family; just the notion of sheer panic and emotional entrapment. I looked around the darkening room and momentarily distrusted the sensation. But it held . . . and relief has rarely felt so overwhelming.

More Hockey Hits
from
Warwick Publishing

Maple Leaf Moments
A Thirty-Year Reflection
by Howard Berger

Sports broadcaster and *On the Road Again* author Howard Berger gives an entertaining, close-up examination of one of hockey's most successful and enduring franchises. A must-read for any fan of the Toronto Maple Leafs.
(ISBN: 1-895629-38-1)

Hot Goalies
By Stan Fischler, with Chico Resch

Professional hockey goaltending has frequently been called "the hardest job in sports." And it is! *Hot Goalies* profiles the NHL's best goalies of today and yesteryear.
(ISBN: 1-895629-96-9)

We hope you have enjoyed this book.
We welcome your comments.
Please contact us at

Warwick Publishing
162 John Street
Toronto, Ontario, Canada
M5V 2E5

Telephone: (416) 596-1555

E-mail: mbrooke@warwickgp.com

* * *

To view our online catalogue,
or to find out
how to submit a book proposal,
please visit us on the web at

www.warwickgp.com